£2-95

The Ashford Book of
WEAVING

The Ashford Book of
WEAVING

ANNE FIELD

BATSFORD

A BATSFORD BOOK

B.T. Batsford Ltd,
4 Fitzhardinge Street,
London W1H0AH

© 1991 Anne Field

First published in New Zealand in 1991
by Tandem Press Ltd
This edition first published 1992

ISBN 0 7134 6990 0

All rights reserved. No part of this publication may be reproduced, stored in a retrieval system or transmitted in any form by any process without the prior permission of the copyright owner. Enquiries should be made to the publisher.

Produced and designed by Shoal Bay Press.
Printed in Hong Kong.

CONTENTS

Introduction   7
Acknowledgments   8

SECTION ONE: THE LOOMS   9

1 Inkle Loom   13
Construction • Warping • Weaving • Finishing • Other methods of tying leashes • Patterns • Uses

2 Rigid Heddle Loom   21
Construction • The warp • Measuring the warp • Warping the loom • Threading • Preparation for weaving • Weaving • Pick-up stick weaving • Block switching • Mock leno • First project

3 Four-shaft Table Loom   45
Construction • Other equipment • Choosing a loom • Rising shed action • Warp length • Planning the warp • Warping the loom • Beaming • Threading • Sleying • Sleying for other setts • Heading • Threading mistakes • Weaving • Weaving a sampler • Binder weft • Warping with the warping mill • Warping with two crosses • Warping with two or more threads

4 Four-shaft Jack Loom   71
Construction • Warping the loom • Threading • Sleying • Heading • Weaving • Shuttles

5 Eight-shaft Table and Jack Looms   85
Eight-shaft table loom • Eight-shaft jack loom • Differential rise and fall • Weaving • Twills • Overshot weaves • Double weave • Surface texture

SECTION TWO: MATERIALS AND TECHNIQUES

6 Yarns   103
Animal fibres • Vegetable fibres • Mineral fibres • Man-made fibres • Synthetic fibres • Finishing of synthetic fibres • Static electricity • Burning test • Blended yarns • Selecting warp and weft yarns • Yarn design • Yarn counts

7 Designing woven projects   111
Designing projects • Cushions • Scarves • Tablemats • Upholstery fabrics • Curtains • Clothing fabrics • Wall hangings • Weaving for exhibitions and shops

8 Pattern drafting   118
Pattern draft • Computers in pattern drafting • Ashford jack loom • Ashford table looms • Reading a draft for a jack loom

9 Finishings 121
Warp finishing • Hemstitching • Blanket stitch • Warp ends darned in • Hemming • Overhand knot • Reef knot • Plaited fringe • Twisted fringe • Philippine edge • Added fringe • Fringes on all four sides • Braids and edging strips • Knitted fringe • Knitting a bias edging • Knitting directly on to a garment • Twisted braid • Finger crochet

SECTION THREE: WEAVING PROJECTS

10 Weaving projects 127
1. Scarves • 2. Tablemats • 3. Cushions • 4. Handspun knee rug • 5. Upholstery fabric • 6. Surface weave jacket fabric • 7. Cotton jacket • 8. Dyed weft stole • 9. Cocoon jacket • 10. Cross-over stole • 11. Inkle Braid braces • 12. Overshot runner • 13. Weft-face hanging • 14. Tapestry hanging •15. Warp-face hanging • 16. Double corduroy rugs • 17. Eight-shaft cotton fabric length • 18. Eight-shaft stuffed cushion in double weave • 19. Jacket with eight-shaft yoke • 20. Eight-shaft knee rug, in double weave.

APPENDICES 193
1. Care and maintenance of looms 194
2. Additonal equipment 195
3. Ashford distributors 196
4. Books for further study 197
5. Glossary 198

Index 199

INTRODUCTION

For over fifty years it has been our pleasure to provide the craftsperson with the best tools for weavers and spinners. It seems a natural progression that the *Ashford Book of Spinning* should be followed by the *Ashford Book of Weaving*.

Again, we were delighted when Anne Field, New Zealand's well-known spinner, weaver, tutor and author, undertook to write it for us. With simplicity and skill she has set out to inform, guide, and extend weavers at all levels of workmanship.

Weaving is simply a warp thread crossed by a weft thread and held in place. This basic concept has been the same since the first primitive human made his/her 'web'. Since then many changes have been introduced and these have made for speed and ease of operating the loom. In our factory, we have been able to adapt old and new concepts to make easy-to-use looms, which leave the weaver free to concentrate on designing and weaving textiles. It is still the weaver who provides the inspiration and imagination to create textile designs.

Weaving is a therapy which can bring personal satisfaction at all skill levels. The beginner, in learning new skills, can use traditional techniques or follow an intuitive exploration of colour, texture and design. As the weaver becomes more skilled, the range widens. The artistic craftsperson has infinite scope.

We wish to thank all who have contributed to the production of this book, and also our staff who make the looms.

We have made the tools to facilitate the art of weaving. To those who read and use this book, we wish you the unlimited joy of handweaving.

Richard Ashford
Walter Ashford

ACKNOWLEDGMENTS

In writing this book I have gathered together much of the knowledge and information that I have acquired over the last twenty years. Bringing this knowledge to you in a useful and readable form has been fun, and I have learned much in the process. Because Ashfords have a wide range of weaving equipment, I was able to cover many weaving skills, including weaving on inkle looms, rigid heddle looms, and four and eight-shaft table and jack looms.

Some of these looms I have reported on in their prototype stage, and made suggestions which have been incorporated into the final design. It is very satisfying to go one step further, and to write about how to use them Once a weaver has the necessary skills and knowledge, he/she can use Ashford weaving equipment to make beautiful and unique fabrics, which can add stimulating colour and texture to the environment.

Of course I could not write this book without help. Once again my husband, Edward, has done the photographic work required, as well as many of the computer-assisted drawings. It says much for our marriage that we can work so closely on a project such as this, and still remain good friends. Lloyd Park took most of the fashion colour photographs.

I also have to thank Birgitte Krogh, Denmark, for her help with the inkle loom section, and Jane McKenzie for her proof-weaving in Section Five. Colin Meynell gave me much help with his computer programme, 'Weave Designer'.

Many of my students and weaving friends have helped me in weaving the projects for Section Three. Again my evening class and study group at Papanui High School have come to my aid, and I am very grateful to them for this help. In particular Ann Clay, Helene Gourlay, Mary Hastie, Lynda Russell, Ngaio Donnell, Marian Gilbert and Jane McKenzie not only did much of the weaving but advised and supported me while this book was being written. Ria Van Lith and Fran Regan (from Australia), both expert weavers, contributed projects Seven and Ten.

Anne Field

SECTION ONE
THE LOOMS

The Ashford inkle loom

The Ashford rigid heddle loom

The Ashford four-shaft table loom

The Ashford four-shaft jack loom

The Ashford eight-shaft table loom

The Ashford eight-shaft jack loom

1. THE INKLE LOOM

AN INKLE LOOM is a small, portable loom used mainly for making narrow, warp-face braids. The warp is the length-wise threads on a loom, and a warp-face fabric is one that has more warp than weft, (the width-wise threads). Only the warp shows on the weave surface. Because the warp dominates, the braids are very strong and can be used as belts, ties, guitar straps, and as trims and edgings on handwoven garments.

I should like to acknowledge the work of Birgitte Krogh, Denmark, an expert inkle loom weaver, in the following instructions.

CONSTRUCTION

Although very simple in construction, the inkle loom has all the features of other looms, that is: a frame to carry the warp ends, a mechanism for lifting the warp threads, and a tension adjustment.

Frame
The frame consists of a rigid timber base, with strong pegs inserted at intervals. The warp is wound around these pegs, in a similar manner to the way threads are wound on to a warping board.

Shed
The shed is the gap in the warp through which the weft threads are placed. This shed is obtained by the use of 'leashes'. The leashes are

1:1 The Ashford Inkle Loom

A   Shuttle
B   Leashes
Peg 3   Tensioner

the loops which pull down alternate warp threads and lock them in place, allowing the rest of the threads to be pushed down or lifted up. The leashes are made from strong, smooth string, and need to be made only once as they last a long time. They remain on peg S while weaving.

A leash is the right length when it pulls the thread going through it down to the same level as the 'open' threads, when pointing out from peg S. A thread not going through a leash is called an 'open ' thread.

Fig. 1:A Correct length of a leash, and two incorrect lengths.

There are three different ways of making the leashes. The easiest way is to make the leashes before you warp the loom as follows. (The other two methods will be described at the end of this section.) As you warp the loom, these leashes are attached to the 'closed' warp threads.

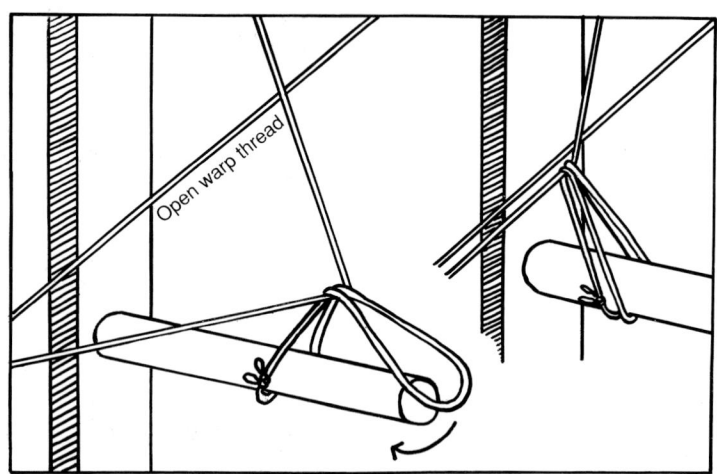

Fig. 1:B Leash

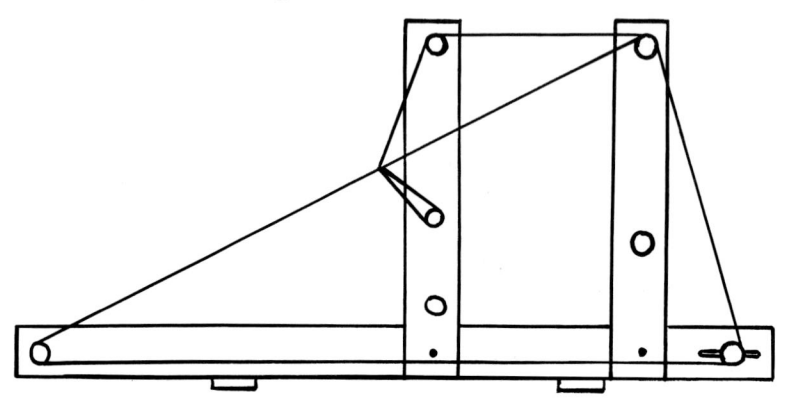

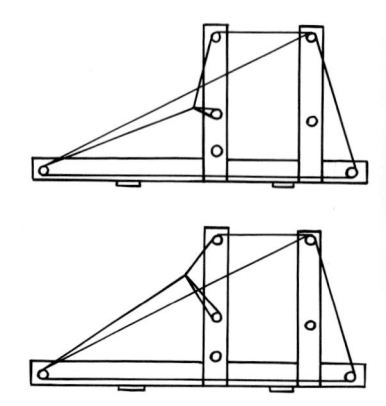

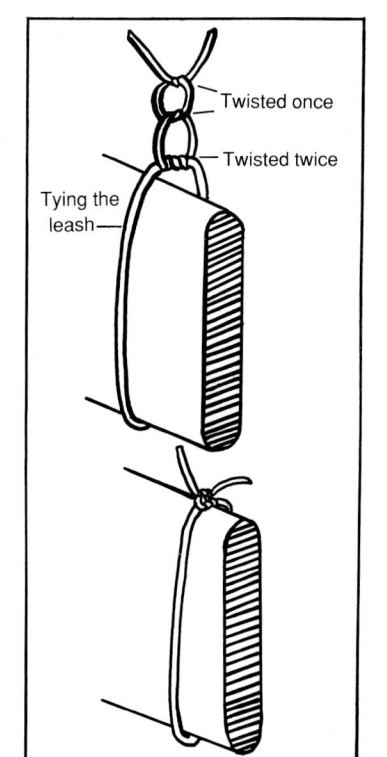

Fig 1: C Tying the leash

Cut several pieces of string 41cm (16in) long. Tie a piece of string around the pegs (or a piece of wood), so the loop it makes is 18cm (7in). Let these leashes hang from peg S as you do the actual warping. Making leashes this way means you do not have to wind the warp into little balls or butterflies first.

14 • THE ASHFORD BOOK OF WEAVING

WARPING

Place the tensioner almost as far back from the other pegs as possible, and keep the threads tight as you warp.

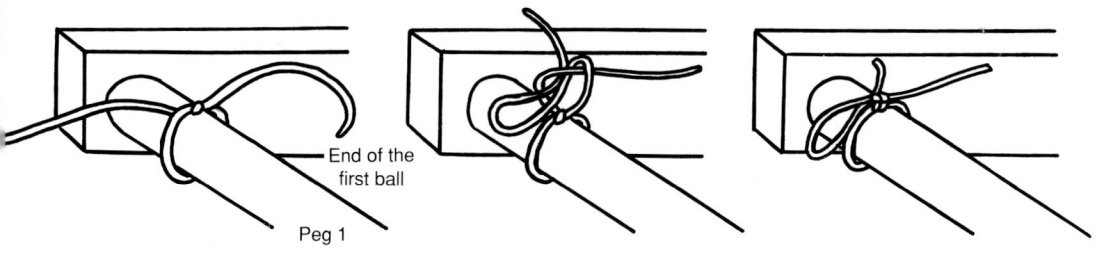

End of the first ball

Peg 1

Tie the end of the first ball (in the colour you want on the edges), to peg 1, so it can easily be undone again. Take the thread directly to peg 2, around peg 3, and back to peg 1. This is the open warp thread. **Without cutting the thread or tying a knot**, take it over peg X and around pegs 2 and 3, the same as the first thread. This is the closed warp thread. Put the leash over this thread, as in **Fig. 1:B**.

Fig. 1:D Beginning the warp

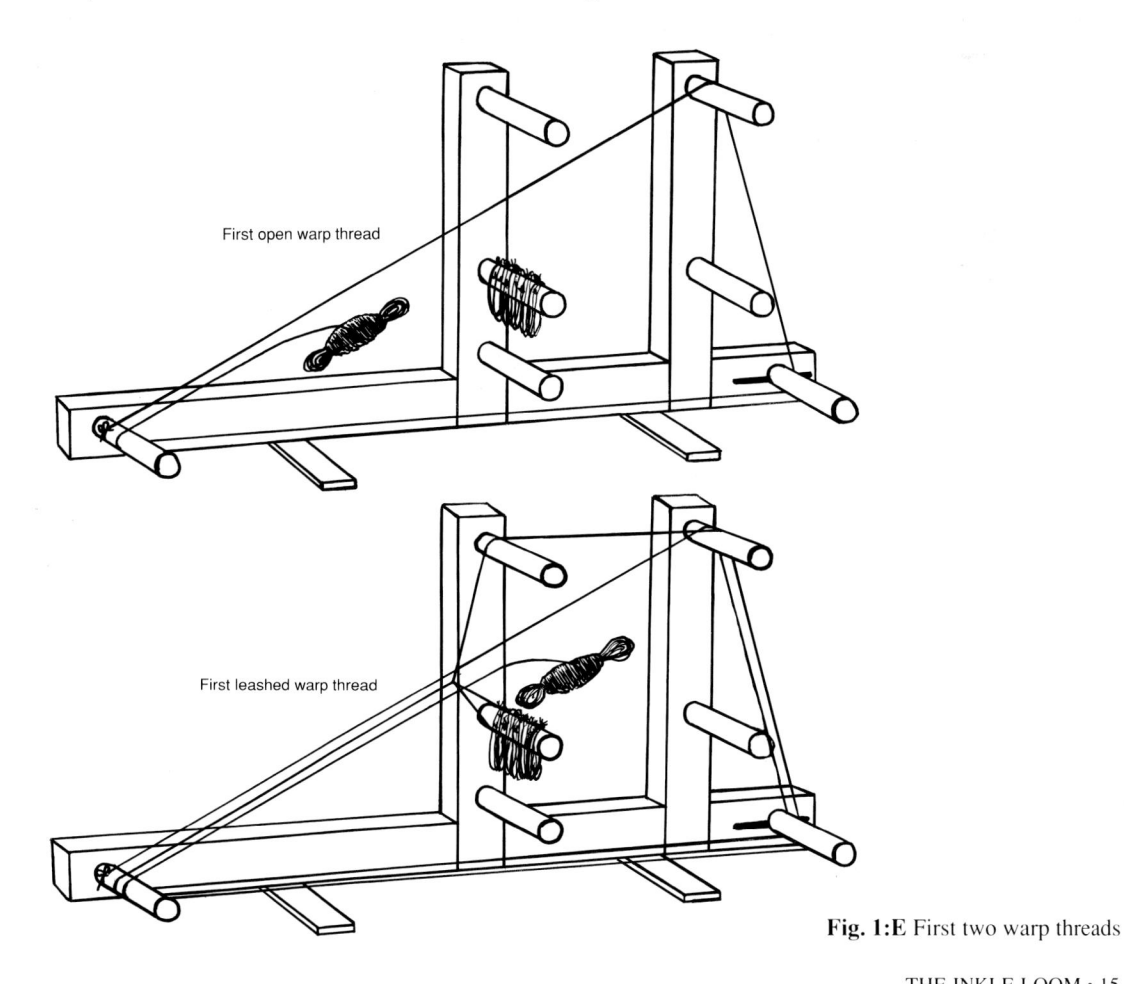

First open warp thread

First leashed warp thread

Fig. 1:E First two warp threads

THE INKLE LOOM • 15

For a longer warp, as in **1:1**, threads may be wound from peg 2 to 5, around 4, then back to 3, and tied at 1.

There is now one open and one leashed warp thread on the loom. Repeat these two threads, with every other thread through a leash, until the warp is as wide as you want it to be. As it is warp-face weaving, the finished braid will only be about half as wide as all the warp threads lying close together on the pegs.

When you change colour, tie the end of the previous colour to the end of the new colour, at peg 1. Do not tie anything onto the loom, and do not undo the first thread yet.

It does not matter whether the last thread is a leashed or an open thread. When the warp is wide enough, undo the end tied to peg 1 and tie it, together with your last thread, at peg 1. It is best if these two are the same colour. The first and/or the last warp thread will always cross some of the other threads, but this makes no difference to the weaving as the threads are in the correct order at the leashes. If you have problems keeping the warp tension even, cut and tie each end at peg 1.

WEAVING

Wind the weft thread on the shuttle. Unless you want a special dot effect, make the weft the same colour as the warp edge threads.

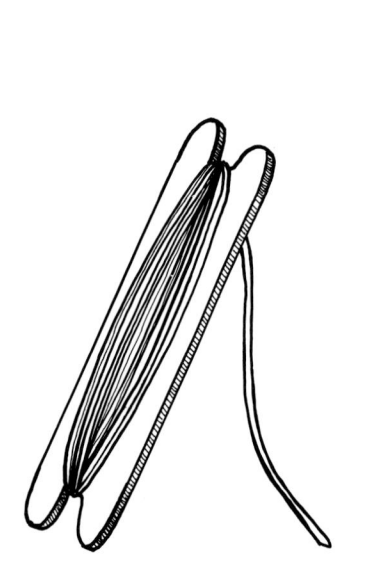

Fig. 1:F Shuttle

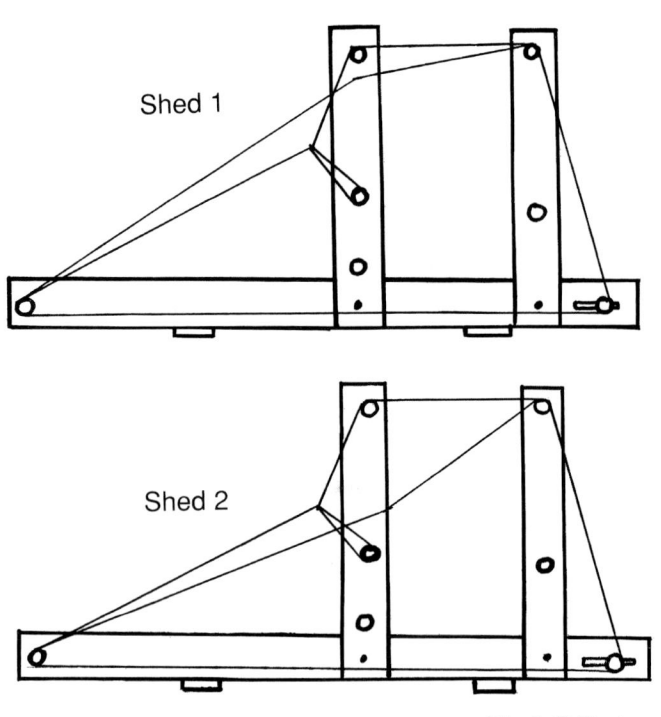

Fig. 1:G Sheds

The shed is the space between the two halves of the warp, in which you place the weft thread. The shed is made by lifting up, or pushing down, all the open warp threads at the same time.

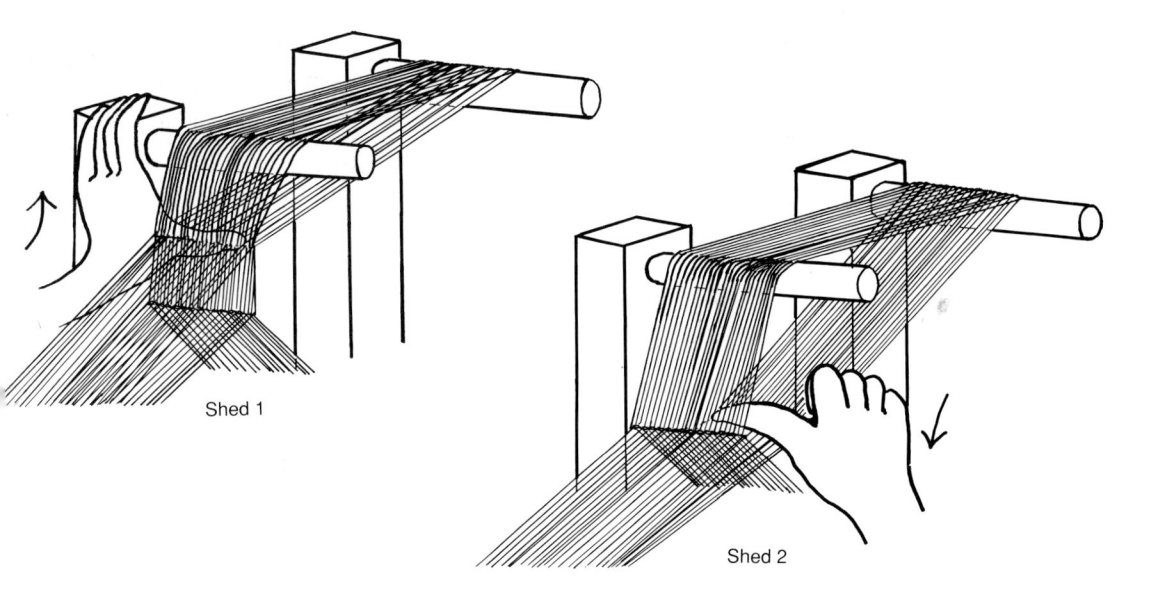

Fig. 1:H Making a shed

Make it a habit to always lift up with the same hand, and push down with the other hand, to prevent undoing the last weft pick (row). When you have the shuttle in your right hand, it is a good idea to make shed 1 with the left hand, lifting the threads with the thumb, and resting the other fingers on top of peg B. This prevents you from lifting the whole loom. When the shuttle is on the left side of the loom, push down the threads with your right thumb or fingers.

Make shed 1, and put the shuttle in the shed from the right to the left. While the shuttle is still in the shed, pull it down towards you until it is close to the knots. Pull the shuttle out of the shed with the left hand, leaving about 10cm (4in) of the weft thread hanging out of the right selvedge.

Make shed 2, and put the shuttle in from the left, with your left hand. Pull the shuttle again until it is as close as possible to the first weft. Then pull the shuttle and weft with your right hand, closing up the warp threads until the weft cannot be seen.

Make shed 1 again, put the shuttle in the shed, and pull it hard down towards yourself. From now on it should be possible to pull it hard without moving the previous weft threads. Repeat this left–right weaving.

Keeping the edges straight

The first 2–3cm (1in) usually looks uneven because the tension is not right, and you may have some crossed threads. This part can be unravelled when the finished braid is cut off the loom.

By following these simple rules, it is possible to keep the edges straight from now on.

1. Keep the warp very tight. A high tension makes the braid and edges look better when finished.
2. Try to keep the same tension on the weft as well. Make it tight enough that the warp threads will slip on top of one another.
3. Every time you pull the shuttle out of the shed, and before you tighten the weft, pull the previous weft thread again. This will even out the little loop that occurs between the two outer warp threads, and is essential when it comes to making even edges.

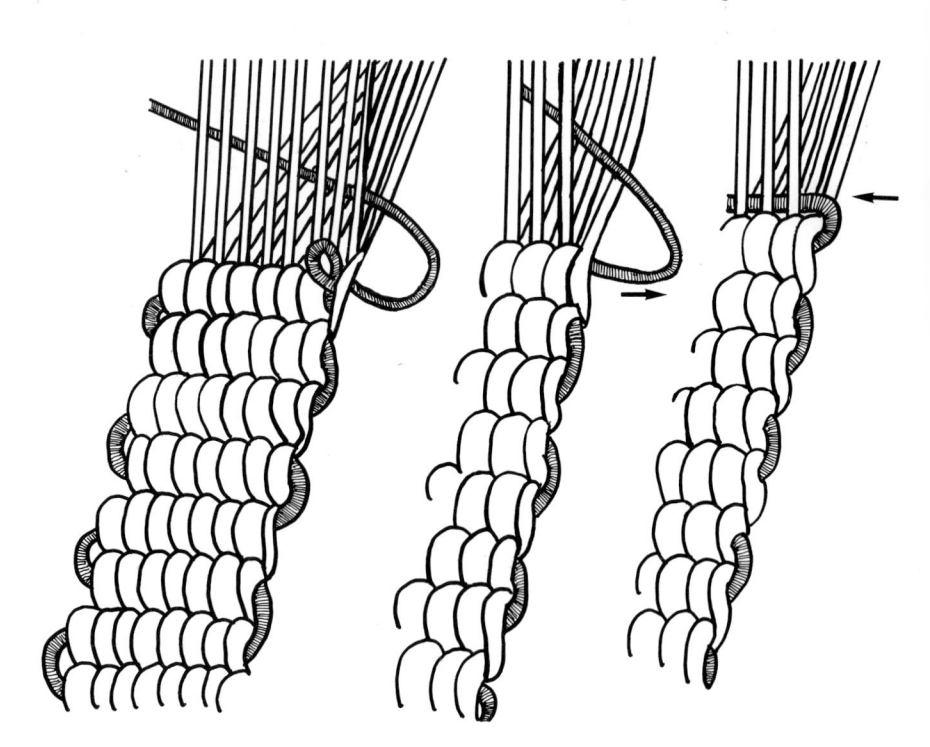

Fig. 1:1 Pulling on the weft

Moving the warp

Continue weaving until there is very little room between the last weft pick and the leashes. Then move the woven braid by loosening the tensioner, pulling the warp towards you until the end of the woven piece is about 5cm (2in) from peg 1, and tighten the tensioner again. Hold a finger in shed 2 while pulling the warp, and push the leashes back to their correct position.

FINISHING

When you cannot move the warp any further, cannot weave any longer, and the knots in the warp are close to the leashes, simply cut the whole piece off the loom. Cut each half of the warp a few centimetres (inches) behind the leashes, without cutting the leashes themselves. Pull the threads out of the leashes, leaving nothing tied to the loom.

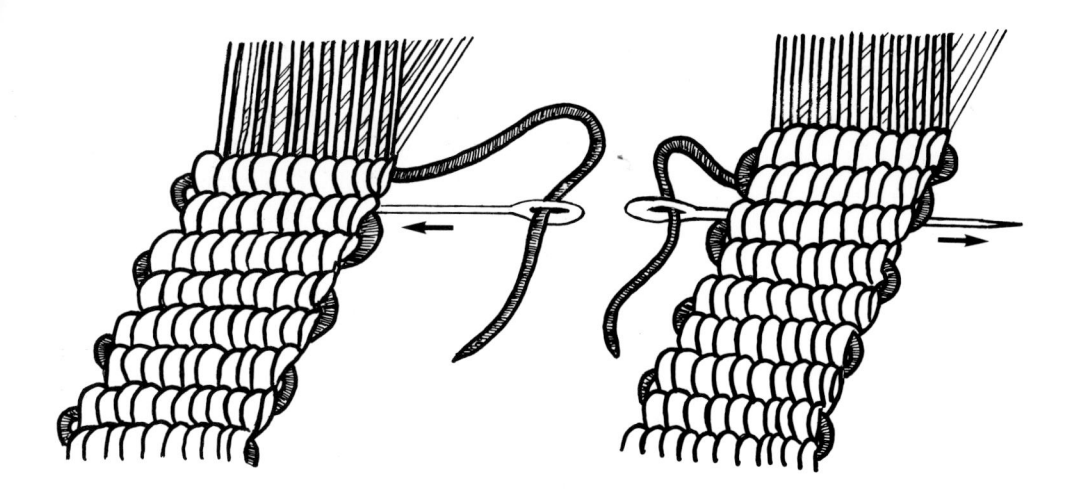

Sew the weft back three or four sheds to prevent the warp threads from coming undone.

Another method of finishing can be done on the loom. On the second to last pick put an unthreaded needle with a large eye into the shed. Change to the next shed, weave the last pick, then break the weft on the shuttle, leaving about 15cm (6in) to thread through the needle eye. Pull the needle and thread through to the opposite side and trim the weft ends.

Do not trim the warp ends very close to the braid. Let them hang loose as a fringe, or plait, twist, or tie them. They can also be glued, or cut close to the braid so you can fold over the end, or tie them around a piece of wood or a bell for a wall hanging. The possibilities are endless.

Fig. 1:J Sewing in the weft

OTHER METHODS OF TYING LEASHES

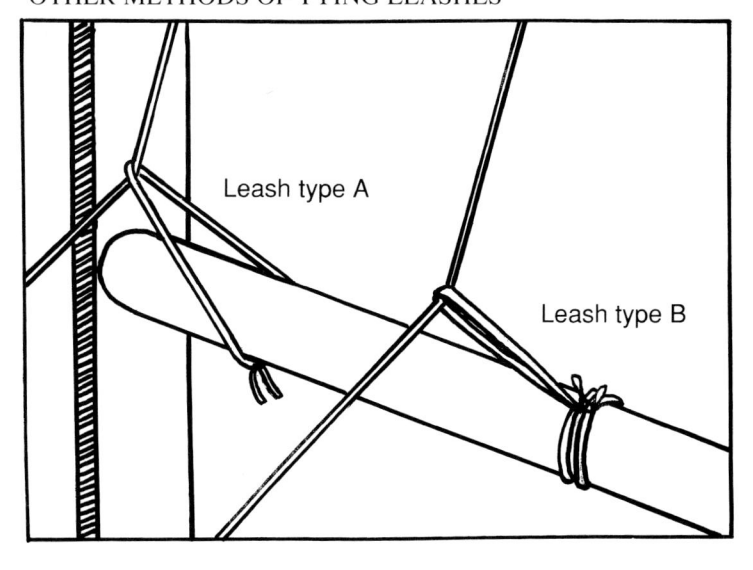

Fig. 1:K Tying leash types A and B

THE INKLE LOOM • 19

Leash A. Cut a piece of string into 30cm (12in) lengths. Tie a length around pegs 4 and S, using these pegs as a measuring guide. Remove the string from peg 4 and let the leash hang loose on peg S until required.

Leash B requires a longer piece of string. Wrap it around a book, a piece of wood, or pegs, to find the right length. Put the leash on peg S with a snitch knot, and check that it is the correct length by putting an open warp thread on the loom and another through the leash.

Both A and B are stationary leashes, which means that once you have finished the warping, you are ready to weave, but the warp yarn has to be wound into little balls or butterflies to pass through each leash.

PATTERNS

Apart from the patterns you can get in different warp colours, there are many pick-up and pick-down patterns, patterns using different colours and thicknesses of warp and weft, and so on. Learn new ideas by talking with other weavers, reading books, and experimenting yourself. There will always be something new.

USES

The inkle loom can make articles other than belts. You can make wall hangings, bookmarks, curtain ties, shoelaces, edgings for clothes, shoulder straps, watch straps, headbands, straps for guitars and cameras, halter straps and animal leashes. You can sew the bands together and make bags, purses, cushion covers, clothes, room dividers, tea cosies, bigger wall hangings, place mats, pot plant hangers and moccasins – you are only limited by your imagination!

In Chapter Ten, Project Eleven will show you how to make a pair of child's braces on the Ashford inkle loom.

2. THE RIGID HEDDLE LOOM

THE FIRST WEAVING CLASS I ever taught used rigid heddle looms, as these were the only inexpensive looms available at that time. In every rigid heddle class of mine since then, at about the third lesson, a rush of excitement hits the students as they realise that they are weaving something that is not only practical, but is original and creative as well. This feeling oftens happens in classes, but it happens earlier with rigid heddle weavers because the results are almost instant. Anyone, no matter how unco-ordinated, can learn to thread and weave on these looms in a short time. The light weight and small size of a rigid heddle loom makes it portable, and its low cost makes it accessible to most people.

Many people use the rigid heddle loom as a stepping stone, later graduating to larger looms and more complicated weaving, but others are quite content to weave on their rigid heddle looms for years. It is not the size or cost of a loom that makes a good weaver, but what you do, using your mind and your hands, that counts. Some beautiful weaving has been done using the most primitive equipment; museums displaying some of the very first pieces of weaving testify to this.

2:1 The Ashford rigid heddle loom
A. Rigid heddle
B. Front roller
C. Back roller
D. Upright for holding heddle: closed position
E. Upright for holding heddle: upper position
F. Upright for holding heddle: lower position
G. Ratchets and pawls

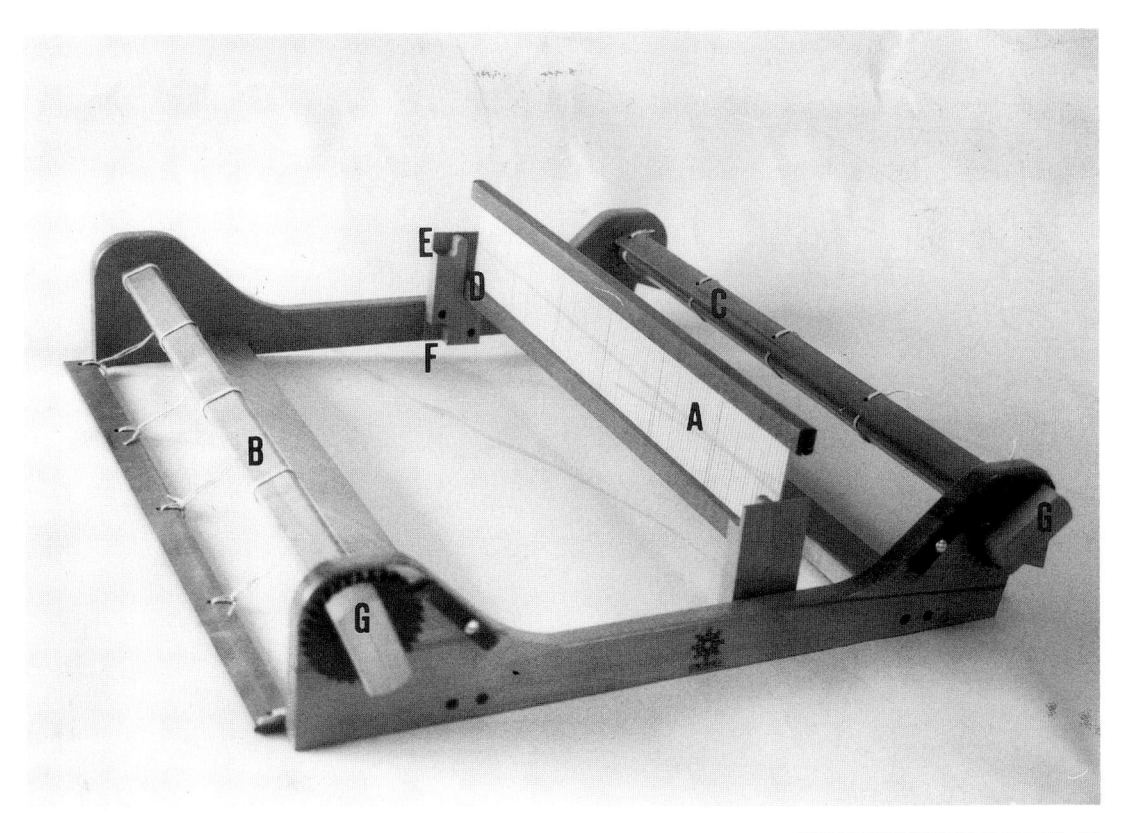

CONSTRUCTION

Rigid heddle looms are quick to thread compared to other looms, but the weaving may be slower. With practice the loom can be threaded and ready to weave in an hour. This does make it attractive to beginners who want to start the actual weaving as quickly as possible. A four-shaft loom will take longer to thread, but is quicker when weaving.

The name 'rigid heddle' is an accurate description of these looms, but it can cause some confusion to beginners. One of my students called her loom a 'higid reddle' the first night of a class, and she was never allowed to forget her mistake. A heddle is the metal, plastic or cord holder of the warp threads, the length-wise threads, on the loom. When weaving, some of the warp threads are lifted by the heddles to form a gap, the shed, through which the cross-wise threads, the weft, are placed. A rigid heddle loom is so named because the heddle (A in **2:1**), is a rigid piece of plastic with alternate holes and slots. When the rigid heddle is lifted, all the threads in the holes rise to form the upper layer of the shed, and the threads in the slots remain where they are to become the lower layer. When the heddle is lowered, all the threads in the holes form the lower layer of the shed, and the threads in the slots remain where they are to become the upper layer.

The heddle shown on the loom in **2:1** is blue and has 40 holes and slots to 10cm. This is shortened to 40/10, and in imperial measurements is 10 to the inch. If you place one warp thread in each hole and slot, there will be 4 threads per cm (10 threads per in). This is probably the most common heddle, but there are others at 20/10 (grey), which has 5 per inch, or 34/10 (white), which has 8 per inch, as shown in **2:2**.

The heddle also governs the width of your weaving. A loom with a 610mm (24in) width heddle will weave a finished piece of weaving

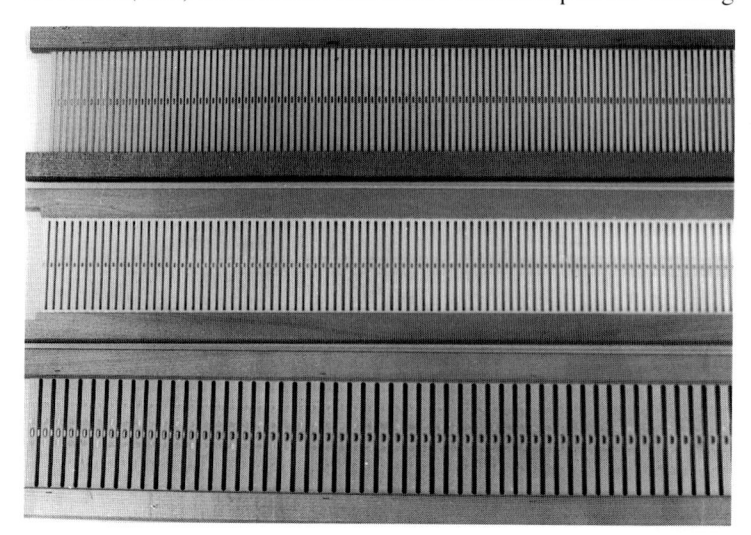

2:2 Heddles

almost that width. Again, this is probably the most common width, but there are looms that are wider (810mm), or narrower (410mm). When buying a loom consider the width carefully. A narrow loom is easy to carry and store, but will weave only scarves and tablemats, not cushions or larger articles without additional seams.

A rigid heddle loom consists of a strong frame which supports the heddle, and also holds the warp, the lengthwise threads. The frame is strong to withstand the pressure of the warp threads wound on at tension. The Ashford rigid heddle loom has a roller/beam combined at each end of the loom. These rollers are of strong timber to prevent bowing. If the rollers do bow, the warp tension is affected, making the outside threads tighter than the central threads. A ratchet and pawl system (G in **2:1**), at one end of both the back and front rollers, extends the warp up to 5 m (16 ft) in length. The unwoven warp is wound onto the back roller, and moves forward onto the front roller as it is woven.

The space between the front roller (which holds the weaving), and the base of the rigid heddle loom is restricted, because of the small size of these looms, and this limits the warp length. If a warp longer than 5m (16 feet) is wound on, particularly with coarse weaving, the front roller will not be able to hold all the finished cloth. On four-shaft looms, which have more space, longer warps can be wound, but 4–5m (13–16 feet) seems to be the maximum warp length for this rigid heddle loom.

When I took my first class in rigid heddle weaving many years ago, I taught the students to thread the looms using the same warping board method I had used for four-shaft looms. After just a few weeks I decided there must be an easier way to thread these simpler looms, and adapted the warping method described in the following pages. It is quick and easy, uses the minimum of equipment, and is suited to short warp lengths.

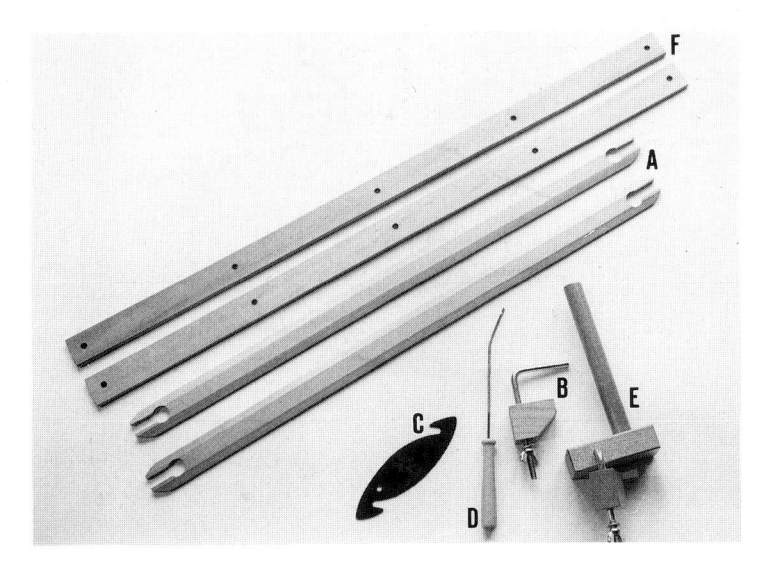

2:3 Other equipment

A. Shuttles
B. Clamp
C. Reed hook
D. Threading hook
E. Warping peg
F. Warp sticks

THE RIGID HEDDLE LOOM • 23

When weaving, you will need shuttles to carry the weft thread, the width-wise threads. Stick shuttles are the most common type of shuttle used with rigid heddle looms. These are straight pieces of wood, with hollowed-out ends.

Included with your loom will be two shuttles and two clamps, one to clamp the loom to the table, and the other for the warping peg. A reed hook and a heddle hook, a warping peg, two warp sticks, string and a booklet on how to thread the loom will be included in the loom package. You will also need scissors, measuring tape, darning needle and pins, notebook and yarns. Chapter Six, on yarns, covers the properties, uses and finishes of most yarns that can be used in weaving.

THE WARP

Before any weaving can be done, the loom must be threaded. This means putting the warp threads on the loom, and you will have to decide what type of yarn to use for the warp and later the weft. The warp yarn will take most of the strain while you are weaving and therefore will need to be reasonably strong. A plied yarn, in which two or more strands of yarn are twisted together, is always stronger than an unplied yarn. One warp thread is called an 'end'.

You will also have to decide how many warp ends to thread to the centimetre (inch). The Ashford rigid heddle looms are sold with a heddle measuring 40 ends per 10cm (10 ends per inch). As this term 'ends per cm (in)' is used frequently in weaving, it is shortened to 'e.p.cm. (e.p.i.)' for convenience. The number of ends to the centimetre (inch), called the 'sett', is determined by the weave construction you want in your finished article, not by the sett of your heddle.

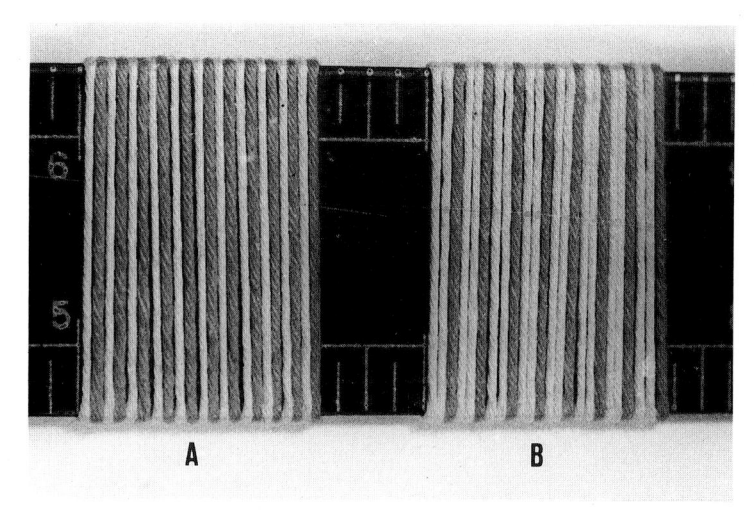

2:4 Sett

A. Balanced weave
B. Weft-face weave
Dark yarn = warp
Light yarn = weft

There are two main types of weave construction that can be woven with ease on a rigid heddle loom: balanced weave and weft-face weave.

Balanced weave

This weave construction has an equal number of warp ends and weft rows to the cm (in). It is a strong, flexible weave. To find the sett for a balanced weave, wind the warp and weft yarn around a ruler for 2.5cm (1 in). Count the number of times the warp yarn goes around the ruler, and this is the correct sett for this type of weave. This ruler method approximates the position of the threads as they would lie on the loom. On the loom, the actual weft threads would cross the warp at right angles, but the ruler method is an accurate way to calculate sett for any thickness of yarn. Do not stretch the yarn as you wind, and lie the threads so they touch one another.

Weft-face weave

This weave construction has more weft than warp, and only the weft yarn shows on the cloth surface. It is a strong, firm weave. To determine the sett for a weft-face weave, wind two of the weft threads and one of the warp ends around 2.5cm (1 in), and count the number of warp turns. This weave has less warp yarn than a balanced weave sett.

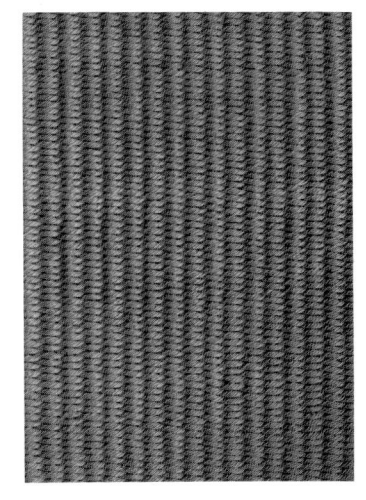

2:5 Balanced weave structure

As this is probably going to be your first piece of weaving on a rigid heddle loom, we will begin with the easiest weave construction, balanced weave. I will take you through the complete sequence, describing how to put on your first warp. This warp will be a sampler, on which you will learn how to use the loom, and how to do some simple weaving techniques. At the end of the sampler, there will be some spare warp to make a small article such as a runner or placemat.

Choose a strong, smooth warp, such as cotton or a firmly plied wool. Calculate the sett by the ruler method as described above. Check the heddle size on your loom. If you are not sure how many holes and slots there are to the cm (in), measure across the holes and slots for 2.5cm (1 in), and count the number. If your heddle is blue in colour and has 10 holes and slots to 2.5cm (10 to the inch), and your yarn sett is 9, 10 or 11 to 2.5cm (1in), then you are in luck. One warp end will go in each slot and hole. If your yarn sett is more or less than the number of holes and slots, something will have to give. Maybe you can change to another heddle, if you have more than one with the loom, or you may be able to thread the holes and slots in a different order. For example, if you have a sett of 5 ends per 2.5cm (1in), and your heddle has 10 holes and slots to 2.5cm (1in), put one warp end in every second hole and slot.

2:6 Weft-face weave structure

It is practical to buy an extra heddle with your loom if they are available. If your loom is supplied with a 10 per 2.5cm (1in) heddle, a 5 or 8 heddle would give a wide variety of setts. A heddle with larger holes enables you to use thicker warp yarns. Check that your warp yarn will run smoothly through the slots and holes. It is better to test this now rather than thread the loom completely, and then find the yarn is too thick and has to be cut off.

MEASURING THE WARP

Now you have chosen the warp yarn and a suitable sett, the next step is to measure the warp width and length. Where the conversion from cm–in does not need to be accurate, I will round off the figures.

Width

Put a permanent mark in the centre of the heddle. Calculate the width of the article you want to weave, adding an extra 2.5cm(1in) for draw-in. This is the amount the article will draw in while you are weaving, and it also allows for some shrinkage in washing. Therefore, if you want to weave a runner 30cm (12in) wide, measure 33cm (13in); that is 17cm (6.5in) each side of the centre mark. You can tie two pieces of wool around the heddle, as in **Fig. 2:A**, to mark the start and finish points. If you do not centre the warp correctly it is difficult to beat evenly.

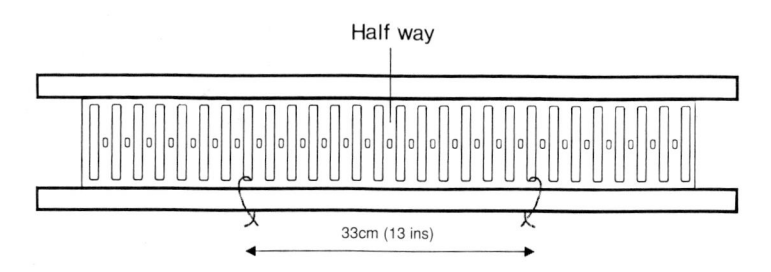

Fig. 2:A Measuring the heddle

Length

To calculate the correct warp length, add the length of the articles to be woven, the fringe allowance, and the wastage, shrinkage, and take-up. The wastage is the amount of warp lost when both ends of the warp are tied to the front and back rollers and is usually calculated at 60cm (24in). The warp is stretched at tension when it is on the loom and will contract when it is cut off. This take-up and the shrinkage during washing is added on as a 10% allowance when calculating the warp length. Wool has a greater take-up and shrinkage than other yarns, and a 15–25% allowance may be necessary. This take-up and shrinkage allowance is calculated on the woven length, and does not include the wastage.

Sample for first project

Length of finished sampler:	91cm (36in)
warp take-up:	18cm (7in) for both articles.
fringe allowance:	10cm (4in)
runner (including fringe):	61cm (24in)
wastage:	61cm (24in)
Total length of warp:	241cm (95in)

This project of a sampler and a runner would require a warp 241cm (95in) long, and 33cm (13in) wide. Jot down these measurements in a notebook, for future reference. Full details, describing how to weave this first warp, appear on page 44. After you have woven a few projects from the last section in this book, you will be able to do your own calculations with ease.

WARPING THE LOOM

The first time you warp the loom you will feel clumsy and uncoordinated, but it does not take long to become quick and dexterous at this task.

2:7 Place the loom on a table, with the heddle in the closed position, and clamp the front support rail of the loom to the table edge. Cut the string supplied with the loom into 61cm (24in) lengths. Double one of the lengths, then, using the threading hook, bring the loop through the hole in the roller at one end. Slip the free end through the loop and pull tight. Attach a warp stick to this cord, at one end only, using a shoelace bow. On another table, placed opposite the front of the loom, clamp the warping peg, lining it up with the centre of the heddle. The distance from the peg to the back stick is 241cm (95in), which is the warp length for this, your first project.

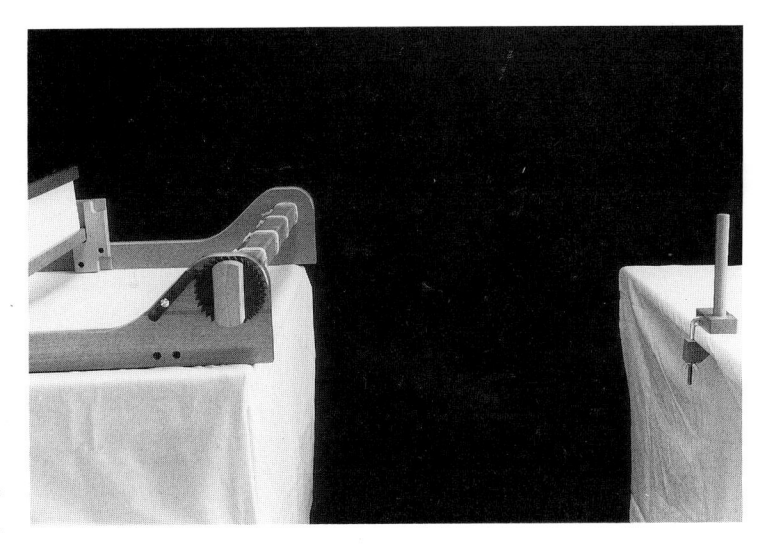

2:8 Place the cone or ball of the warping yarn on the floor at the back of the table holding the peg. If you are using balls of thread, place them in a box to stop them from rolling all over the floor. Bring the yarn over the back of the table and tie it to the warping peg.

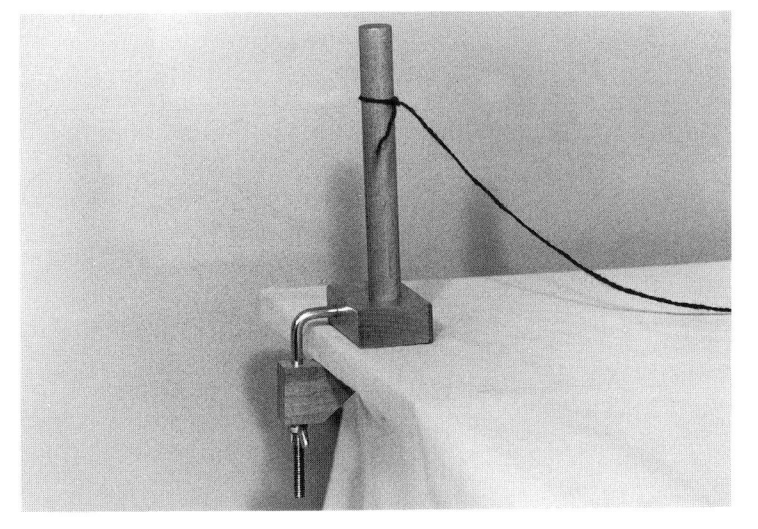

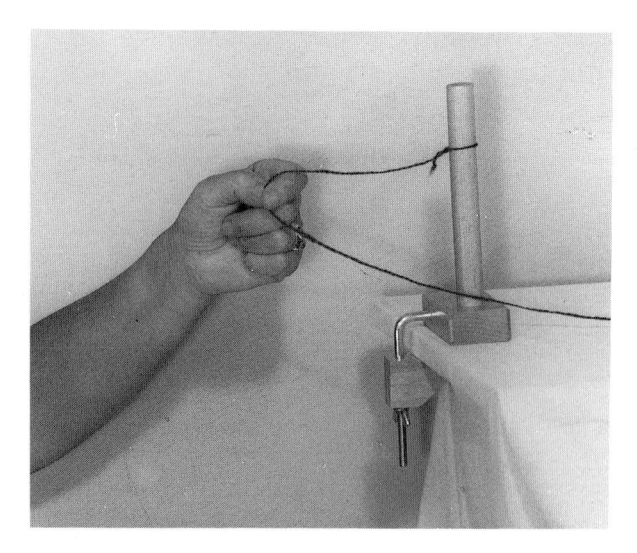

2:9 Take the doubled loop formed by lifting the yarn between the tie (on the peg), and the cone or ball, and take it along the table to the loom, letting it run smoothly over your fingers.

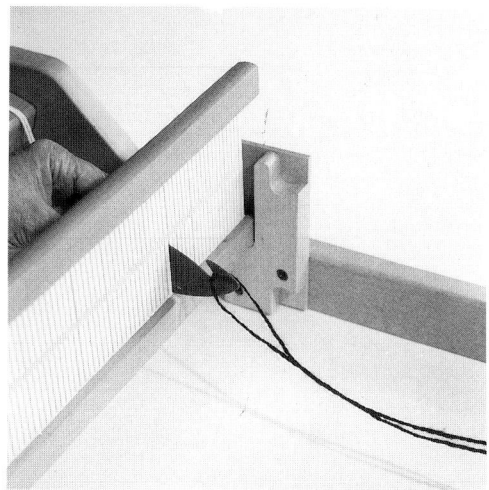

2:10 Put the loop through the slot in the heddle you have designated as the beginning of the warp, using the reed hook as shown. Start at the side where the stick is attached to the back roller.

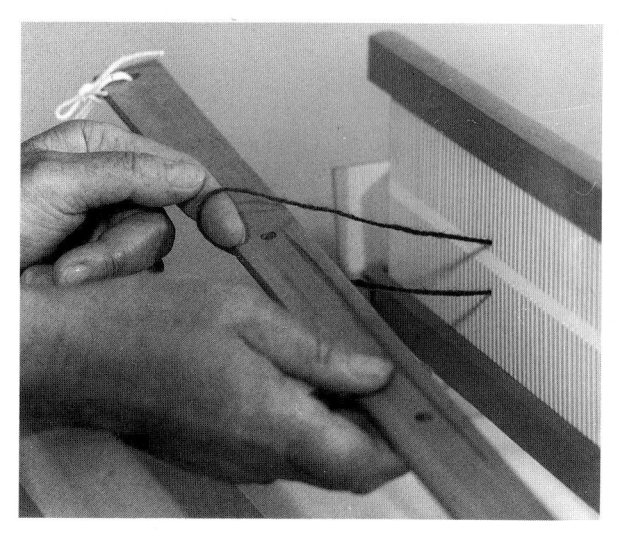

2:11 Pull the loop through the slot and slide it over the free end of the back stick and along the stick until it is lined up with the slot.

2:12 If you are working on your own, tie a string loop, and slip the stick into this loop to hold the stick in position while warping. If you have help, the loop can be slipped onto the stick by your assistant. To ensure all the warp ends are the same length, make sure the stick is parallel with the back roller.

For your first projects it is better to thread the outside two threads through one slot to form a selvedge. This will show as a doubled end on each side of the finished weaving. Later, when your weaving is more confident and your selvedges are better, this doubled end can be discontinued.

Take the required number of loops from the peg to the loom, threading each loop through the slot until the correct width is reached. Threading the warp through the holes is done at a later stage. If you find a knot or need to join the yarn, make sure the knot is either at the peg or the loom end of the warp. If it is left in the middle of the warp, the knot will not pass easily through the slots or holes, and will show in the finished weaving. At this stage, the warp ends will be slightly uneven in length, but this will be corrected when the warp is wound on.

2:13 Thread loom to required width.

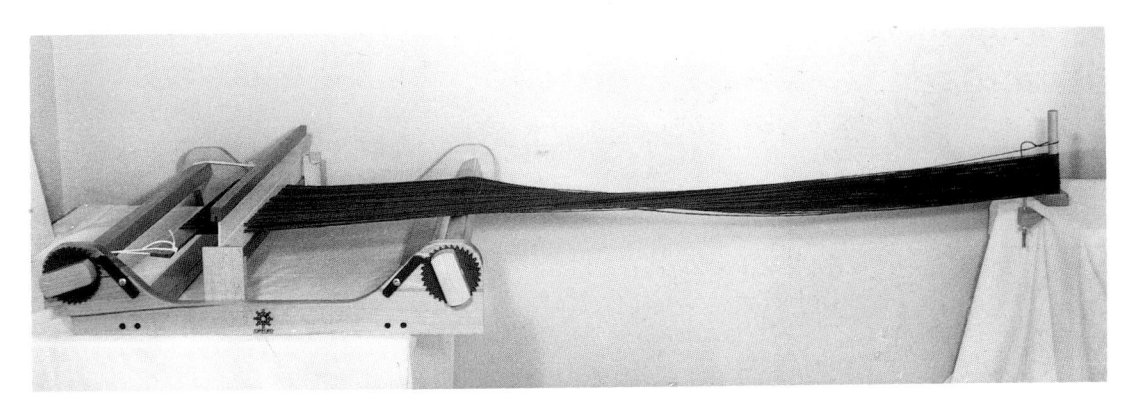

2:14 When you have threaded the required width, finishing with the doubled selvedge ends again, take the last thread to the peg and tie it on. Spread the warp evenly along the back stick and then tie the stick to the back roller at the other end, and in the centre to prevent bowing. This stick should be parallel with the back roller, and attached to the roller in the same manner as the first tie, but using reef knots and the 60cm (24in) lengths of string.

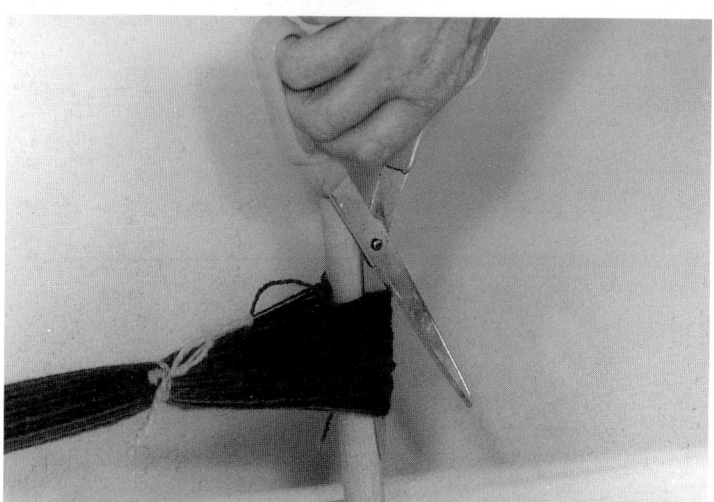

Fig. 2:B Reef knot

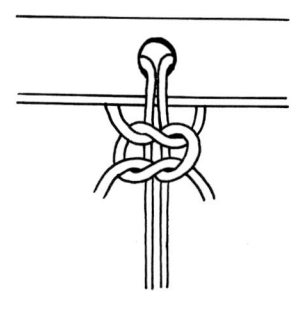

2:15 Return to the peg end of your warp, and tie the warp a few cms (in) from the peg. Cut through the warp at the peg.

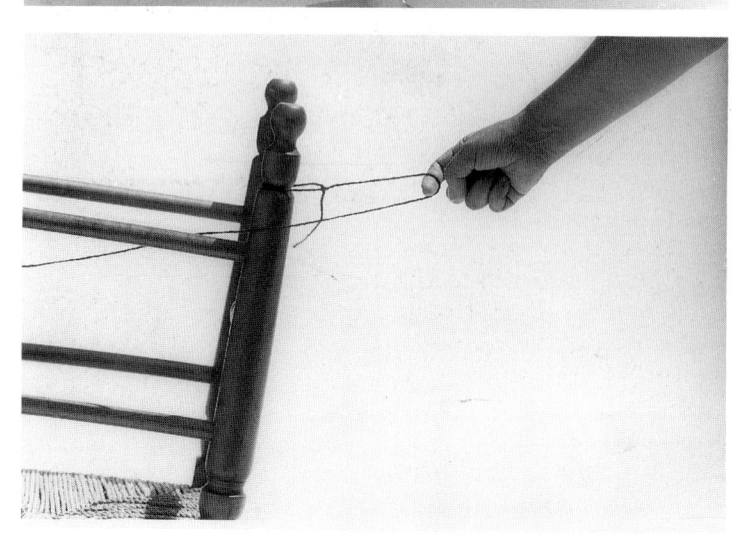

2:16 If you do not have a warping peg, a chair can be placed upside-down in the correct position, with one front leg used as a warping peg.

Winding on the warp

This is easier to do with two people, particularly the first time. One person holds the warp at the front of the loom, and the other turns the ratchet that winds the warp onto the back roller.

2:17 The person at the front of the loom grasps the warp firmly, making sure it is centred correctly and not pulling to one side. He/she must ensure that each end goes through the slots in the heddle at the same tension, with no knots or tangles impeding the progress. It is usually necessary to comb the warp lightly with the fingers to remove tangles, although a good shake can undo most snags.

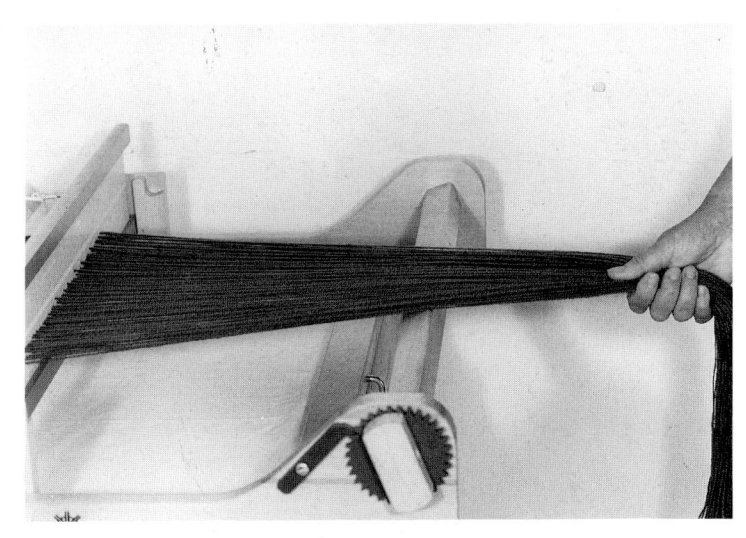

2:18 The person at the back of the loom turns the ratchet to wind the warp onto the back roller. The ratchet is self-locking; that is the warp will not unroll when the tension is released. Check that you are rolling on the correct way. When you stop winding, the ratchet will self lock, with the pawl holding it firmly. Do not wind the warp on unless it is being held at tension by the person at the front of the loom. Turn the ratchet until one complete layer of warp is around the back roller.

Place a sheet of brown paper across these first warp threads on the roller to prevent the next layer from sinking into the previous one and making the warp tension uneven. Do not use newspaper, as the print can come off, and it is too soft. Make sure the selvedge ends do not slip off the edge of the paper. If they do, the tension on the selvedge ends will become so loose that it is impossible to weave on this warp, and it will have to be rewound.

Winding on the warp is a most important part of weaving. If the warp is wound incorrectly, mistakes will occur on the loose threads when you begin to weave. Wind on slowly and carefully.

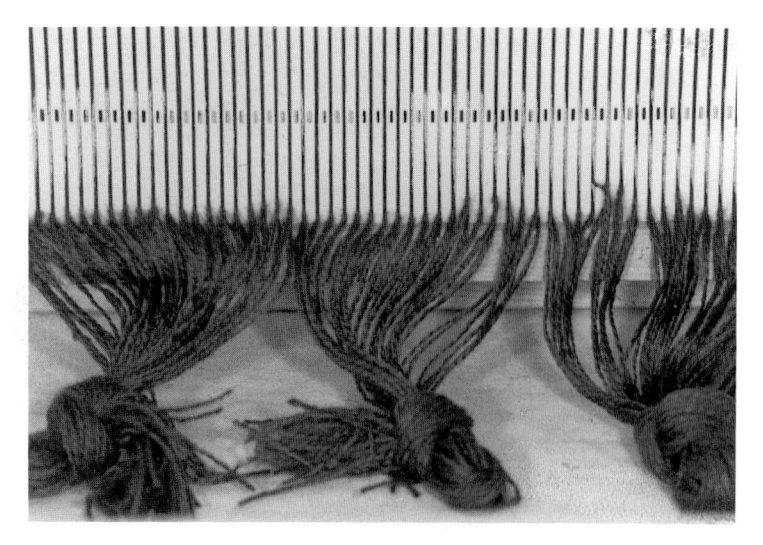

2:19 When the end of the warp is about 30cm (12in) from the front of the heddle, stop winding, cut the holding tie, and tie a slip knot (**Fig. 2:C**) in the remaining warp to prevent it from slipping through the heddle.

Fig. 2:C Slip knot

Threading

The next step is to place one thread from each slot into the adjacent hole in the heddle. Undo the slip knot. It is a good habit to begin at the right-hand side when threading, as most pattern drafts are read from the right.

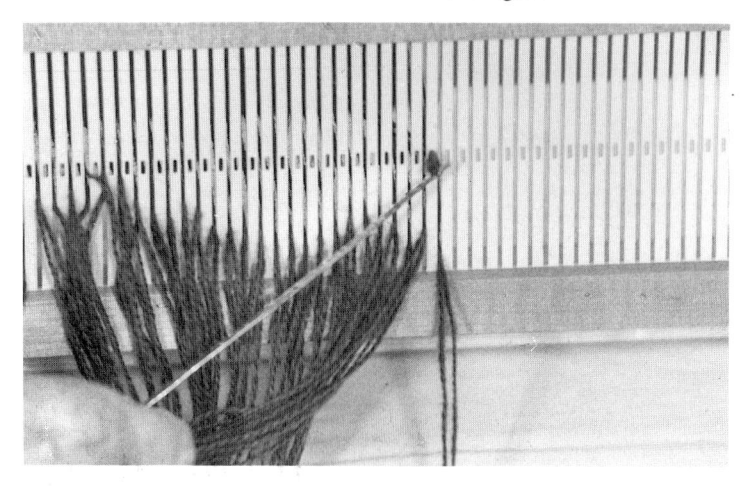

2:20 Hold the two warp ends from the first slot in one hand in front of the heddle, then reach behind the heddle and gently pull out one end (or two for the doubled selvedge ends) from the slot. Put this end through the hole to the left of the slot it came from. It does not matter which of the ends you pick out of the slot. Use the threading hook supplied with the loom. Good lighting will help at this stage, as threading can be a strain on the eyes.

Continue across the loom according to the sett you chose earlier. You may be threading every hole, or every second or third hole. Because one end, in the slot, is in the correct place already, only the hole has to be threaded, and this does not take long. Check every 5–8cm (2–3in) to make sure you are threading correctly. Tie these checked ends with a slip knot to indicate this, and to ensure that the warp will not slip back through the heddle.

If you have made a mistake, do not take handfuls of warp out of the heddle slots and holes to start again, as you will lose the sequence in which they were wound on. Take one thread out at a time and put it in the correct place.

32 • THE ASHFORD BOOK OF WEAVING

Tying warp ends

2:21 Tie the front warp stick to the front roller, using reef knots, and put the pawl into the front ratchet to prevent any movement. Undo the slip knots and tie the warp ends from the front of the heddle onto the stick. Do not tie too many ends in one knot; four to six at once is enough. Start the knots at the centre of the loom and work outwards, leaving the selvedge ends until last as these should be tied tighter than the rest of the warp.

Use the triple twist knot (**Fig. 2:D**). This knot is the same as the beginning of tying a bow, but with an extra twist to make it more secure. Pull the knot tight against the stick to prevent it coming undone. With very slippery yarns, it may be necessary to complete the bow on top of the triple knot.

The tension should be even across the warp. Test this by running the back of your hand over the warp. Tighten any loose sections by pulling on the knot. The correct tension for weaving is achieved by turning the front ratchet. The warp should be tight enough to hold the heddle in position when using the lower shed position, while allowing the heddle to be placed in the upper position without straining the warp ends. Some weavers prefer a tighter warp than others.

Now the process of dressing the loom is complete, check that everything is correct. Compare your threaded loom with the photograph of the dressed loom (**2.22**).

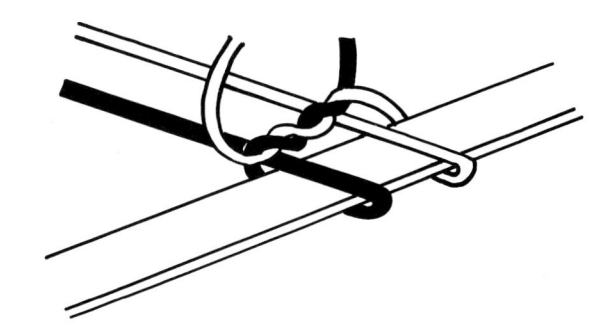

Fig. 2:D Triple knot

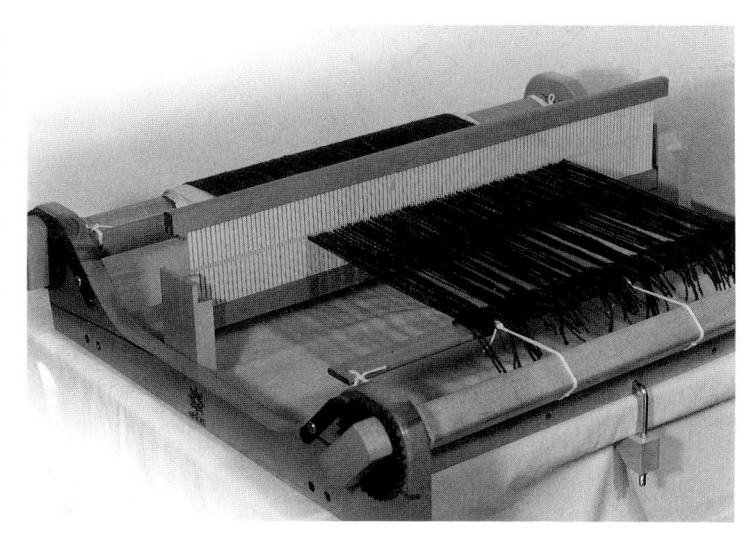

2:22 Loom after completing threading, with heddle in closed position.

THE RIGID HEDDLE LOOM • 33

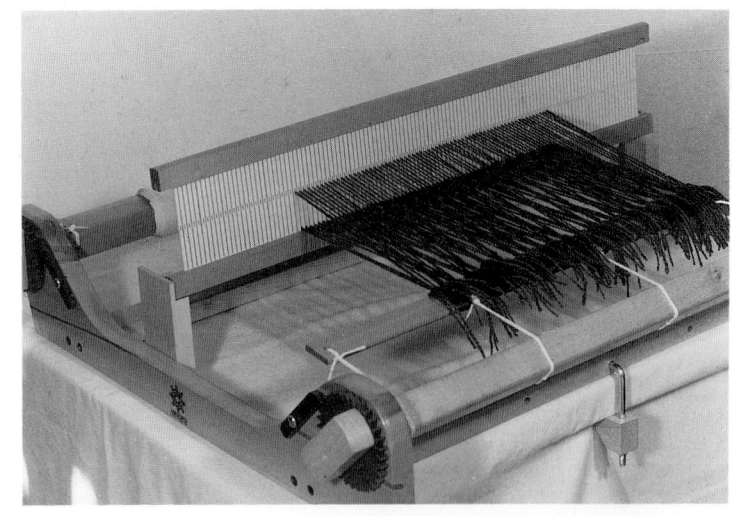

Place your heddle in the three positions, upper, lower and closed. When the heddle is in the upper position, the upper layer of warp is stretched tighter than the lower layer. The upper layer is being pulled upwards by the heddle to form a shed.

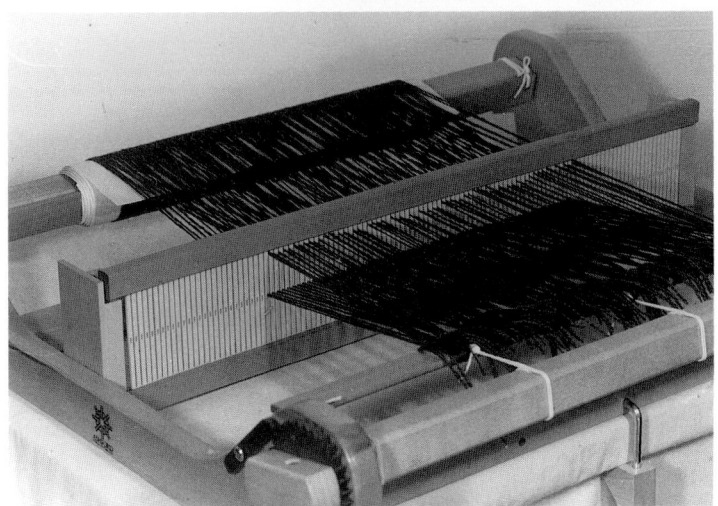

2:23 Heddle in upper position.

Similarly, when the heddle is in the lower position, the lower layer is tighter than the upper. Because of this tension difference, leave the heddle in the neutral or closed position when you are not weaving. Do not place objects such as books, or balls of yarn on the warp, as this will cause it to stretch.

2:24 Heddle in lower position.

PREPARATION FOR WEAVING

Now exciting things begin to happen, and you can begin the actual weaving. The heddle alternates between the upper and lower positions. The shuttle carrying the weft yarn passes over every second warp end for one pick, and under that end for the return pick. A 'pick' is a single row of weft yarn. Some techniques require a closed shed, with the heddle in the central, neutral position.

Before you start weaving, place the loom and yourself in a comfortable position. The loom can be set up with the slot at the back of the loom fitting over a table edge, and the front of the loom resting in your lap, while you sit down to weave.

Another alternative is to clamp the loom to a solid, steady table with two clamps to prevent the loom moving while you weave. You may either sit or stand to weave.

Heading

Before you can begin weaving, a heading must first be woven (**Fig. 2:E**). This will close the gaps left when tying the bundles of warp ends to the front stick. You can now see why it was better to tie only a few ends into one knot, as this means less heading. The heading is also used to check that there are no mistakes in the threading, and that the tension is even, before starting on the weaving proper.

Wind 8–10 turns of a very thick yarn on to the shuttle. Place the heddle in the upper position, and put the shuttle through this upper shed. Pull the heddle towards you, using both hands, thus beating the yarn against the knots. Weave three more picks in alternate sheds before beating again with the heddle, giving several sharp taps to beat the weft into place. If the gaps between the knots have not disappeared, repeat the last three picks again. The weft can be left in loops at the selvedge, as this will make it easier to cut out this heading, when removing the weaving from the loom. This method of weaving a heading wastes very little warp, and is not bulky.

Common mistakes that can be rectified here are:

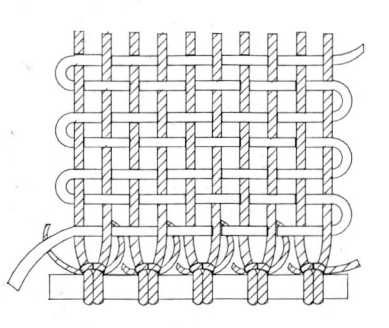

Fig. 2:E Heading

Loose warp ends

If sections of the warp are loose, the weft will curve upwards over this section, and will not beat down in a straight line across the warp as it should. Tighten these loose ends by pulling on the knot.

Missing ends

These have either broken during the winding on of the warp, or have been put into the wrong hole or slot. If the thread has broken, add in another warp end, the same length as the rest of the warp. Tie this added end to the front stick. Weight the back of this end (a bulldog clip or clothes peg is ideal) to bring this warp end to the same tension as the rest of the warp. If the missing end is in the wrong hole or slot, move it to the correct place. However, if this involves moving the missing end across a few cm (in), this will cause a difference in tension and may create tangles in the shed while you are weaving. It would be better to replace another warp end in the empty slot or hole, and weight it.

Selvedge

If the selvedge does not pack down as firmly as the rest of the weaving, the selvedge ends are not tight enough, or are sett too closely for the thickness of the weft. For the former, tighten the selvedge ends at the knot. For the latter, re-thread the selvedge ends in the heddle wider apart and re-knot.

It is always frustrating to find mistakes at this stage when you are about to begin weaving at last, and excited at what lies ahead. However, if these mistakes are left, a line or gap will appear through every piece of weaving you will do on that warp, and this is even more frustrating.

It always seems as though mistakes occur in the centre of the warp, where they are most difficult to get at, and never at the edges where they would be relatively easy to fix. Do be patient enough to stop and fix these mistakes now. It is worth the effort.

WEAVING

Fill a shuttle with your chosen weft yarn. With a stick shuttle, it is best to wind the weft on with a figure-of-eight movement which builds up the sides of the shuttle without overfilling it (**Fig. 2:G**). Fill one side of the shuttle, then the other, and finish with some turns around the centre. If the shuttle is overfilled it will not slide easily through the shed. Choose a shuttle that is slightly longer than the width of the article you are weaving, then you will not need to insert your fingers into the shed to pull the shuttle through.

Place a stick through the shed to separate the heading from the weaving, change sheds and put your shuttle through. It helps to avoid mistakes if you develop a rhythm. Enter the shed at the right-hand side when the heddle is in the lower position, and from the left for the upper position. With some techniques this rhythm is not always possible, but plain weaving, using one shuttle, is easier when woven in this manner.

Put the shuttle smoothly through the shed at its widest part, close to the heddle. Make sure there is enough yarn unwound from the shuttle to cross the entire warp width, letting the shuttle pull through without the yarn jerking and tightening the selvedge.

There are three important points to remember here:

1. Leave about 5cm (2in) of the weft end hanging out from the selvedge, and turn this in by taking it around the outside warp end and tuck it back into the same shed. Never leave loose ends of weft hanging out, as it is very tedious darning these in afterwards, and they tend to show in the finished work. Break the weft, rather than cutting it, as this leaves a tapered end.

2. The weft yarn has to pass over and under the warp ends and some extra weft must be left to compensate for this weft take-up. If there is no slack, the weaving pulls in and gradually narrows. Apart from spoiling the appearance of your weaving, the strain on the selvedge ends will cause them to break. To allow for this take-up, put the weft

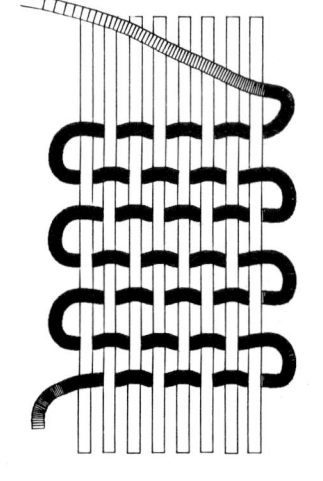

Fig. 2:F Weft take-up 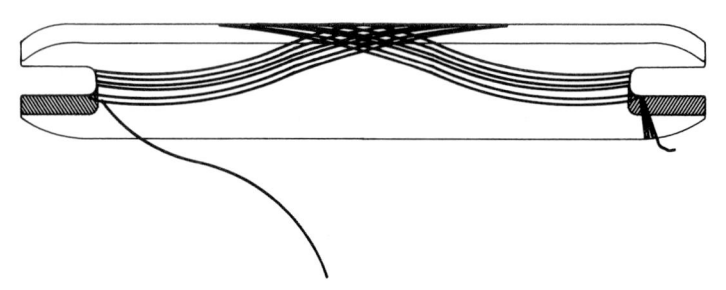   **Fig. 2:G** Winding a shuttle with a figure of eight

through the shed at an angle so it emerges at a point about 5cm (2in) higher than where it entered the shed.

3. The rigid heddle, when used as a beater, has a tendency to drag the last pick back when returning the heddle to the upright for the next pick. This will make an open, loose weave structure. To ensure a close weave, change heddle positions when the heddle is against the last weft pick. That is, put the weft through the upper shed, beat, and as the beater touches this weft pick, push down, and change to the lower heddle position and return the heddle to the upright. The opposite happens when changing from the lower to the upper shed.

Practise weaving, watching these three points – they will quickly become habit.

After you have woven about 7–10cm (3–4in), pause and look carefully at your weaving. Is the beating even? When beating, the heddle should be grasped evenly with both hands, and pulled forward, keeping the heddle parallel with the front stick. It is very easy to exert more pressure with one hand than the other. Try to achieve the same force of beating with each weft pick. This force will depend on how firm and strong the finished article is to be.

Check that the weaving is not pulling in too much at the sides by placing the heddle against the weaving. The selvedge ends should travel in a straight line from the weaving to the corresponding holes and slots. The edges of your weaving will probably be uneven at this stage, but this will improve with practice as you develop a rhythm and become more relaxed.

Remove the stick that separated the heading from the weaving proper before you move the woven fabric onto the front roller. If you wish to hemstitch the beginning of this article, do it now, following instructions on page 121. It is a good idea to do plain weave until you feel your edges are reasonably straight, and your weaving is even.

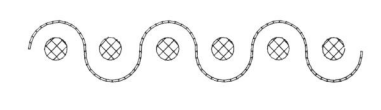

Fig. 2:H Cross section of plain weave

Joining weft threads

When you start a new shuttle of the same colour, just overlap the new thread about 2.5cm (1in) over the old thread. A thread that has been broken by pulling apart, will show up far less in the weaving than a thread that has been cut, as the former has tapered ends.

To join in a different colour, break off the original colour 2.5 (1in) from the selvedge. Tuck this end into the next shed, lay in the new colour to overlap the old by 2.5cm (1in) and continue weaving. If you are weaving stripes the weft can be carried up the selvedge for a few picks, but this can give untidy edges to your weaving.

Separating articles on the loom

If you are weaving more than one article on the same warp – for example, four tablemats – separate them as you weave. Finish the end of the first mat by hemstitching, or any other finish you wish, place a stick across the warp in the next shed, and change sheds.

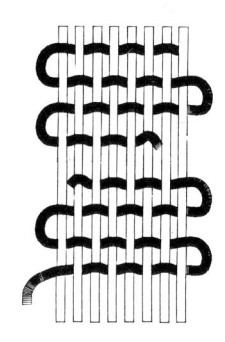

Fig. 2:I Joining weft threads

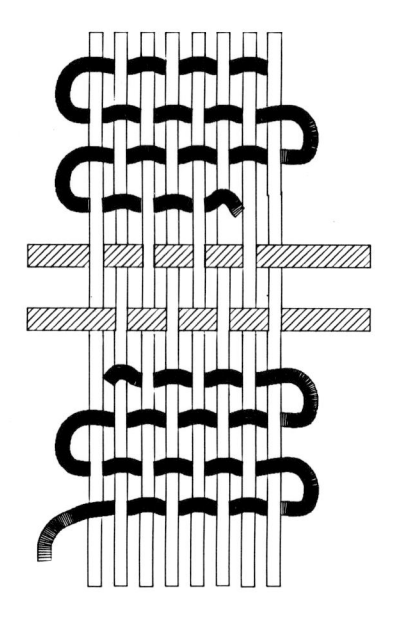

Fig. 2:J Separating articles on the loom

Place another stick across, and change sheds ready for the first pick of the new piece. It is easier to remove two sticks than one. The distance these sticks are apart will determine the length of the fringe. Always leave slightly more than you think you will need, as the warp is at tension and will contract when the tension is released after the piece is removed from the loom.

After weaving about 5cm (2in) on the new piece, remove the sticks and hemstich or finish the article.

Broken warp ends
When a warp end breaks, measure out a matching piece of warp yarn, long enough to stretch from your weaving to the back roller (about 60cm or 24in). Thread this replacement end through the heddle, replacing the broken end in either the hole or slot. At the back of the loom, as close to the back roller as possible, tie the replacement thread to the broken end, using a bow knot. Place a pin in the weaving at the point where the broken end emerges from the weaving, and secure the replacement end around the pin, at the same tension as the rest of the warp, with a figure of eight. If this is not done in the correct order, that is, the bow first, then the figure of eight, it is difficult to get the tension right.

Continue weaving until the bow reaches the heddle. The original end should then be long enough to be replaced back in the weaving, around a pin, after removing the replacement thread. If it does not reach to the weaving, just re-tie the bow further back. Both ends of the replacement thread will be darned in when the weaving is removed from the loom.

If a knot in the warp yarn appears, treat it exactly the same way. Remove the pins before the weaving is wound on, or they will catch on subsequent layers of weaving.

replacement end
broken warp end

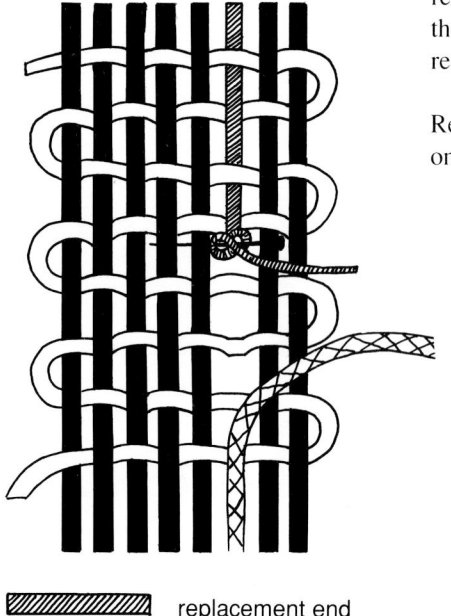

Fig. 2:K Broken warp end

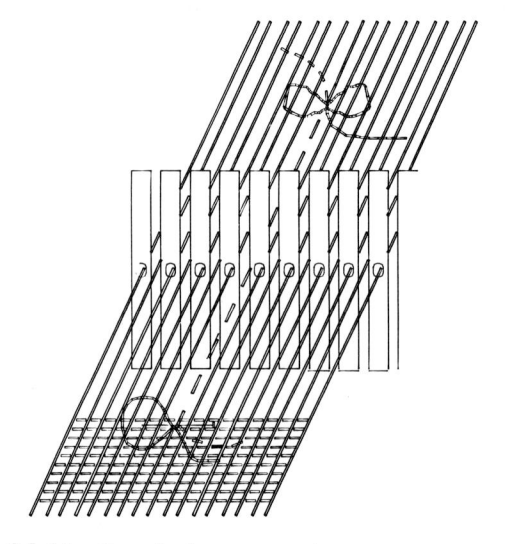

Fig. 2:L Mending a broken warp end

If you have many broken ends, particularly on the same end, check that this warp end is the same tension as the rest of the warp. If it is tighter or looser, this could cause breakages. If a selvedge end keeps breaking, it may be that the weaving is drawing-in too much. In this case, leave more slack in the weft before beating.

Bringing the weaving forward
You will notice the shed narrowing as your weaving moves towards the heddle. When the shed is too narrow for the easy passage of the shuttle, put the heddle in the closed position, release the back ratchet, and turn the front ratchet. Wind the woven cloth onto the front roller, making sure the last pick of weaving, also called the 'fell' of the cloth, comes within range of the heddle. Check that the tension is the same as before. You may need to insert a stick to cover the knots for the first turn of the front roller, as these knots can cause bumps in the cloth, which will affect the tension.

Measuring the weaving
It is a good idea to mark every 15cm (6in) to indicate just how much weaving you have done. You can do this by tying a contrasting thread to the selvedge. Do not unwind your weaving from the front roller either to measure or admire it. It is very difficult to wind it back on evenly, and at the same tension. Because your weaving is stretched tightly on the loom, it will contract and measure less when it is removed from the loom. It is usual to allow about 10% for this warp take-up.

Loose selvedge ends
On a rigid heddle loom the selvedge ends have a tendency to become loose as your weaving progresses. This does not happen to the same degree on other types of looms, and appears to be caused by the relatively narrow shed of most rigid heddle looms. To minimize this, do not overfill your shuttles, and use shuttles slightly longer than the warp width. It does help to tie the selvedge ends at a tighter tension than the rest of the warp when you are tying the warp onto the front stick during the loom threading process. If the selvedge ends do slacken, making weaving difficult, pack these ends with wads of paper at the back of the loom. These wads will need to be replaced every time you move the warp forward. Another common cause of loose selvedges ends is that they have slipped off the paper at the back of the loom. Also check the front of the loom. If you have woven several tablemats, the unwoven warp you have left as fringes may have slipped off at the front roller.

Removing the finished weaving from the loom
You can continue weaving until the back stick is about 10cm (4in) from the back of the heddle. Stitch or finish the end of the last article, then cut the warp, leaving plenty for the last fringe. Never

cut the weaving closer than about 5cm (2in) from the last weft pick, as this will leave a very weak finish. Undo the pawl from the front ratchet, and pull the weaving off the loom. When you reach the heading, cut through the loops at the edge of the heading, and pull the heading threads out. Undo the knots at the front rod, or cut them if you have left the correct amount for a fringe.

Take a good, analytical look at your finished piece. Hold it up to the light to check for even beating. If streaks show through, the beating is not even. Mend any flaws, such as broken ends. If there are any skipped warp or weft ends, where the shuttle has not gone over or under in the right place, mend these. Take a thin piece of matching yarn, and darn, following the correct over and under positioning of the skipped thread. Cut this replacement thread close to the weaving, but do not cut out the skipped thread. This mend will disappear into the fabric when it is washed.

Finish the piece by washing, following the washing instruction for your particular yarn as outlined in Chapter Six. It is only when the piece is washed and pressed that the true characteristics of any woven piece can be evaluated. Washing causes the warp and weft to merge and become a single entity, and true fabric is formed.

Record any problems and details about that piece for future reference. Recording the weight of a finished article is very helpful, as this will tell you how much yarn to buy for a similar project in future, and can save much yarn wastage. Tape or staple small snippets of yarn into your record book, as this is invaluable for future projects, and record the amount of shrinkage. If possible, I like to weave a small sample at the end of a warp, and keep this as a reference. My record books are indecipherable to anyone else, as they cannot read my writing (even I cannot read it at times), but they are a necessary and worthwhile part of the weaving process.

PICK-UP STICK WEAVING

The use of pick-up sticks extends the rigid heddle loom to beyond the usual two shafts, and is one of the most exciting innovations that has happened to this loom. The hole and slot method of lifting and lowering alternate threads is a limiting factor on rigid heddle looms, as two adjacent warp ends cannot be raised together. One end is in a slot and the other in a hole, which forces the ends to move against each other. A pick-up stick can hold ends out of this alignment, and many interesting patterns can be made.

Pick-up stick weaving can be done on either a balanced weave, or a weft-face weave background. If a balanced weave background is chosen, the pattern picks will be further apart than with a weft-face weave background. Choose the most suitable background for the article you are weaving.

A pick-up stick can be a warp stick, a pointed stick, or a shuttle, as in **2:25**. The stick should be 2.5cm (1 in) wide, and slightly longer than the article being woven. The pattern weft should be a little thicker and softer than the background weft. This pattern weft floats across the background, and is not really an integral part of it, so it does not matter if different types of yarn, such as cotton and wool, are used as pattern and background weft. Keep the weft floats short, if the article is to be subjected to heavy wear.

Only the warp ends in the slots can be picked up, as these are movable; the ends in the holes are fixed. Therefore, when picking up these slot ends, it is easier to put the heddle in the lower position, thus bringing all these slot ends to the surface and readily accessible.

Basic technique
Weave the required amount of plain weave, finishing with the shuttle emerging from the upper shed. Put the heddle in the lower position, and with the pick-up stick at the back of the heddle, pick up the required number of ends in the upper layer.

In **2:26** the first four ends from the left are picked up, the next four are missed out and so on across the warp. Slip these ends onto the stick. Turn the stick on its edge and push it against the back of the heddle, as in **2:25**. You can see how an extra shed has formed, by raising these picked-up ends above the others. The weft is put through the shed at the front of the loom, as usual, not at the back of the heddle, where all the picking-up is happening.

2:25 Pick-up stick weaving

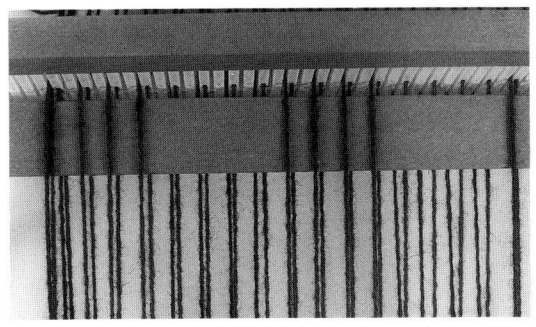

2:26 Stick lying flat against heddle

Basic pick-up weaving has three steps:
First pick: Stick on edge, pattern weft, heddle in lower position.
Second pick: Stick laid flat against the back of the loom, background weft, heddle in lower position.
Third pick: Same as second, but heddle in upper position.

When weaving these three steps it can be seen that it is only for the first pick that the ends are held out of alignment to form the pattern shed. In the second and third picks, all the ends return to normal, as the stick is pushed back away from the heddle.

Repeat this sequence a few times. Then look closely at the cloth structure. If you push the pattern weft out of the way, you will see underneath, the plain background weave. It is this plain background which gives the cloth strength. The pattern thread simply floats across the surface, intersecting every now and then with the background, but not really forming part of it.

To form this strong background, it is necessary always to weave at least two picks between each pattern pick. More than two can be woven, but if only one background pick is woven, there will be long warp floats on the underside of the weaving. Unfortunately these will not be seen until the weaving is removed from the loom, when it is too late to do anything about it.

Variations

The pattern picks can be woven in doubled or twisted threads, and also in novelty yarns. This is a economic way of using expensive yarns, as these will be woven only in every third pick, but will always be on the surface of the weaving. Fleece wool, either carded or in locks, is very effective used in this way. The fleece wool or yarn can be pulled up to form loops on the surface of the weaving.

The pattern area need not extend the complete width of the weaving as it can form blocks, and the number of ends picked up onto the pick-up stick does not have to be constant. You can pick up two, then one, all the way across. You can also control the size of the blocks, making the blocks larger, then smaller, as was done in the centre of the photographed sample in **2:27**.

This technique is suitable for tablemats, runners, cushions, borders on scarves, stoles, fabrics, and wall hangings.

BLOCK SWITCHING

By using more than one pick-up stick, very interesting patterns can be made. Weave the required background, put the heddle in the lower position, and pick up two ends, miss two, all the way across, using a pick-up stick at the back of the loom as before. Weave the three picks as detailed in basic pick-up weave, four times. Leave the first pick-up stick pushed flat at the back of the loom. Use another stick, and with the heddle in the lower position, miss two ends and pick up two. That is, you are picking up the opposite ends to before. Weave the basic three picks four times again, but only moving the second stick. Take the second stick out, and repeat the first block again, using the first stick.

Variations

More than two sticks can be used at once. You will note that only the stick nearest the heddle can be used. The distance between the back of the loom and the heddle governs the number of sticks; usually about four is the limit. The blocks can be equal in size or of different sizes.

MOCK LENO

This is a pick-up technique which needs only one stick and one shuttle. It is best woven in a balanced weave, with a warp and weft in the same yarn. This is a quick technique, as you do not change shuttles.

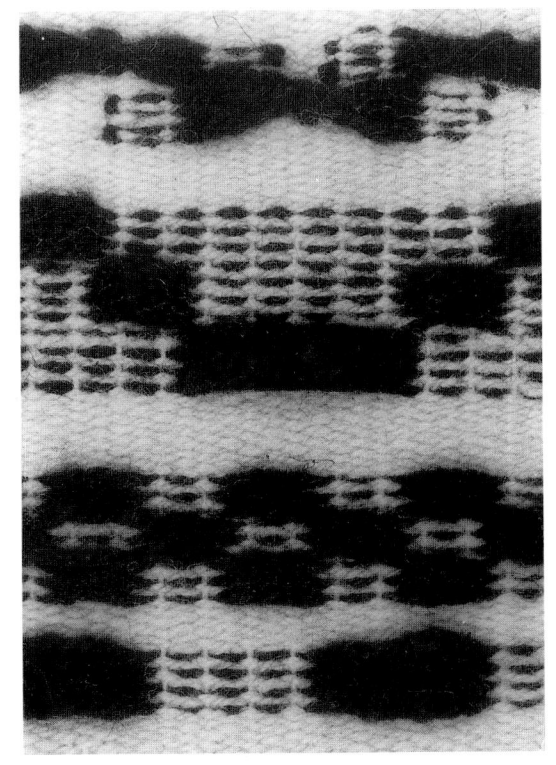

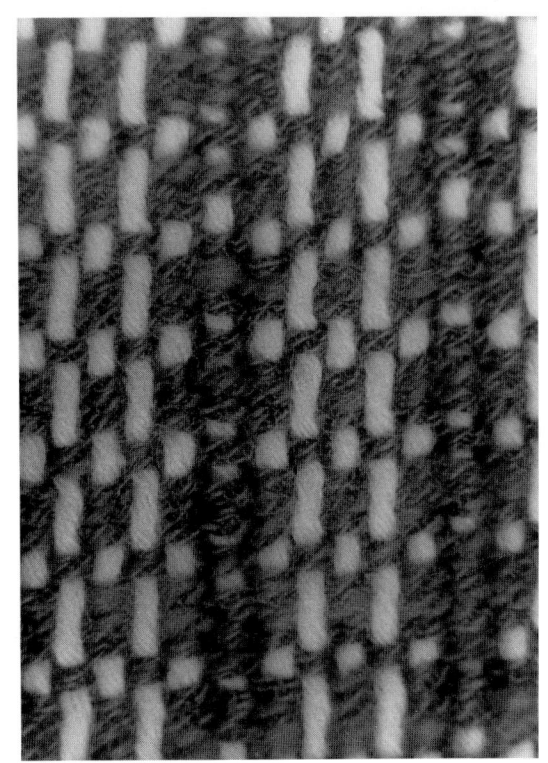

2:27 Variations of pick-up weaving   **2:28** Mock leno

Weave a heading in a balanced weave, finishing with the weft emerging from the upper shed. Put the heddle in the lower position. With the stick behind the heddle pick up two ends, miss one, all the way across the top layer. Push the stick, lying flat, against the heddle. Weave five picks in the background weft, starting with the heddle still in the lower position. On the sixth pick, in the upper position, move the stick to the back of the loom, enabling all the ends to return to their normal position. Beat this sixth pick lightly.

The texture of this weave will not show up until the article is washed, and the fabric relaxes. When pressing the finished article, use a very light pressure to avoid flattening the surface texture, caused by the floats.

FIRST PROJECT

Warp: strong, smooth wool (or cotton), in a neutral shade.
Weft: Same as warp.
Combined weight of yarn needed for warp and weft: 500g (18 oz)
    Also some contrasting yarns and colours
Weave construction: Balanced weave
Sett: Wind the yarn around the ruler to calculate the correct sett, as on page 25.
Warp length: 241cm (95in)
Warp width: 33cm (13in)

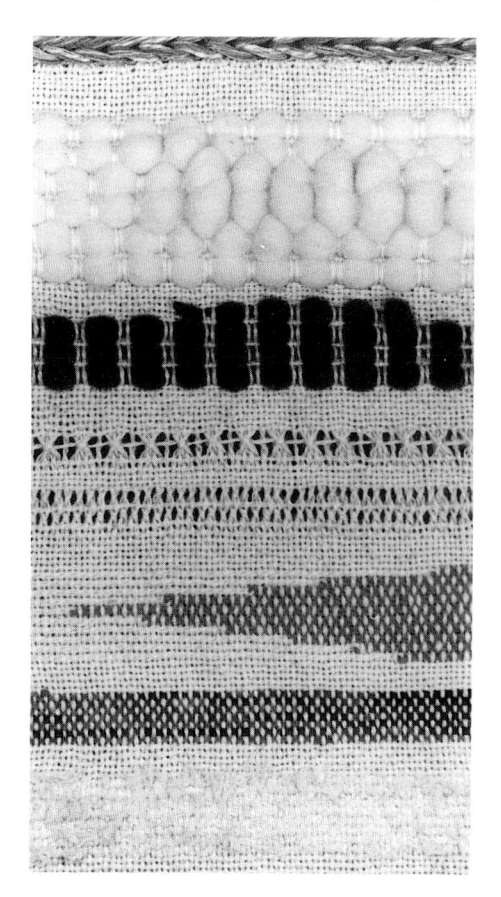

2.29 First project

Weaving instructions
This warp will be used for a small sampler and a runner. Weave for 8–10cm (3–4in) in plain weave, using a weft yarn the same colour as the warp. Then fill a shuttle with a contrasting colour, and weave stripes against the background colour. Try a few cm (in) using novelty yarns. Now branch out into some other techniques. Details of how to do these techniques appear in Chapter Ten. I suggest:
    Linked weft: page 132
    Leno and/or Brooks bouquet: page 134
    Pick-up weaving: pages 40–43
    Chaining: page 132

When your sampler reaches 91cm (36in), you will probably have reached saturation point. If you try too many new techniques at once, you will become confused, and unable to remember how to do them.

Hemstitch the end of your sampler, following the instructions on page 122. Place two sticks as spacers and begin weaving the runner. Choose one technique from the above list that you enjoyed the most, and plan how best it can be used in a runner 50cm (20in) long. Perhaps you may choose to weave a runner with leno borders 5cm (2in) from each end. You could weave a runner with two rows of chaining, in a contrasting colour, at each end. Some design ideas are included in Chapter Seven.

Finish the runner with hemstitching, or whatever finishing you think is appropriate. Cut it off the loom then wash as per instructions for your yarn type in Chapter Six. The very beginning of the sampler can be finished by knotting with an overhand knot, as on page 122. This will give you experience with two types of finishing in this project.

Then you may sit and gloat at your first piece of weaving. I do not think I have ever felt so satisfied as I did when I finished my very first piece. Now I know it was very peculiar in appearance. It was shaped like an hour glass, and had little loops from the selvedges in the first few picks. But I can remember the satisfaction it gave me. I hope you now share that feeling?

For your next few projects, look through the selection in Chapter 10, and choose from them. You may not be able to obtain the exact yarn as specified, but you can still weave the articles by choosing your own yarn, noting whether the weave structure is balanced or weft-face, then following the instructions on page 25 to get the correct sett. Thread the loom according to this sett, and your weaving will be structurally strong, although the yarn may be finer or thicker than the yarns shown in the project.

Once you have woven a few pieces, following a set of instructions, it is easy to branch out and design your own projects.

3. THE FOUR-SHAFT TABLE LOOM

THE FIRST LOOM I BOUGHT in 1967 was a four-shaft table loom. I did not know that was what it was called then, and I had to look through a book until I found a drawing of one that looked like mine. Then I had to assemble the loom, and thread it up. I can still remember the tangle I got into with that first warp. So this section of the book is what I needed all those years ago: a straightforward explanation of how the loom works and how to thread it.

The four-shaft table loom can be misjudged when it is used for purposes for which it was not designed. If it is understood and used correctly within its limits, it can give endless satisfaction and produce excellent weaving.

Advantages
1. Shafts can be lifted simply and quickly, and no changes in the tie-up between shafts and handles are necessary.
2. It is transportable.
3. It takes up little space, and can be folded down and stored away when not in use.
4. Each shaft is independent, allowing a wide variety of patterns to be used.
5. It is a sensible choice for a first loom, as it is easy to understand and use.
6. It can be used as a sampler loom for the larger, complex looms.

Disadvantages
1. Size limit. It can be no wider than 610-810mm (24-32in) if it is to remain portable.
2. The loom has a light frame, not suitable for heavy beating.
3. Because it is a rising shed loom (more about that later), it is not suitable for weaving floor rugs that require a tight, inelastic warp.
4. The warp length is limited to approximately 10m (33 ft).
5. The shuttle has to be put down after each pick to manipulate the shafts.

CONSTRUCTION

Basically the loom consists of a frame which holds the warp, the length-wise threads, at tension. To this frame are added two rollers with ratchets at one end of each roller to extend the warp. During the weaving process, the warp moves from the back to the front roller.

Weaving is the interlacing of the warp with the weft, the width-wise threads. Alternate warp threads are lifted to allow the weft to pass through. The lifting mechanism on the Ashford table loom is contained in the 'castle', a box-type structure set into the loom frame. Within the castle are four sets of needle-like wires, called heddles. Each heddle has an eyelet to hold the warp thread, and the

3:1 The Ashford four-shaft table loom

A Rollers
B Ratchets
C Castle
D Heddles
E Handles
F Beater
G Reed

heddles are strung onto frames, or shafts. The shafts are attached to handles on the top of the castle, and these handles move the shafts up and down. A Texsolv system of cords and pegs is used to connect the shafts and handles. This cord will not stretch and can be adjusted to ensure the shafts remain at the correct height.

A beater, containing a reed, is pivoted at the front of the loom frame. There are two metal bars protruding from each loom side, which allow for a change in pivoting positions. When the last weaving pick (the 'fell') is close to the front of the loom, use the pivot position nearer to the front of the loom. This ensures the beater always strikes the fell of the cloth at right angles. The reed spaces out the warp, and also pushes or beats the weft rows (picks) together. The reed also determines the maximum width you can weave. If your reed measures 610mm (24in), then your weaving will be that width, less the amount of weft take-up. Weft take-up is the amount your weaving will pull in, and it usually comes to about 2-3cm(1in).

OTHER EQUIPMENT

You will need a raddle, shuttles, threading and reed hooks, warp and cross sticks, and clamps (if you are clamping the loom to a table), which are all supplied with the Ashford loom, together with a booklet describing how to warp it. A warping board or mill is essential for winding the warp prior to putting it in the loom. You will also need scissors, a darning needle, pins, tape measure, and sheets of strong brown paper.

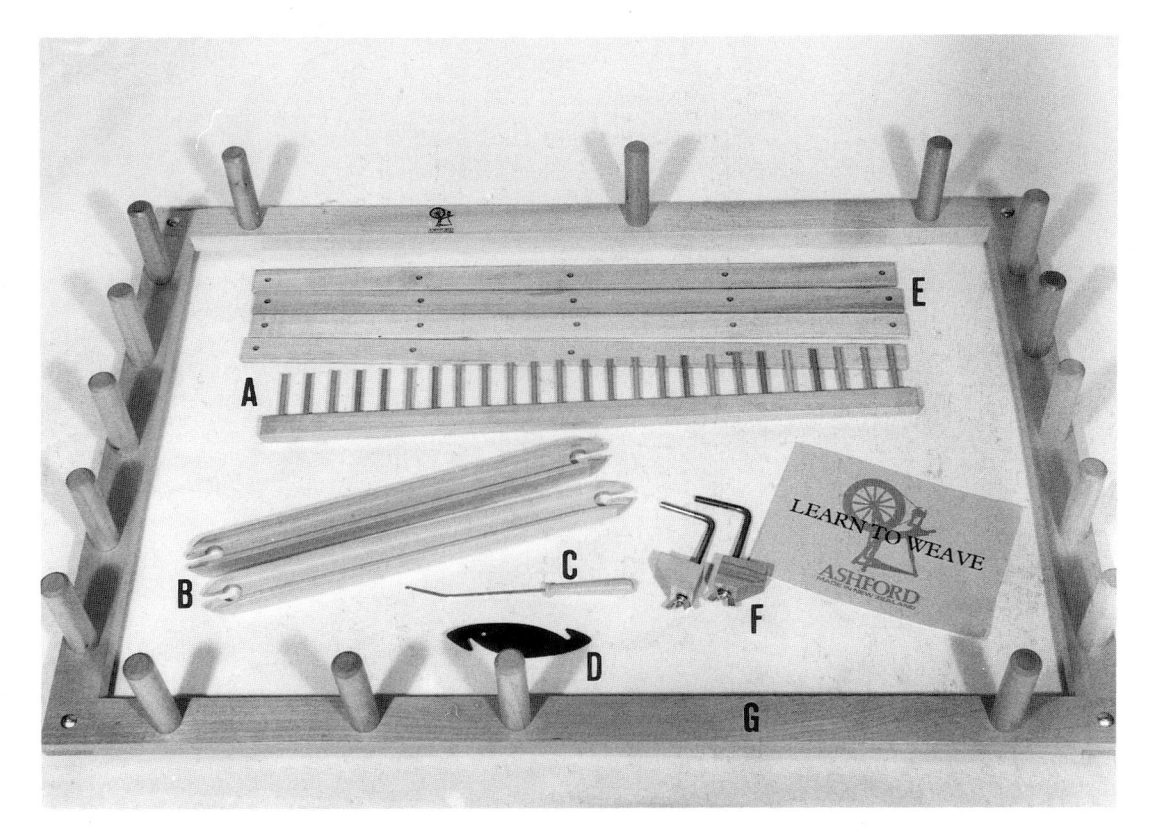

CHOOSING A LOOM

Ashford table looms come in three sizes: 410mm (16in), 610mm (24in) and 810mm (32in). The width you choose depends on what you want to use your loom for. The smallest size is suitable for a sample loom, when you have other, larger looms to work on. The 610mm (24in) loom is the most popular, as it is easy to carry. If you need a loom to take to classes, or you will be moving the loom from room to room, this size is the best buy. The 810mm (32in) loom can be moved, but it is difficult to manoeuvre through doorways and into small cars. It is best used if you want to weave wider fabric widths.

RISING SHED ACTION

All table looms are rising shed looms. To form a shed, the gap between the warp threads through which the shuttle is thrown, the shafts are pulled upwards. The lower layer of the warp remains stationary.

When the upper layer is pulled up, these warp threads become tighter than the lower layer, and this causes the warp to buckle when weaving. To prevent this the shafts, in their lower or closed position,

3: 2 Other equipment
A Raddle
B Shuttles
C Threading hook
D Reed hook
E Warp and cross sticks
F Clamps
G Warping board

Fig. 3:A Upper and lower warp layer.

↕ These distances should be equal

— — — — Horizontal warp line

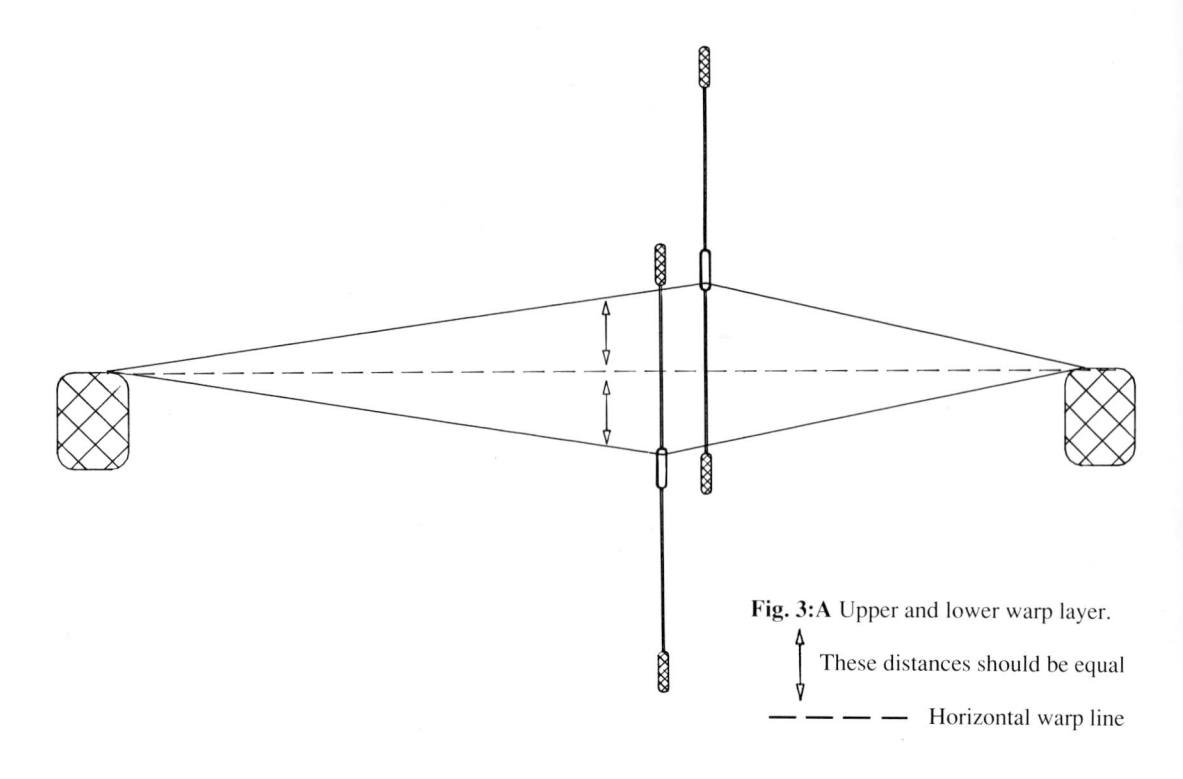

are set with the heddle eyes **lower** than a horizontal line extending from the front to the back beam. The warp never actually sits on this imaginary horizontal line, shown as a dotted line in **Fig. 3:A**.

If a very tight, inelastic warp such as linen is used on the full width of a rising shed loom, the lower layer of warp will pull upwards under the warp pressure, and narrow the shed.

The Ashford table looms have metal heddles, as this weight helps to keep the shafts down in their correct position.

WARP LENGTH

The amount of warp that can be wound onto the loom is governed by the distance between the front and back rollers and the table top. The space under the front roller is most important, as the woven warp, which is thicker than the unwoven warp, is wound on here. Much depends on the thickness of the warp yarn, but 10m (33 ft) is about the limit.

PLANNING THE WARP

Before the warp is wound on to the loom certain decisions have to be made. Firstly choose the yarn for your warp. Chapter Six will help you differentiate between yarn types. I will assume this is your first experience with a table loom, and therefore will go through each stage carefully. As in the rigid heddle section, I suggest you put a sample warp on to begin with. This will get you used to the loom, and introduce you to some simple weaving techniques.

For this sample warp choose a strong 2-ply wool or cotton in a neutral colour. You will need about 500gm (1lb). The weave structure for this sample warp will be balanced weave, as this is the most common and useful weave.

Plain weave, where each warp end intersects with each weft thread, as in darning, is the simplest of all weave structures. By changing the relative density of the warp and weft, we can make three structural changes within this group to form a balanced weave, a weft-face weave and a warp-face weave.

Calculating sett

Having chosen the weave structure, the next step is to find the correct sett for our yarn. This is done by using the ruler method. Wind your warp and weft yarns around a ruler for the given length, making sure the threads lie flat and just touch. This approximates the position of the threads as they would lie in the weaving, and it allows us to estimate how many ends to the cm(in). In **3:3** the warp yarn is the light-coloured cotton yarn, and the weft is the dark colour.

Balanced plain weave (see 2:5)
Wind the warp and weft yarn around a ruler for 2.5cm (1in). Count the number of times the **warp** yarn goes around and this is the correct sett for a balanced plain weave (sometimes called a 'tabby' weave). In **3:3A**, the warp yarn goes around the ruler eight times.

Weft-face weave (see 2:6)
Wind two of the weft and one of the warp threads around 2.5cm (1in), and count the number of warp turns. In **3:3D**, the correct sett for these yarns would be 5 ends per 2.5cm (1in).

Warp-face weave
Wind the warp yarn around 1.25cm (0.5in), and multiply by three. In **3:3C** the number of turns is ten, and this multiplied by three gives a correct sett for this warp thread, at 30 ends per 2.5cm (1in).

3:3 Sett

A. Balanced plain weave
B. Balanced twill weave
C. Warp-face weave
D. Weft-face weave

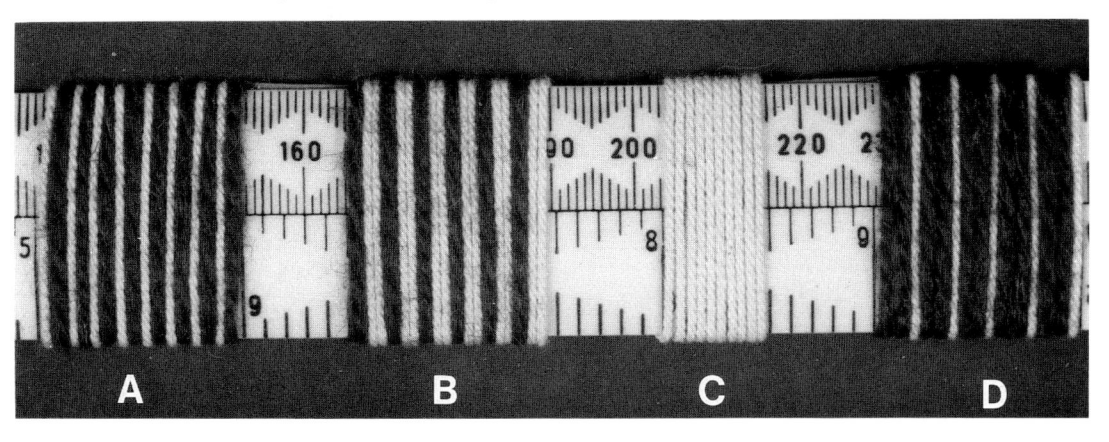

3:4 Warp-face weave sample

Balanced twill weave
As twill weaves are so popular, I will include the sett for this weave structure here for future reference. With twill weaves, the warp and weft intersect every second warp end, so wind two warp threads to one weft thread around 2.5cm (1in) on the ruler. In **3:3B**, the number of warp turns is twelve. There will always be more warp ends for a twill weave than for a plain weave.

As your sampler will be woven in balanced weave, follow those instructions for calculating the sett of your yarn. Your sett may vary from the sett of the yarn used in the sampler illustrated in this section, and if so you will need to change the following figures slightly. I will base my calculations on the yarns used in **2:5** and the warp will be sett at 8 ends per 2.5cm (1in). This is abbreviated to e.p.cm (in).

Estimating warp length
The warp length includes the length of the article/s to be woven, plus fringes, if any, and warp-take-up and wastage. Warp take-up is the amount the weaving will shorten when it is removed from the loom and the tension released. It also includes shrinkage, and 10% is the usual allowance. A soft wool yarn may need as much as a 15% take-up allowance. Wastage is the amount of warp lost when both ends of the warp are tied onto the loom, and 61cm (24in) is the usual amount.

Estimating warp width
Calculate the width of the article you want to weave, adding an extra 2.5cm (1in) for draw-in. This is the amount the article will draw-in while you are weaving, and it also allows for some shrinkage. Multiply the width by the sett, and this is the number of of warp ends you will require.

The following instructions for a sampler will illustrate how you go about making your calculations. On the sampler you will learn how to use the loom, and how to do some simple weaving, in both plain weave and twill. The spare warp allowed for the tablemats will give you some experience in weaving actual articles. For a sampler 92cm (36in) long, and allowing enough of the warp for you to weave two tablemats on the end, the warp plan would be as follows:

Length

sampler	92cm (36in))
fringes (5cm (2in) at each end)	10cm (4in)
article (2 tablemats, including fringes)	81cm (32in)
warp take-up	20cm (8in)
loom wastage	61cm (24in)
Total	264cm (104in)

Width

finished articles	30cm(12in)
add draw-in	3cm (1in)
Total	33cm (13in)

Sett: 3 e.p.cm (8 e.p.i.)
Total number of warp ends 3 x 33 = 99 ends (8 x 13 = 104 ends)

The warp for this project will be 264cm (104in) long and 33cm(13in) wide, with a total of 99 (104) ends.

It is in calculations like this that the conversion from metrics to imperial cannot be exact and appears confusing. Eight ends per inch is actually 3.15 per centimetre, but this figure is too clumsy. When taken to the nearest number, the figures differ. However, as no weaver uses both imperial and metric measurements, the difference will not matter. If your reed and loom are measured in the metric scale, use those figures. If imperial measurements are used in your loom, use those.

WARPING THE LOOM

Warping is the process of putting the warp ends on to the loom. The threads are first wound on to a warping board or mill, which holds the warp ends so each end is the same length as the others. They are then transferred to the loom. For this first project I will describe the use of the warping board and at the end of this chapter I will explain how to use a mill. Both are equally easy to use.

There are many different ways of winding a warp, and each weaver has his or her own favourite method. The method I will use in this section is one I have used in my classes for many years, and it seems to suit most beginners. At the end of this chapter I will describe other methods and their uses, but I suggest you stay with this one method until you are completely familiar with it. When I first began weaving, it took me a year before I could warp my loom without looking up the instructions, so do not despair if you cannot remember everything at once. Just take each step at a time, and it will gradually come to you. And it takes practice to wind a good warp, so do not worry if you feel very unco-ordinated for your first warp.

Some points to remember while warping are:
1. If you are right-handed, your right hand carries the yarn around the pegs while the left hand holds the yarn directly over the cone or ball, and tensions it. These hand positions prevent the yarn from jerking as it unwinds and help to produce an evenly-tensioned warp.
2. If the yarn has to be joined, or has a knot in it, make sure this knot is at peg A or D, not in the middle.
3. Push the warp to the base of the pegs at intervals while warping.
4. The tension should not be too tight, as this pulls the pegs over at an angle, making the upper threads shorter than the lower.

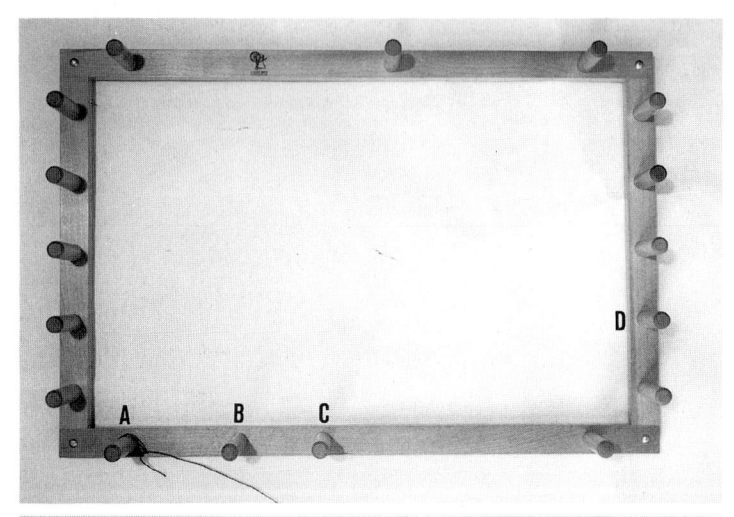

3:5 Place the warping board on a table, or hang it on the wall at a suitable height. Put the warp yarn on the floor, about midway across the board, and bring the yarn end up and tie it onto peg A. If the yarn is in balls, place the balls in a box to prevent them running all over the floor.

3:6 Carry the yarn past the inside of peg B and the outside of peg C to the right hand peg and then to peg D. This is one end and the distance is 274cm (108in). This is the nearest to our planned length of 264cm (104in). Always take the measurements **up** to the nearest peg measurements.

* The warping board in these photographs is 91cm(36in) in width, between the outside pegs.

3:7 Bring the yarn back from peg D to peg A for the second end, this time passing peg B on the outside. The cross that has formed between pegs B and C will keep the ends in order when they are removed from the board.

Repeat this sequence three more times, until you have eight ends wound onto the board. Four will be to the outside of peg C and four will be inside it.

3:8 At the position shown, tie in a counting thread in a contrasting colour around these eight ends. Use a snitch knot as shown in **Fig. 3B**. This marks 2.5cm (1in) of your width, as the sett for this warp was 8 ends per 2.5cm (1in). Only 12 more bundles to go.

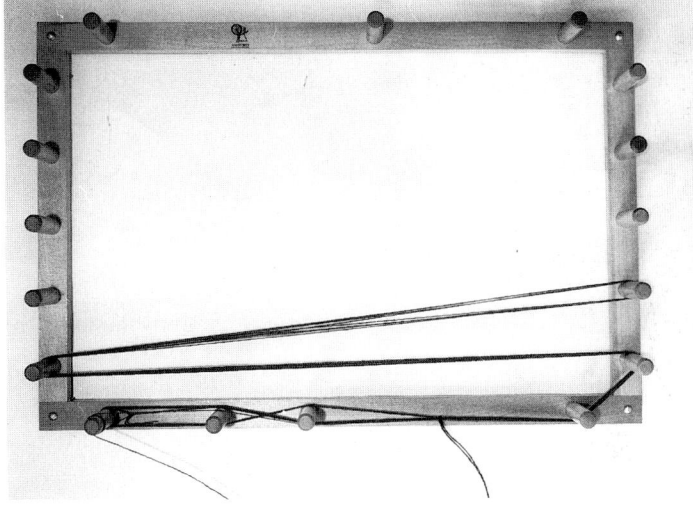

3:9 Repeat this sequence until you have all thirteen bundles of eight wound onto the board. Knot the last end to peg A. Then put a contrasting tie around the cross as shown.

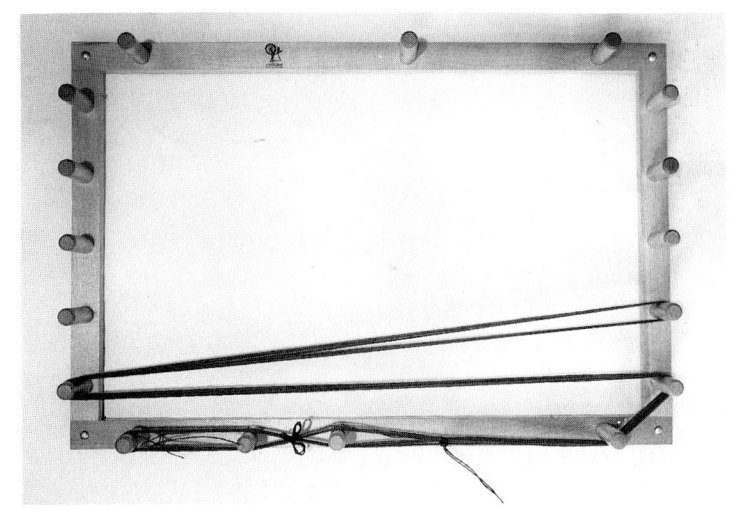

THE FOUR SHAFT TABLE LOOM • 53

3:10 Tie a contrasting thread around the ends at peg D.

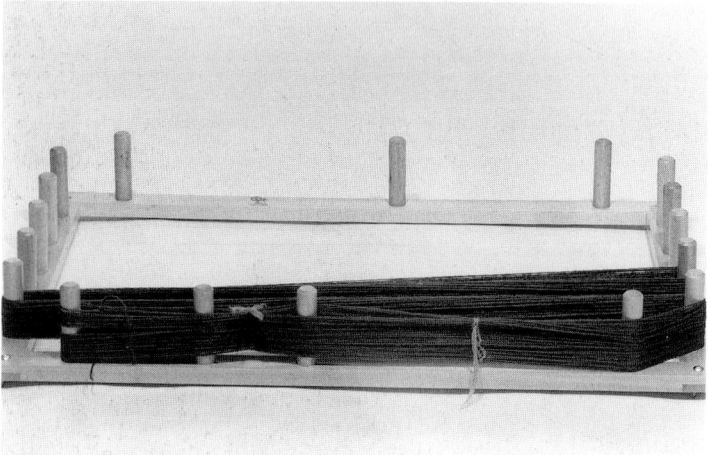

3:11 Your completed warp should look like this.

3:12 Take the warp off the board, beginning at peg D, and chaining as you go. To chain, put your hand through the loop at peg D, lift the warp off the peg, and grasp firmly. Pull about 23cm (9in) through the loop, then continue chaining until you reach the counting tie. Do not pull the last length of warp through the loop, as this prevents it undoing later.

54 • THE ASHFORD BOOK OF WEAVING

If you are winding a wide warp, with thick warp yarn, I suggest you wind the warp in two or four sections, treating each section as a separate warp, with its own counting ties, etc. This prevents a build up around the pegs, and keeps the warp ends all the same length.

BEAMING

Clamp the loom to a solid table with the clamps provided, or use a loom stand, which can be bought separately, and bolt the loom to this. Remove the reed from the beater and replace it with the raddle. The raddle is simply used as a spreading device while the warp is being wound onto the back roller. Check that the shafts are in the lower position, and the heddles are pushed to each side. There is a pin on the side of the loom which fits into a hole drilled into the loom and the beater, which will keep the beater upright.

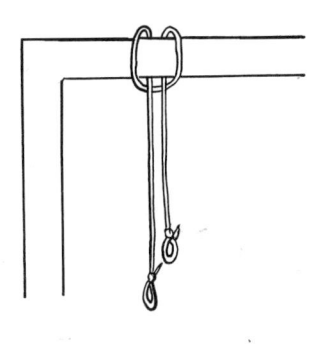

Fig. 3:B Loops attached to castle

3:13 Take the chained warp to the back of the loom, and slip the loop from peg A onto the stick which is attached to the back roller at one end only. Remember to include the first and last warp ends. Re-attach the stick to the roller at the other end, but do not re-tie the two centre ties.

Cut two pieces of string about 114cm (45in) long, and tie a loop at the ends of these lengths (4 loops). Attach the strings to the back of the castle at the top with a snitch knot, leaving one loop hanging 2.5cm (1in) lower than the other as in **Fig. 3B**. These loops should be on approximately the same level as the heddle eyes.

3:14 Put the cross-sticks, the sticks with holes drilled in, through the warp at each side of the cross. Slip the ends of these sticks into the prepared loops hanging from the castle. The cross-stick nearer to the heddles will be in the lower loops. Tie these sticks together at each end, leaving a gap of about 2.5cm (1in), to prevent the warp from slipping off. Remove the cross tie.

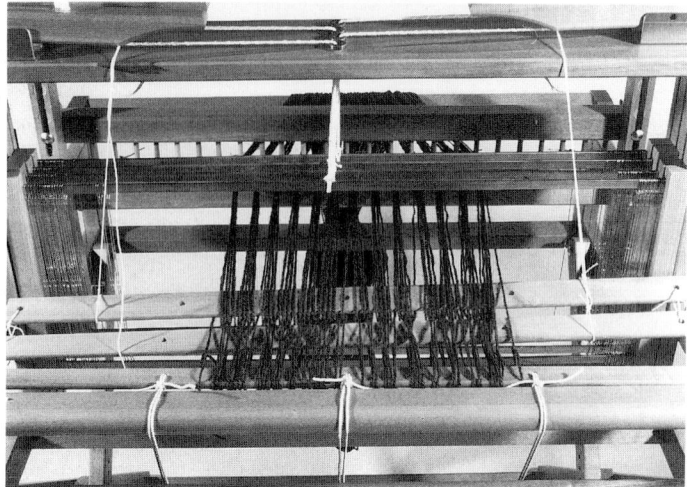

3:15 Go around to the front of the loom, and place the warp ends in the raddle spaces, making sure the warp is centred correctly. I usually place a mark in the centre of the raddle, and work from the centre out. Each group of eight ends is placed in one space in the raddle. Undo the counting tie as you work. The ends must be placed in the raddle in the same order in which they came out of the cross. If they have become twisted, usually because the counting tie was grouped around the wrong ends, return to the cross to find the correct order.

Replace the beater cap to hold the warp ends in the raddle. At the back of the loom, spread the warp on the back stick until it is the same width as it is in the raddle, and re-tie all the ties attaching the stick to the back roller.

3:16 Check that your warp looks the same as this one.

3:17 Have an assistant hold the warp at the front of the loom at an even tension, and without any bias to left or right. Shake the warp to loosen any tangles, but do not comb the warp out with your fingers. The less the warp is handled, the easier it will be to wind on. The warp will unchain as it is wound on If there are any loose threads which do not tighten up after giving the warp a good shake, take the loose ends and lift them out of the warp. Place them in the hand that holds the warp, keeping them the same tension as the rest of the warp.

3:18 The person at the back of the loom turns the ratchet to wind the warp onto the back roller. Check that the ratchet is turning the correct way and will not slip. The pawl should hold the ratchet steady between turns. Turn the ratchet until the back stick has done one complete turn of the roller. Then insert strong brown paper between the warp and the roller. This paper prevents each warp layer from sinking into the previous layer, and spoiling the tension. Make sure the brown paper is wider than the warp width, and that the warp does not slip off the paper.

3:19 When the end of the warp approaches the raddle, cut through the warp at the end tie (the tie that was at peg D). During the winding process, the cross has moved over the cross sticks from one end of the warp to the other. Remove the beater cap, and lift the warp out of the raddle. The beater and the raddle can now be removed from the loom. Divide the warp in half, and tie a slip knot (**Fig. 2:C**) in each half of the warp in front of the cross sticks.

3:20 The warp can be held on and wound by one person without an assistant. Take the warp under the front beam and over the castle. Hold it firmly, not pulled to one side, and turn the ratchet with your free hand.

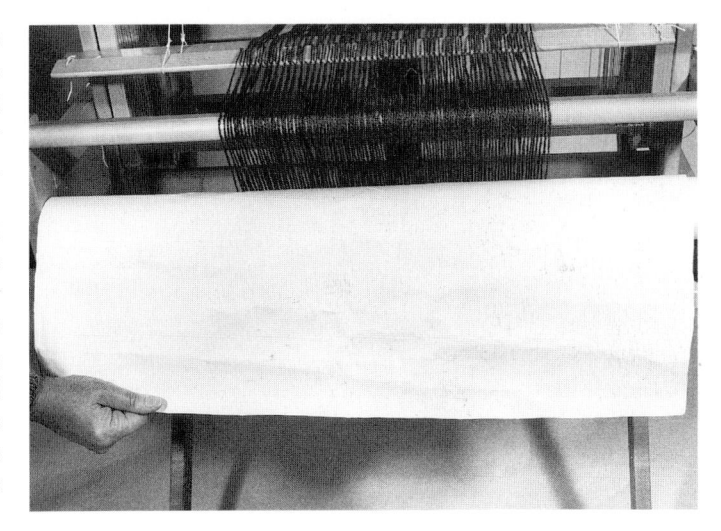

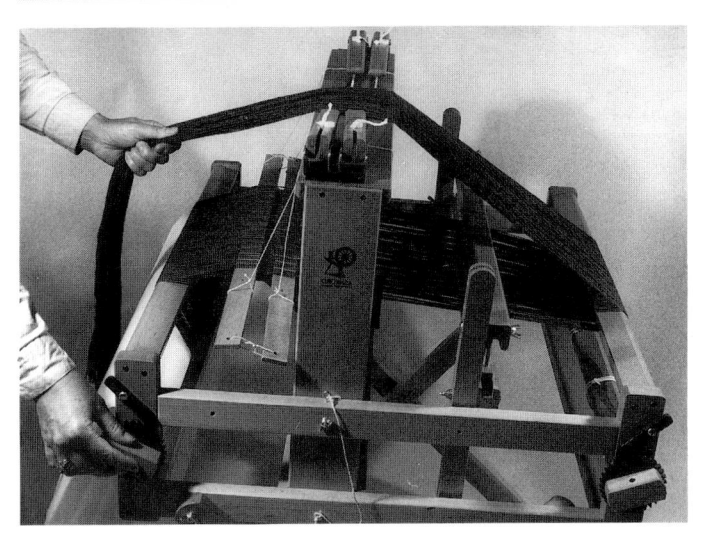

THE FOUR SHAFT TABLE LOOM • 57

THREADING

Sit at the front of the loom, and push 13 heddles (one-eighth of the total number of warp ends), from the right side of the loom to the centre on each shaft.

Pick up the first end at the right edge of the warp at the cross-sticks. Put this end through the heddle eye on shaft 1, using the heddles that have been pushed to the centre, and starting with the heddles to the right of this group (**3:21**)

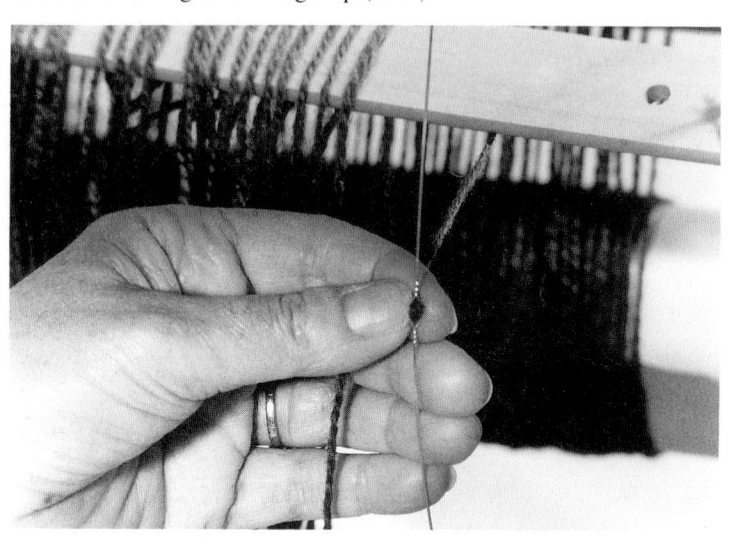

3:21 Threading the first heddle

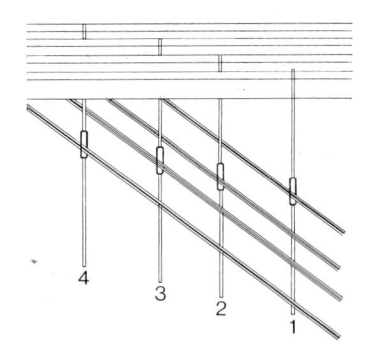

Fig. 3.C Threading the heddles

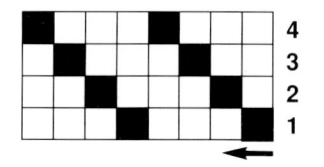

Fig. 3:D Straight draw

The second end goes through on shaft 2, the third end on shaft 3, fourth on shaft 4, fifth on shaft 1 again, and so on. With the front cross-stick slightly lower than the back stick, it is easy to see the order of the warp in the cross. To make threading the heddles easier, bend the end of the yarn over and thread the bent end through the heddle eye. Some weavers find the threading hook easier to use than their fingers.

The plain threading we are using would be shown on a graph as in **Fig. 3:D**. This pattern is called a straight draw, and is read from right to left, with shaft 1 at the lower end of the graph.

When eight ends have been threaded, check that they are in the correct heddle eyes and tie them loosely in a bundle in front of the heddles, with the ever useful slip knot (**Fig. 2:2**).

When half the warp is threaded, use the heddles on the left, which do not need to be counted out first. If you are threading the full width of the loom but not using up all the heddles, the spare heddles take up space needed by the warp if they are pushed to the side of the loom. Spread these out between the threaded heddles, with one or two empty heddles between each threaded one.

SLEYING

3:22 Place the reed back in the beater, which is then replaced back in the loom with the locking pin to hold it upright. Mark the centre of the reed and untie the slip knot. Begin in the centre of the warp and, using the plastic reed hook, bring one end through each dent (space) in the reed. This process is called 'sleying' the reed.

Put the outside two ends through one dent to form a selvedge, and remove the cross sticks.

3:23 Attach the front stick to the front roller using the string included in the loom package, which has been pre-cut to the correct length, and a reef knot. Tie the warp ends to the front stick with a triple knot (**Fig. 2:D**) with four warp ends in each bundle. If more are grouped together, more heading is required and this wastes the warp.

Check that the tension is even by running the back of your hand across the warp. If necessary, tighten the warp bundles by pulling on the triple knot. Raise each shaft in turn to check that the threading is correct.

SLEYING FOR OTHER SETTS

Your Ashford loom is sold with a reed which has 8 dents to 2.5cm (1in), so one end is placed in one space to give you the 8 ends to the 2.5cm (1in) as required in the sample warp above. This is probably the most common reed used in weaving, and is suitable for beginner weavers. If you want to buy another reed, choose one that will complement the first one. A reed with 10 dents per 2.5cm (1in), is a useful addition.

It is not necessary to always put just one warp end in each dent. With an eight dent reed, 2 ends can be put into each dent to give a sett of 16 ends per 2.5cm (1in) and so on. The following are some common spacings if you want to put fewer ends in the 8 dent reed:

For 6 ends per 2.5cm (1in): thread 3 dents, then miss one.
For 5 ends per 2.5cm (1in): thread 2 dents, miss 1, thread 2, miss 1, thread 1, miss 1.
For 4 ends per 2.5cm (1in): thread every second dent.

HEADING

It is necessary to weave a heading at the beginning of each warp to spread out the warp ends evenly and to close the gaps left when knotting the warp to the front stick. It is also useful to check the threading and tension at this stage.

Tighten the tension by turning the front ratchet. A reasonable tension is achieved when there is no strain in lifting the shafts, but the warp is tight enough to form a clear shed, Wind about 2-3m (2-3yds) of coarse yarn around a shuttle.

1st pick: Open the shed by lifting shafts 1 and 3. Shaft 1 is nearest to the front of the loom. Place one pick (row) of weft through, and beat it against the knots. Drop shafts 1 and 3.
2nd pick: Shafts 2 and 4 lifted; no beating.
3rd pick: Shaft 1 and 3 lifted; no beating.
4th pick: Shafts 2 and 4 lifted, beat these three picks onto the first pick.

Leave the weft yarn protruding from the selvedges in small loops, as it is easy to cut these loops and remove the heading when the weaving is taken from the loom. If these first four picks are not sufficient to close the gaps, repeat the last three picks. Beating after three picks instead of the usual beating every pick, closes up the gaps very quickly and does not waste warp.

When the heading is complete, check the tension. If parts of the warp are too loose, the weft will bulge upwards; if parts are too tight, a hollow will form. Adjust the triple knots until the weft is lying in a straight line. With most yarns the triple knot is sufficient but if they begin to slip, as they may do with a slippery warp yarn, tie a bow on top of the triple knot.

3:24 Weaving a heading

THREADING MISTAKES

These have a bad habit of appearing in the centre of the warp, never on the outside where they would be easy to fix. Even with careful checking, the odd mistake will happen and it is better to fix it now than to have it showing up throughout the entire warp.

Mistakes in the heddles

If there is one warp end not in the heddle eye, but entered in the reed, and the sequence is correct, pull that end out of the reed and leave it hanging over the back of the loom. Re-sley the reed from that point.

If the end is on the wrong shaft; i.e. you may have threaded 1,2,2,4, instead of 1,2,3,4, remove the incorrect end from the heddle and reed. Tie a string heddle in the correct place on shaft 3, making sure the heddle eye matches the height of the other heddle eyes. Tie this replacement heddle with reef knots around a pencil to make the heddle eye (**Fig. 3:E**).

Replace the warp end through the replacement heddle, back in the reed, and re-tie the end to the front stick. Throughout this re-threading, check that the end is in its correct position at all stages.

Mistakes in the reed

Sometimes the ends are out of sequence in the reed, causing the ends to cross and block the open shed. Replace the ends in the correct sequence. Missed dents, or too many ends in one dent require re-sleying.

Fig. 3:E Replacement heddle

WEAVING

This is the time you have been waiting for: the actual weaving process itself. It is very satisfying, after all the work involved in setting up the loom, to see articles taking shape.

Take a shuttle that is slightly longer than the weaving width of 33cm (13in). If the shuttle is a stick shuttle, fill it with a weft yarn which is the same as your warp yarn, using the figure of eight action described in **Fig. 2:G**. A shuttle with raised wooden edges, as in **3:2**, slides through the shed easily, as the wooden edges run smoothly across the warp and the ends of the shuttle slope upwards. Wind the weft yarn around the centre of this shuttle. Do not overfill either type, as this can stretch the shed, and slow down the passage of the shuttle. Place a narrow stick through the shed formed by lifting shafts 1 and 3.

When learning to weave, it best to form good habits from the very beginning. One good habit to get into is to try and match the movement of the loom handles with the shuttle movement. This can make complex weaving patterns much easier to remember. For this beginning sampler, we will begin on the right, with the right handles, which lift shafts 2 and 4, acting together with the shuttle being inserted into the shed from right to left.

First pick: Lift shafts 2 and 4, and enter the shuttle from right to left. Leave 2.5cm (1in) of weft yarn hanging out at the beginning of the pick (row). Take this short end around the outside warp end and tuck it back into the shed. All weft ends should be tidied up like this, as it prevents much tedious darning in afterwards. The weft should be broken rather than cut as this leaves a tapered end.

Angle this weft pick to emerge from the shed at a higher point from which it entered the shed, as in **Fig. 2:F**, to allow for the draw-in which occurs as the weft intersects the warp, shown in **Fig. 2:H**. If the weft is not angled, the weaving will gradually narrow and strain the selvedge ends which may break. The thinner the weft, the less the angle, as a thin weft has less draw-in than a thick weft. Beat this first weft into place with your right hand on the beater, from which the locking pin has been removed. The left hand has taken the shuttle from the shed and placed the shuttle on top of the heading.

Second pick: Change the shed by dropping shafts 2 and 4, and lifting shafts 1 and 3. Place the next weft pick through the shed from left to right, angling it as before, and beat it with the left hand.

Continue with this sequence, lifting shafts 2 and 4, and then 1 and 3, for about 8–15cm (3–6in). This sequence will cause every second warp end to rise for the first pick, and every alternate end to rise for the second pick.

Fig. 3:F shows this weaving sequence in graph form. The weaving graph for a table loom has three sections. The top left section is the threading sequence, read from right to left, with the first block indicating that the first warp end is threaded on shaft 1. The lower right section is the lifting sequence, read from the top down.

The lower left section is the draw-down: a diagram on graph paper of the woven cloth. The black squares indicate where a warp thread is on the cloth surface. A white square is where a weft end is on the surface.

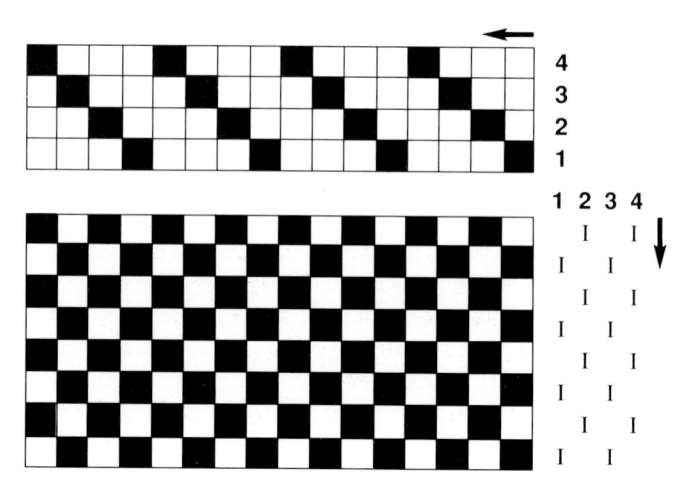

Fig. 3:F Weaving graph

If you want to know more about pattern drafting, turn to Chapter Eight, for this explanation is intended to be just enough to get you started with weaving.

When you have woven 8–15cm (3–6in), take a look at your weaving, and count the number of picks in 2.5cm (1in). Are there the same number of weft picks as there are warp ends? If so, you are doing very well for a beginner, and you will have an equal amount of warp and weft showing on the surface of your weaving. If there is more warp than weft, you are not beating hard enough, and if there is more weft than warp you are beating too hard.

The edges will still be rather uneven, but this will improve with practice. If your weft yarn is tugging at the selvedge, this will also cause uneven selvedges. Make sure enough weft is unwound from the shuttle before you put it through the shed. If you enter the shuttle with the weft unwinding from the outside end of the shuttle, this means you will not have to turn the shuttle over after each pick to unwind the yarn.

When the fell of the cloth, that is, the last weft pick, is so close to the reed that the shed is narrow and difficult to weave, the warp must be moved on. Release the back ratchet and wind the warp forward until the fell is about 2.5cm from the front beam, but still within beater range. Tighten the tension until it is the same as before. Frequent moving on is better than trying to force the shuttle through a very narrow shed.

Ideally the beater should tap the fell of the cloth at right angles. This is why there are two positions for the beater. As the weaving moves closer to the reed, move the beater to the position nearest to the shafts. There are two sets of pivoting bars attached to the lower loom sides for this purpose.

You may need to insert a stick over the knots on the front stick, as these knots can press against the first turn of the weaving around the front roller. If left, these bumps can cause tension problems.

To join a new weft thread, see **Fig. 2: I**. Separating articles on the loom, and mending broken warp ends are also described in Chapter Two. Measuring instructions are given on page 39.

WEAVING A SAMPLER

After weaving the first few cm (in) in plain weave, try some of the techniques from Chapter 10, such as linked weft (page 132), leno/Brooks bouquet (pages 134–35), chaining (page 132), surface weave (page 146), and distorted warp (page 148). Then try some twill weaves. A twill weave forms the threads into diagonal lines which should be beaten to a 45 degree angle. Plain weave and twills form the basis of most weaving structures. There are various types of twill:

1. 2/2 twill, where the warp and weft float over two ends (**Fig. 3:G1**).
2. 1/3 twill, where the weft floats over three warp ends and under one

(**Fig. 3:G2**). This weave is not balanced, and the weft predominates, giving a weft-face cloth.

3. **3/1 twill.** This is a reverse of the 1/3 twill as the weft floats under three warp ends and over one (**Fig. 3:G3**). A warp-face cloth is formed on the surface.
4. **Swiss twill.** This is a combination of a 2/2 twill and a 1/3 twill (**Fig. 3:G4**).
5. **Zig-zag twill.** The diagonal line is reversed from a left to a right twill (**Fig. 3:G5**). At the reverse point, the warp will float over three weft picks instead of the usual two.

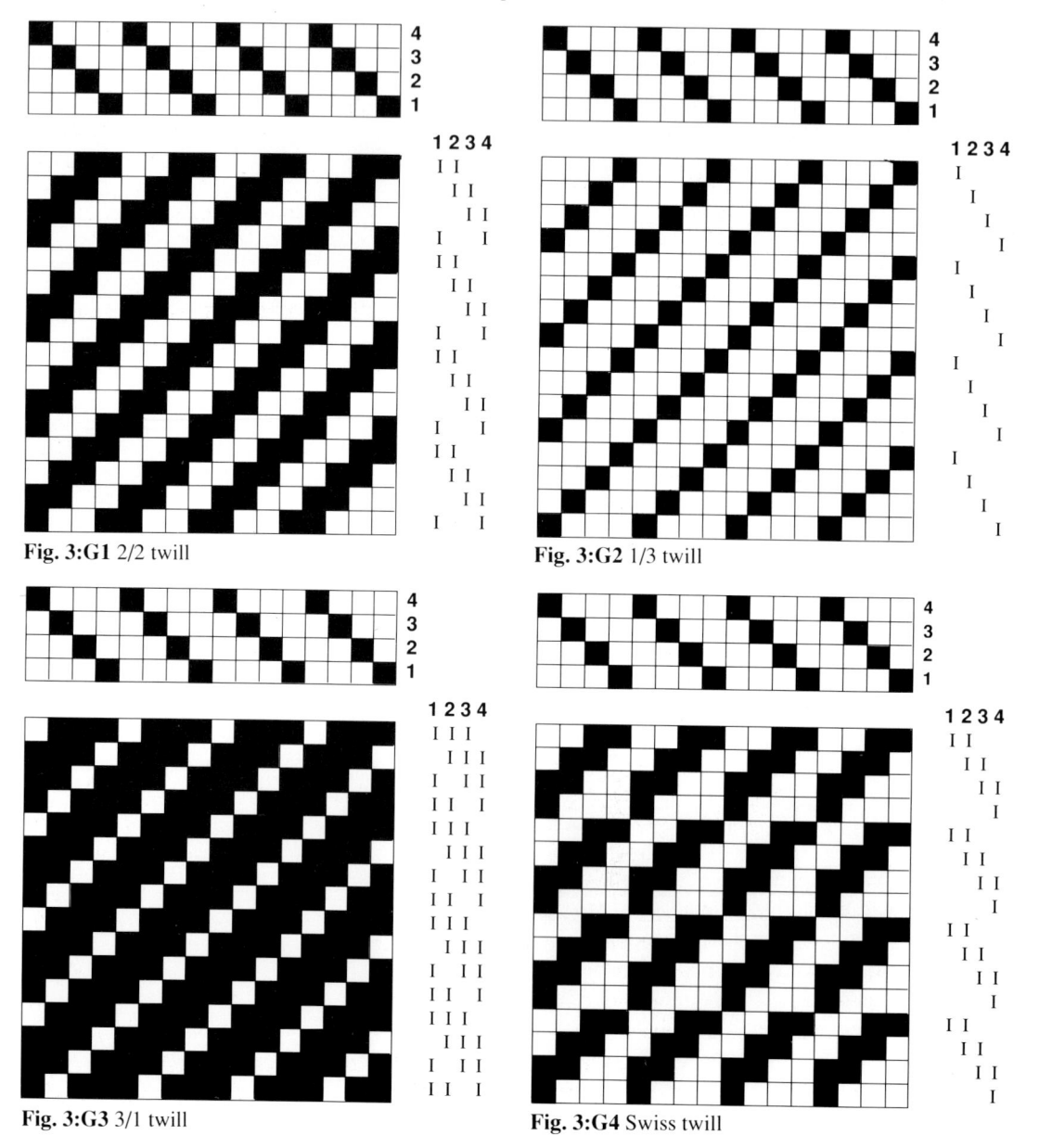

Fig. 3:G1 2/2 twill

Fig. 3:G2 1/3 twill

Fig. 3:G3 3/1 twill

Fig. 3:G4 Swiss twill

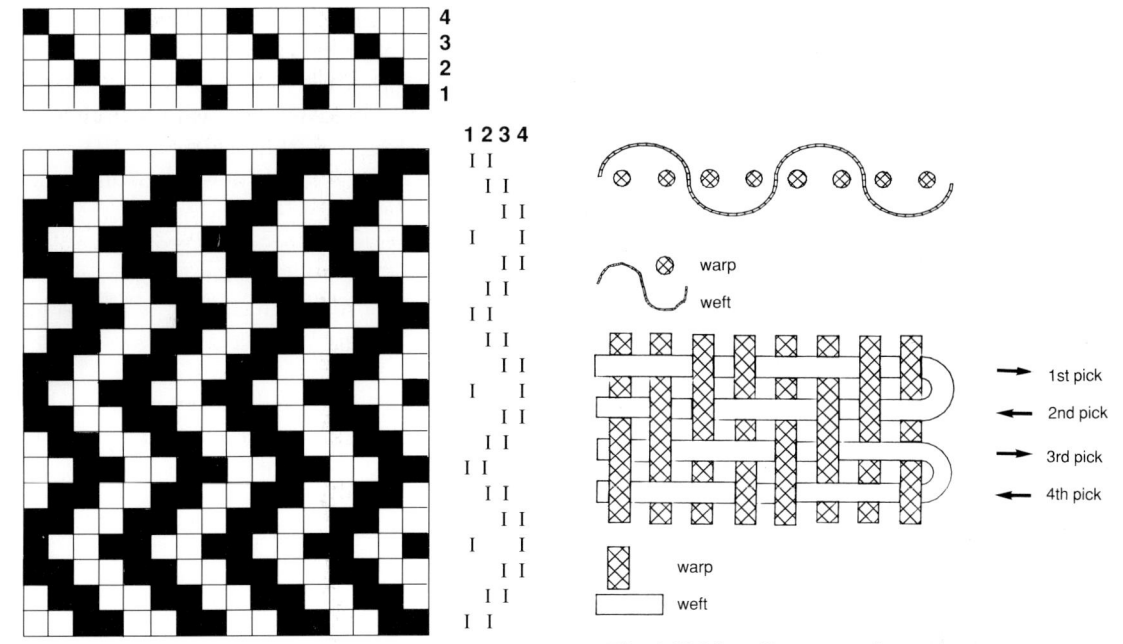

Fig. 3:G5 Zig-zag twill

Fig. 3:H 2/2 twill cross section and weave structure

Try some of these twills, putting a dividing line of two picks of a contrasting colour to separate each twill. Sometimes you will find that a warp end becomes missed out at one selvedge when weaving twills. To correct this, simply break off the weft yarn, and start from the other side.

For zig-zag twill, this spare selvedge end will be woven in on either the 'zig' or the 'zag' but not both, and nothing much can be done about this, apart from taking the shuttle under or over the offending end by hand.

You will notice that the weaving feels different in the twill areas than it does in the plain weave section. This is because the structure of each area is different. The twill weave is more flexible, and has more bulk than the plain weave. There are fewer intersections in a twill compared to a plain weave, and it is not usual to combine the two structures in one cloth. This is why we usually sett a twill weave closer than a plain weave, as discussed on page 50.

BINDER WEFT

One combination of twill and plain weave is essential to weavers. This is where a binder weft in plain weave is used between the twill or pattern weft. This binder is necessary with overshot patterns, some of which are given in Chapter Ten.

The binder weft is usually the same as the warp yarn. It strengthens the cloth, and is woven on shafts 1 and 3, 2 and 4. In **Fig. 3:I1** the binder weft has been included in the lifting sequence. However, most drafts are written as in **Fig. 3:I2**, without the binder shown,

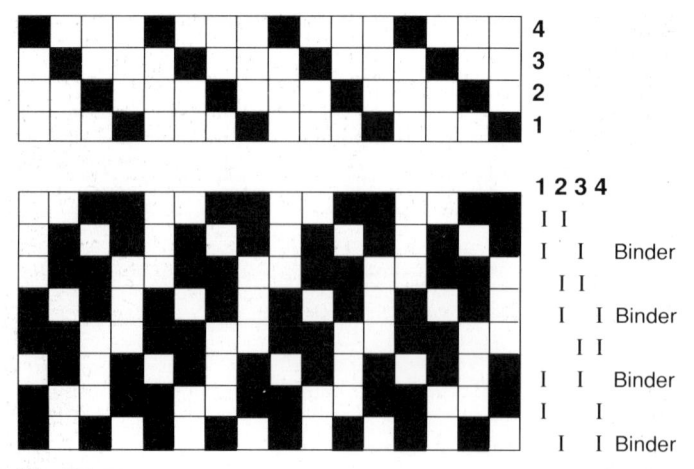

Fig. 3I1 Binder weft

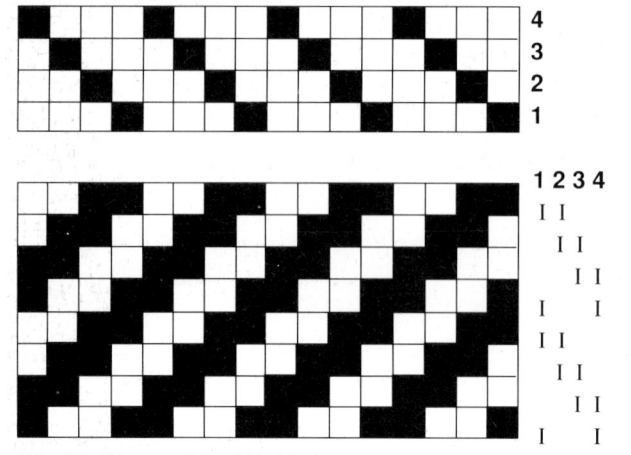

```
1 2 3 4
I I
I  I    Binder
I I
I  I    Binder
I I
I  I    Binder
I I
I  I    Binder
```

Fig. 3I2 Weave with tabby binder

```
1 2 3 4
I I
  I I
  I I
I   I
I I
I I
  I I
I   I
```

and just a note somewhere on the draft to indicate that a binder is necessary.

Weave about 8cms (3in) on your sampler, following **Fig. 3:I1**. Use as a weft yarn some of the warp yarn. For the pattern weft, use a slightly thicker and softer yarn. The effect will not be very interesting, but this exercise is a good starting point and will help you to understand more complex weaves later.

It is when weaving these two-shuttle weaves, with one shuttle weaving a plain weave on shafts 1 and 3, 2 and 4, and the other shuttle weaving a pattern on the twill shafts of 1 and 2, 2 and 3, 3 and 4, 4 and 1, that the order of the weft picks can easily become confused. I think the most helpful piece of weaving advice I was ever given relates to this confusion.

On page 61 I described how to relate the shuttles to your hand movements. In order to keep the binder weft in the correct plain weave sequence, simply note which side the shuttle is on, and then move the shaft handles on the same side. Therefore, if your shuttle is on the right of your weaving, move the handles which raise shafts 2 and 4. If your shuttle is on the left, raise shafts 1 and 3. If you find you are working with the shuttle and the loom handles on opposite sides, you will know you have made a mistake, and this can quickly be rectified.

The binder does strengthen the fabric considerably, and will cause the pattern to be more spread out. Compare this pattern you have just woven to the earlier 2/2 twill without a binder, and you will see the difference. Another advantage of using a binder weft is that it allows you to weave the same pattern weft more than once, without undoing the previous picks: that is, you can weave the pattern weft on shafts 1 and 2 for three picks, with the plain weave binders in between. Remember that the binder should alternate between the two plain weave sequences, even if the pattern weft is a repeat. This variation allows a very wide range of patterns to be woven.

Try some variations on your sampler as an experiment.

When you have reached the end of your sampler, you will be ready to weave the last of this warp into two tablemats. If your enthusiasm has carried you away, there may only be enough for one tablemat, but this does not matter. Finish the end of your sampler with a few picks of plain weave, then hemstitch the end, as described on page 121 in Chapter Nine.

Place two sticks across the warp, one in the shed formed by lifting shafts 1 and 3, and the other in the alternate shed of 2 and 4. Make sure a gap of about 10cms (4in) is left, and this will form fringes on the pieces of weaving. These sticks are removed when the weaving is wound forward on to the front roller.

Think about the techniques you wove in the sampler, and choose one technique you enjoyed doing. Weave the two tablemats, each 41cm (16in) long, using this technique, leaving the same gap between the two tablemats for a fringe.

Project Two, in Chapter Ten, describes how to weave tablemats in some detail. Finish the tablemats by hemstitching, or any other finishing technique described in Chapter Nine. The tablemats will become smaller when they are taken off the loom, so do not worry if they appear extra large at this stage.

Cut the last tablemat off the loom, leaving a 5cm (2in) fringe at the end, and follow the instructions in Chapter Two, page 40 for cutting the weaving from the loom.

For your next project, look through Chapter Ten and choose one of the projects described therein. If you do not have exactly the yarns as described, choose one that is similar

3:25 Sampler

THE FOUR SHAFT TABLE LOOM • 67

and gauge the correct sett by following the instuctions on pages 49–50, for either balanced weave, balanced twill, weft-face, or warp-face weave. The project instructions will tell you which is the type of weave structure to aim for.

Once you have woven some of the projects in Chapter Ten, you should be ready to design your own weaving projects, with the help of the design ideas in Chapter Seven, and the books listed in the Appendix.

WARPING WITH THE WARPING MILL

Most weavers who regularly wind long warps use a warping mill rather than a warping board. As I see it, there are two advantages. First, the mill uprights hold the warp, not the pegs as on a warping board: the uprights cannot move under pressure as the pegs sometimes do. Secondly, the mill does the turning, and your hands remain steady, unlike the warping board where your hands take the warp around the board.

3:26 The Ashford warping mill is collapsible. Remove the two cross pieces that hold the pegs, and push the uprights together for storage.

3:27 Before winding a warp, place one cross piece at the top of the mill. Measure out a length of yarn the same length as your warp length. For the sampler and as an example in the following photographs, we will use a warp 264cm (104in) long. Tie the beginning of your guide yarn to Peg A, over peg B, and under peg C. One complete turn of the warp yarn around the mill measures 1.5 m (59in).

3:28 Take the guide thread around the mill until the end is reached, and then bolt the second cross piece to the mill uprights with peg D being the correct distance, 264cm (104in) from peg A. Always bolt the crosspiece in beyond the end of the guide cord, rather than before it.

It is infuriating to reach the end of a warp on the loom and find that the last of a set of six tablemats is 10cm (4in) shorter than the others, so overestimate your warp length.

68 • THE ASHFORD BOOK OF WEAVING

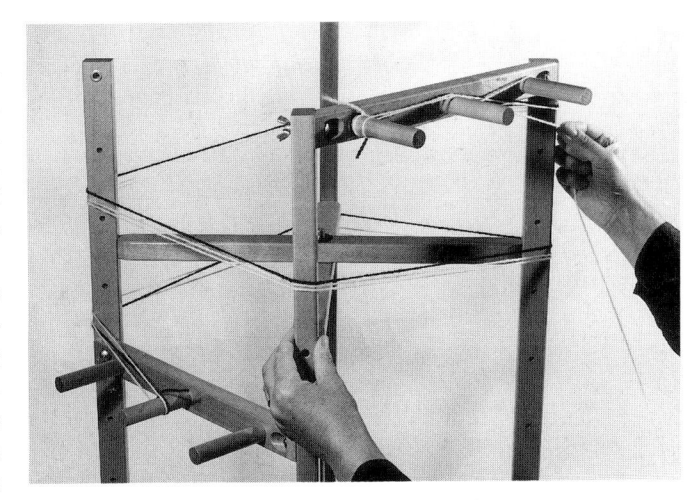

3:29 Attach the end of your warp yarn to peg A, and follow the guide cord around the mill, spinning the mill with one hand, and guiding the warp with the other hand. The second end, returning to peg A, goes over peg C and under peg B, in exactly the same manner as **3:7** on a warping board. The cross therefore is exactly the same. Wind the complete warp, following the instruction for counting ties, etc, as on pages 52–4 for a warping board. When removing the warp from the mill, it may be necessary to unbolt the lower cross piece to take the warp off peg D, prior to chaining.

The Ashford mill can hold a warp length of 15m (49 ft), but the thickness of the warp yarn does make a difference. I would suggest winding the warp in two or even four portions, if the yarn is thick. This prevents a build up on the mill, which can cause the last warp ends to be longer than the first ends. If you are winding the warp in four sections, remember to put counting ties and the cross tie in on each section. Treat each section as a separate warp, and you cannot go wrong. The guide cord will ensure each section is the same length.

WARPING WITH TWO CROSSES

This method is best used with a 'sticky' warp, that is, one that will not move easily over the cross sticks while it is being wound onto the loom. In this category are bouclé yarns, closely-sett warps such as a warp-face warp, tie-dyed warps, and fine wool warps sett closely. Wind all these warps with a cross at both ends of the board or mill.

3:30 Warp wound with two crosses

When putting the warp on to the loom, slip the loop from peg A on to the back stick as usual, and re-attach the stick to the back roller. Instead of putting cross sticks through the cross, simply tie a piece of cord from each end of the back stick, through the cross. This tie will make sure the ends are in their correct order at the back of the loom.

Continue warping as usual, using the raddle as before. When winding on, this back cross does not travel up the warp but will wind on to the back roller.

THE FOUR SHAFT TABLE LOOM • 69

3:31 Cord through cross

When the front cross from peg D reaches the front of the loom, remove the raddle. Put the back cross stick in the warp as normal (**3:19**), moving the cross back behind the heddles until the stick can be attached to the loops hanging from the castle. This cross should move back easily. The front part of the cross should then be moved back behind the heddles: this is not as easy.

Undo the cross tie, put the cross over the fingers of the left hand (if right-handed), and transfer the warp to the right hand, pushing down on the cross as you do so. This will loosen the cross, and move the cross back down the warp behind the heddles. Slip the front cross stick through the warp, and hang the stick in the front loop. Cut through the warp at the end, and it should be in the same position as in **3:19**. Moving the cross back can be avoided if the cross is made 61cm (24in) from the end of the warp when it is wound on to the warping board or mill.

WARPING WITH TWO OR MORE THREADS

This technique greatly reduces the time spent in winding a warp on to the board or mill. The warp is wound in the usual way, but two or more threads are held in one hand. As long as these threads are separated by your fingers, they will not twist around each other. I have wound as many as four threads at once, but I find two or three the easiest number to handle. With four ends at once, I seem to run out of fingers.

3:32 Winding with two threads

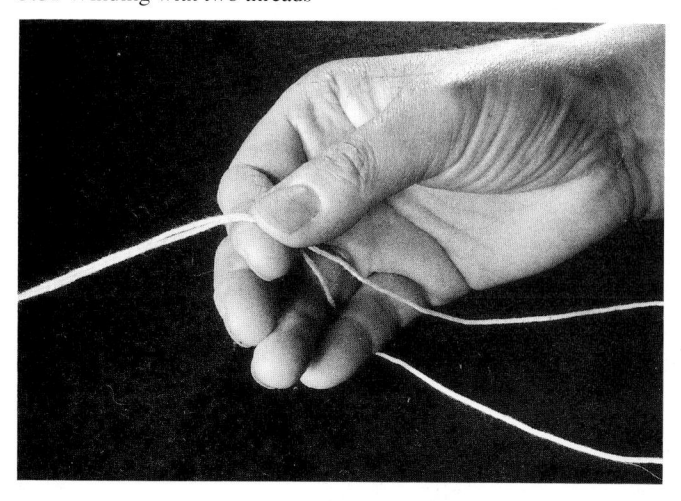

The threads will be doubled in the cross. Do not split this pair while raddling. When threading the heddles, it does not matter which thread of the pair comes first, but the pairs must be taken in order. As the tension must be the same on both threads, have them running from the same type of container or package. I often buy yarn in two or three smaller cones, rather than one large cone, to facilitate this method of winding.

4. THE FOUR-SHAFT JACK LOOM

ONCE MY STUDENTS tell me they have bought a floor loom, I feel they are well on the way to becoming serious weavers. Weavers buy floor looms for various reasons and the most common is that floor looms usually weave a wider width than table looms, and can store more woven fabric. This means that you can weave bigger pieces because the warp length can be extended, and your weaving becomes more efficient, with more articles on each warp. There is also less wastage if more articles are woven on one warp: it is much more efficient in both yarn usage and time to weave thirty tablemats at once instead of six.

Another advantage is that the shafts are raised by your foot pressure on treadles, thus freeing your hands for the actual weaving. You do not put the shuttle down to change shafts, and this not only speeds up the weaving process, but gives a rhythm to your weaving. This rhythm makes weaving on a floor loom less tiring and also improves the evenness of your beating.

A table loom, with its independent shaft action, has each shaft lifted singly. On a floor loom, one treadle can be tied to two or more shafts, enabling you to lift these shafts together. This does make your weaving quicker.

4:1 The Ashford four-shaft jack loom (970mm, 38in)

A Castle	I Warp beam
B Beater	J Cloth beam
C Reed	K Breast beam
D Ratchet lever	L Back beam
E Brake lever	M Heddles
F Treadles	N Spacer
G Parallel lamms	O Friction brake
H Jacks	

THE FOUR-SHAFT JACK LOOM • 71

Because the loom is longer from front to back than a table loom, the shed is bigger and this means you can throw a shuttle across the complete loom width. A shuttle race, a ledge underneath the beater, supports the thrown shuttle.

Of course a floor loom is more costly than a table loom, and it takes up more floor space. The back beam and warp roller on the Ashford floor loom can be swung in towards the shafts when moving the loom from room to room, and the compacted loom will then fit through doorways. The two widths of the Ashford loom, 970mm (38in) and 1100mm (45in), make it unsuitable for transporting to classes, and a table loom is best for this.

CONSTRUCTION

The Ashford floor loom is called a 'jack' loom, because it is the action of the jacks, or levers, which raise the shafts. These jacks are underneath the shafts, and connected to both the shafts and the treadles, via lamms. A lamm is a pivoted lever to which are attached the treadle cords. The Ashford loom has parallel lamms suspended from the shafts. A parallel lamm has the advantage that all tie-up cords are the same length, and when any treadle is depressed, the jacks of that shaft raise the same distance.

The jacks are metal. When the treadle is depressed, the outer edges of the levers, marked A in **Fig. 4:A**, drop, and the inside edges rise. This pushes up the hinge (B), which is connected by metal pins to the centre of the shaft. The shafts are set in guide rails and can only move straight up or down. When the treadle pressure is released, the shaft will drop back to its original position aided by gravity. As the connections from lamms to shafts are metal, there are no stretching problems as can occur with cord connectors, and adjustments are seldom necessary.

4:2 Jacks

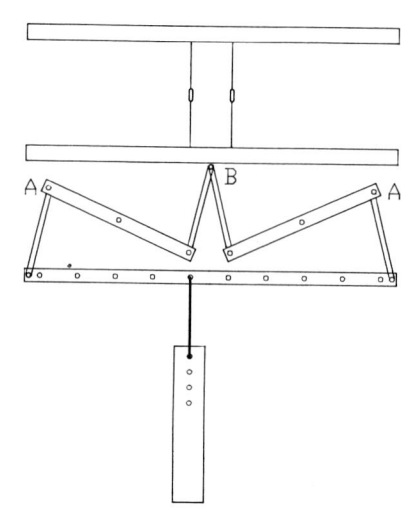

Fig. 4:A Jack mechanism on an Ashford loom

Because the shafts are pushed up from beneath, the castle, the upper support structure, is minimal. The loom will not dominate a room in the same way as a loom with a heavy over-structure, as the loom is the same height as much of the furniture. I like demonstrating on this loom, because I can talk over the top of the loom to interested spectators.

Beater
The beater is underslung, and pivoted from the lower loom sides. There are three holes in the beater sides where it is attached to the loom sides. This allows for adjustment of the beater up or down. The lower warp layer should lie on the shuttle race to allow for the smooth passage of the shuttle, and different yarn types will sometimes raise or lower this warp line. The beater is also adjustable forwards or backwards, to ensure the beater strikes the fell of the cloth (the last weaving row or pick) at right angles.

Rising shed action
A jack loom is a rising shed loom. All the shafts, in the rest position, lie below the horizontal warp line, which is the line the warp would take if it were stretched in a straight line between the breast and back beam. To form a shed, some of these shafts are pushed above the horizontal warp line. When weaving, the lower layer of warp threads remains stationary, and only the upper layer moves. This can be a distinct advantage when the weave structure calls for more sinking than rising shafts. To make one shaft rise, leaving 3 shafts stationary, takes little foot pressure from the weaver, and the action is fast. Because there is less warp movement on a jack loom, there is also less friction on the warp.

The upper layer of the open shed should pull upwards approximately the same distance as the lower layer is held below the horizontal warp line, keeping the tension the same on each layer. If the warp is pulled too high, that warp layer will be tighter than the

Fig. 4:B Warp line at rest

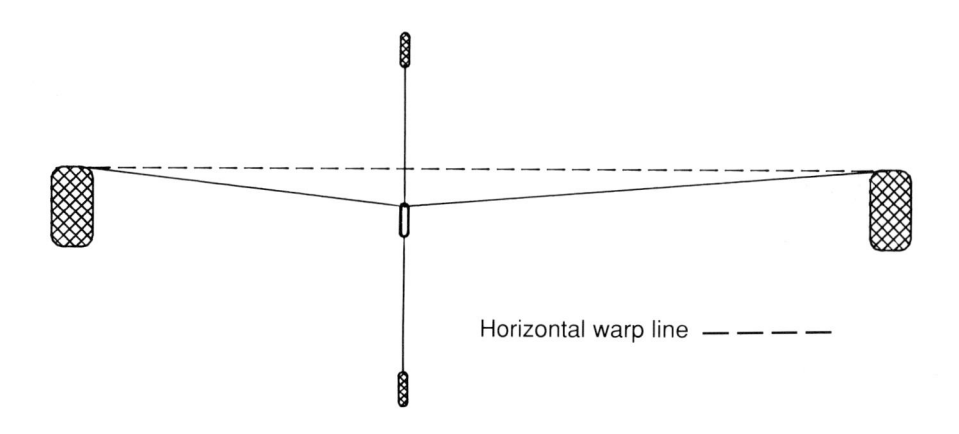

Horizontal warp line — — —

lower layer; if pulled too low, the tension will be looser than the lower layer. These tension differences will equalize as the warp layers are constantly reversing, but some types of weave, such as weft-face weaves, do need an even tension on both warp layers. The horizontal warp line on a jack loom is an imaginary line, as the warp never lies in this intermediary position.

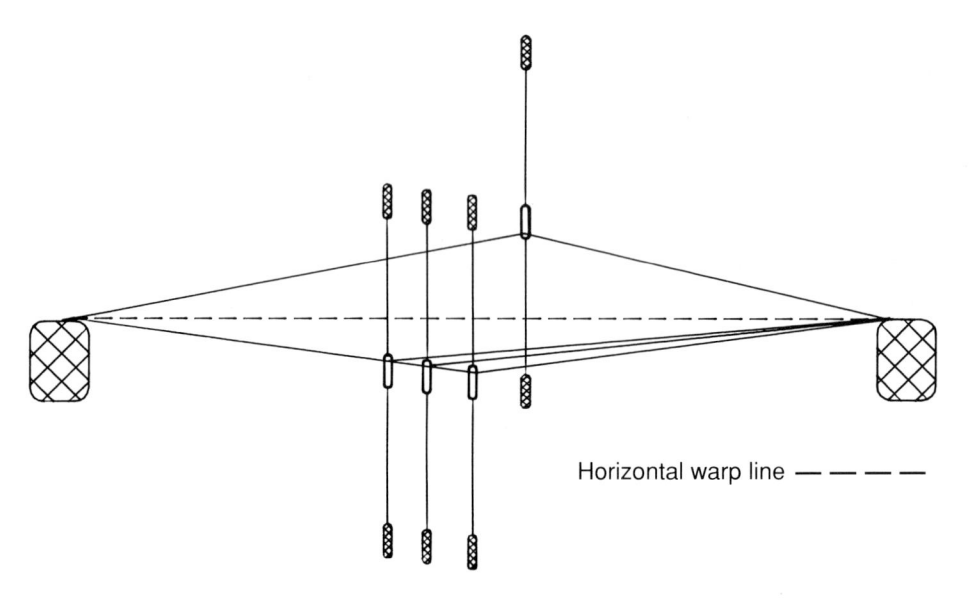

Fig. 4:C Warp line with one rising shaft

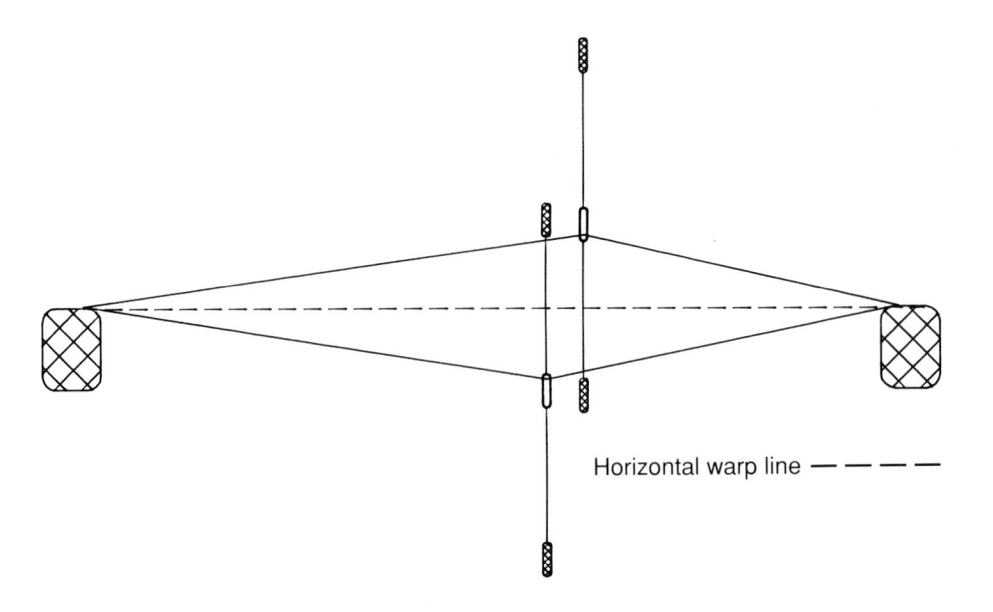

Fig. 4:D Upper and lower warp layer

74 • THE ASHFORD BOOK OF WEAVING

When the shafts are stationary, they must be kept below this imaginary horizontal warp line. The horizontal warp line is the natural position of the warp, and when a warp is in position on the loom, the ends want to return to this central position. Some weight or force is needed to keep the shafts at the correct position. On the Ashford jack loom, the weight and position of the metal heddles and frames holds the warp down.

A warp made of an elastic yarn, such as wool, poses no problems on a jack loom as the warp will stay at the correct, sunken position. However, a strong, inelastic warp, such as linen, particularly if it stretches the full width of the loom, can cause the warp to bounce up from its sunken position. Next time you put a strong, wide warp on your loom, test this theory. Loosen the warp, and note how it stays in the correct, sunken position. Then tighten the warp, and see how it lifts up. This not only narrows the shed when weaving, but will cause the lower warp line to lift above the shuttle race, making it more difficult to throw the shuttle across the shed.

If you do want to weave floor rugs on your Ashford jack loom, I would recommend the use of a cotton, not a linen warp, as cotton has more elasticity. In Chapter Ten, I have included a project for double corduroy floor rugs, which are suitable for a rising shed loom. The other factor to take into consideration is the heavy beating which is necessary when weaving most floor rugs. Again, a collapsible loom does not have the rigidity of other floor looms, and you may be putting too much of a strain on your jack loom. A pile rug, such as the one in ChapterTen, does not need beating as heavily as some other rugs such as a fleece rug, and places less strain on the loom itself.

Treadles

The treadles are front-slung, that is, they are pivoted from the front of the loom. There are two more treadles than shafts, therefore, on the four-shaft jack loom, there are six treadles. This gives you four treadles for weaving twills, and two treadles for weaving plain weave. In Chapter Eight is a full description of the various tie-ups, but I will cover one common tie-up here.

The twill tie-up shown in **Fig. 4:E** is on the four outside treadles, with the plain weave tie-up on the central treadles. Notice which foot is used for each treadle. When you are weaving a straight 2/2 twill, with a treadling sequence of 1 and 2, 2 and 3, 3 and 4, 4 and 1, your feet are moving in a walking sequence, known as 'walking the treadles'. This enables you to use the right and left feet alternately, which is less tiring and less likely to cause errors.

The tie-up shown in **Fig. 4:E** would be depicted on a weaving draft as in **Fig. 4:F** (over). On this floor loom weaving graph, the top right section is the tie-up draft, and it depicts in graph form which shafts are tied to which treadles. You can see that the left hand treadle, A, is tied to shafts 1 and 2, and so on. The treadling

Fig. 4:E Tie-up

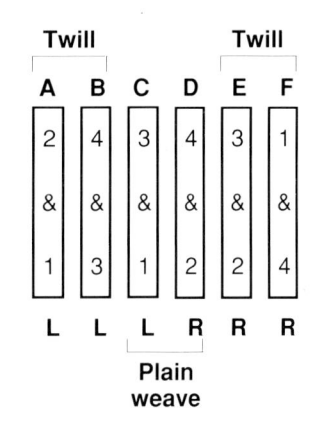

Twill				Twill	
A	B	C	D	E	F
2 & 1	4 & 3	3 & 1	4 & 2	3 & 2	1 & 4
L	L	L	R	R	R

Plain weave

L = left foot
R = right foot

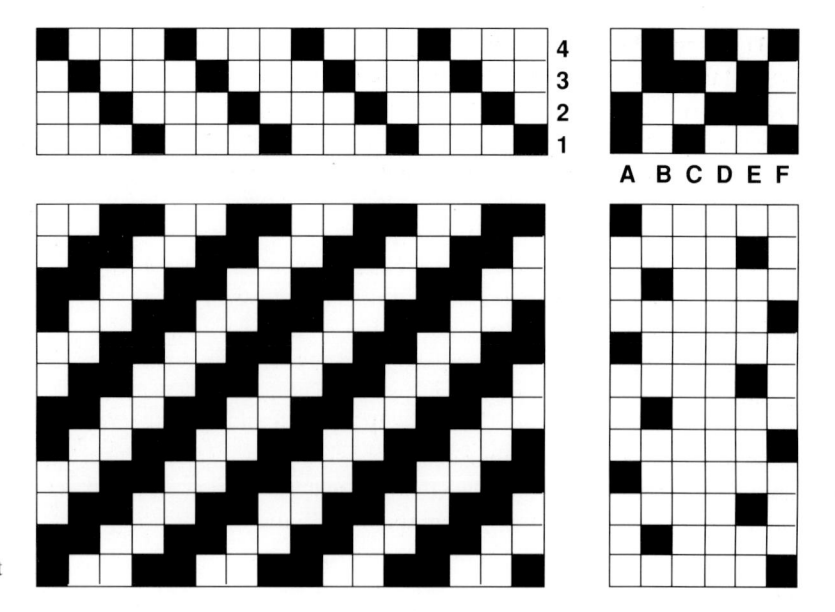

Fig. 4:F Weaving Draft

sequence, in the lower right section, tells you which treadle to depress, and is read from the top down. The top left hand section is the threading draft, and the lower left-hand section is the drawdown; a diagram on graph paper of the woven cloth. A black square indicates where a warp thread is on the surface. A white square depicts a weft thread on the surface. Chapter Eight covers pattern drafting in some detail.

To change the tie-ups from lamms to treadles, just slide the cords out of the slots in the treadles and into the new slots. To make it easy to change tie-ups, it is a good idea to have all the cords tied to the lamms to begin with. Therefore, each lamm will have four cords each. For one project, only 1, 2, or 3 cords will be tied to the correct treadles. The others will just hang down from the lamms.

As the treadle-to-lamm tie-ups are so simple to change, look at your weaving sequence when you begin each project, and change your tie-up to suit that sequence. If you find your feet accidently straying to the two centre treadles when you are supposed to be using the twill treadles only, a good tip is to tie the two centre treadles together, with a piece of cord, making them inoperable.

Brake system

The Ashford jack loom has a ratchet and pawl on the cloth beam, and a friction brake on the warp beam to tension the warp while weaving. This friction brake allows fine adjustments to be made to the warp tension, controls spin-off, and gives some elasticity to the warp. Spin-off is what happens when you release the tension, and too much warp runs off the warp beam. This is most irritating, because you then have to go to the back of the loom and re-wind the warp on to the warp roller.

The friction brake is a metal cable, wound three times around the brake drum, which is attached to one end of the warp roller at the back of the loom. One end of the cable is attached to a hook on the loom side, the other end is attached, via a turnbuckle, to a lever which extends to the front of the loom. Adjustments are made to the brake tension by tightening or loosening the turnbuckle. A very firm warp is needed for some warps, such as a cotton rug warp, and a looser tension for a light wool warp for weaving fabric.

To loosen the warp when moving the weaving forward on to the cloth beam, press the brake lever with your foot, and advance the warp by lifting the ratchet lever. Hold the smaller pawl, the one not attached to the ratchet lever, down to engage the teeth. Remove your foot from the brake lever and tension the warp using the ratchet lever. All this can be done from your sitting position at the front of the loom.

If the brake grabs and will not release, check the following points:
1. Adjust the turnbuckle so there is about 30mm (1in) of sideways movement in the wire cable halfway between the drum and the turnbuckle.
2. Check that the cable is wound evenly on the brake drum and is not crossed over.
3. Check that the cable has side clearance on the brake drum. Over-tightening sometimes causes the cable to flatten and wedge itself on the sides of the drum. The cable may need to be replaced if this has happened.
4. When the drum is manufactured and zinc plated, a rough finish can occur which should be smoothed off either with a fine file or emery paper.
5. A smear of light oil on the brake drum may also assist the brake to function properly.

4:3 Friction brake

Apron
A cloth apron connects the warp and cloth beams to the warp stick which holds the warp ends. On a table loom cords make this connection, but on a floor loom the distance between the beams and the warp sticks is much greater. If cords were used for this longer connection, the cord would build up around the beam, and push up through the warp and woven cloth, to cause tension problems. A stick slots through a hem in the apron end, and a warp stick is attached to this apron stick with short ties.

Other equipment
Included with your Ashford loom will be two ski shuttles, threading and reed hooks, cross sticks, warp sticks, and a weaving guide. You

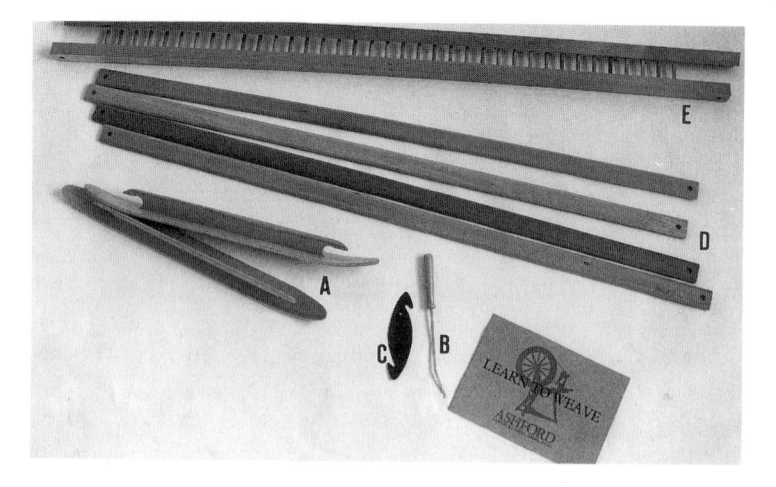

4:4 Other equipment

A Ski shuttle
B Threading hook
C Reed hook
D Warp sticks
E Raddle

will also need a raddle the same size as the loom width, scissors, tape measure, and a warping board or mill. As you will probably be making longer warps on the floor loom than on a table loom, I would suggest that a mill, which holds a longer warp length, is more suitable than a warping board.

WARPING THE LOOM

There are probably as many methods of warping a loom as there are weavers, and it can be confusing for the beginner to be faced with so many options. The method I use for threading a floor loom is basically the same as the one I use for warping table looms, described in Chapter Three. This method threads the loom from the back to the front, and I suggest you use this method until you have become familiar with it. Then you can change it to suit yourself.

Planning the warp

If this is your first weaving experience, I suggest you put a sample warp on to your loom as your first project. This sample will show you how the loom works, and teach you some simple techniques. If you have some weaving experience, begin with one of the simpler projects in Chapter Ten.

For the sampler warp, follow the instructions in Chapter Three, on planning a warp (pages 48–51). This covers all the necessary information on weave structure, sett, and warp length and width.

Making a warp

To save my repeating information, refer to Chapter Three, pages 51–55. If you have a warping board follow those instructions; if you have a warping mill, see pages 68–69.

Beaming

Remove the reed from the beater. Place the raddle in position at the back of the castle, with its cap removed. There are two holes drilled in the back of the loom castle for the raddle supports. Screw the supports to the castle, then slip the raddle over the metal pegs. Push the heddles to the sides of the shafts. If the heddles do get in the way of the warp as it is being wound on, tie a piece of cord around the heddles and the loom side to make more room. Tie a warp stick to the back apron stick at one end only, with a section of the string supplied with the loom, cut to 50cm (20in).

Take the chained warp to the back of the loom, and slip the loop from peg A on to the warp stick, including the first and last ends. Re-attach the stick to the apron stick, at the other end only. Put the warp chain over the raddle, through the shafts, and hang it over the breast beam.

Place two cross sticks, the sticks with holes drilled at each end, through the warp at each side of the cross, and tie the sticks together at both ends, leaving a gap of about 2.5cm (1in). Secure the cross sticks by tying the front cross stick to the raddle at both ends.

Follow the instructions in Chapter Three, pages 56–57, which tell you how to put the warp in the raddle, and how to wind the warp onto the warp beam. Enter the ends in the raddle from the back of the loom, replace the raddle cap, and tie the cap on to the raddle to hold it firmly. The handle on the warp roller is wound on in an anti-clockwise direction. If the warp beam slips, tighten the turnbuckle on the brake cable. If the warp beam will not turn, loosen the turnbuckle, or smear light oil on the gog groove.

If you have no assistant to hold the warp while you are beaming, take the warp under the beater, under the breast beam, and back over the shafts to the back of the loom. You can hold the warp, turn the handle, and insert layers of paper, on your own. It just requires patience and a few contortions. If we had three hands it would be much easier! It may be necessary to return to the front of the loom now and then to shake the warp and loosen it up.

4:5 Warp in position

4:6 Attaching the cross sticks

In New Zealand we have Venetian blinds made with thin metal slats, which are excellent for placing between the warp layers, instead of brown paper. You may not call these blinds by the same name, but look out for them. They can be trimmed to the size of the warp beam with scissors, and their curved shape fits neatly around the warp beam.

THREADING

Follow the instructions from page 58 for threading the heddles. The breast beam should be removed from the loom to allow easier access. The bottom beater rail can also be unscrewed to allow you to sit closer to the heddles for threading. I have a special low stool I sit at when threading the heddles, which puts my eyes at the heddle eye level. It does save a lot of back ache.

Tie the back cross stick to one end of a cord attached to the loom castle, with the cross sticks at heddle eye height. This will hold the cross sticks and the warp in a position near the heddles, ready for threading. The front cross stick will hang slightly lower than the back stick, and this makes it easier to see the cross. Remove the raddle, and the ties holding the cross sticks to the raddle.

SLEYING

Place the reed back into the beater, and tie the beater to the castle to keep it in an upright position. Follow the instructions on page 59 for sleying the reed, and tying the warp ends to the front stick. The front stick is attached to the apron stick in the same manner as the back stick.

HEADING

The heading is woven as on page 60. With the treadles tied up according to **Fig. 4: E**, shafts 1 and 3 are lifted by depressing the left of the centre two treadles (treadle C). Shafts 2 and 4 are lifted by depressing the right of the centre two treadles, (treadle D). Check for mistakes in the threading or sleying (page 61).

WEAVING

I suggest you weave the sampler techniques set out in Chapter Three, with plain weave, twills, and binder weft. By the time you have finished this sampler you will be familiar with the loom, at ease with the various weaving actions, and able to read the weaving drafts. The 2/2 twill draft is shown in **Fig. 4:F**.

The treadle to lamm tie-up will be changed when weaving **Figs G3, G4, and G5**. This will show you how easy it is to change the tie-ups, and to slide the cords from one slot to another. It may help to put sticky labels on the treadles, naming each treadle, A, B, C, etc. according to the weaving drafts.

Fig. 4:G1 Plain weave

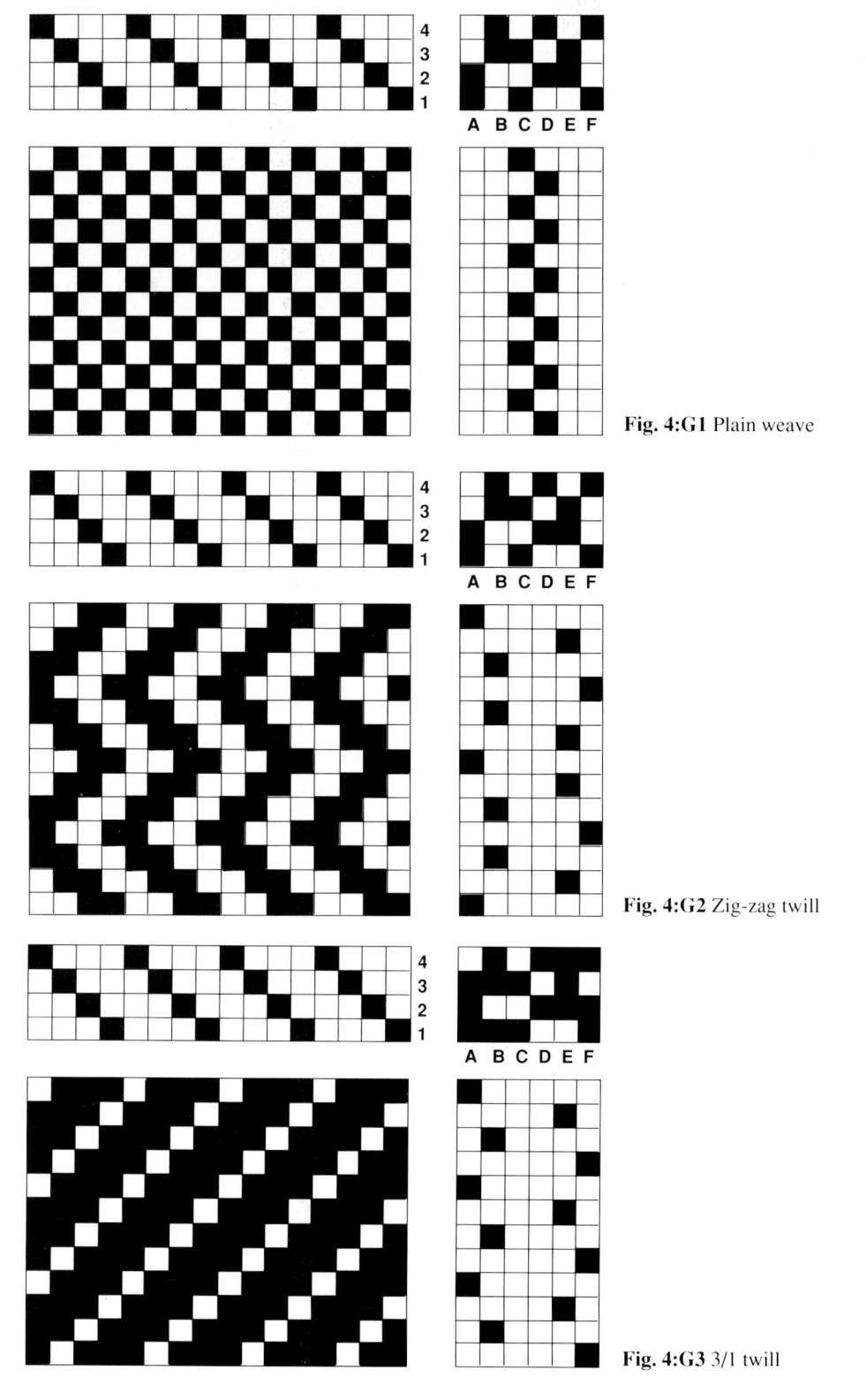

Fig. 4:G2 Zig-zag twill

Fig. 4:G3 3/1 twill

THE FOUR-SHAFT JACK LOOM • 81

Fig. 4: G4 1/3 twill

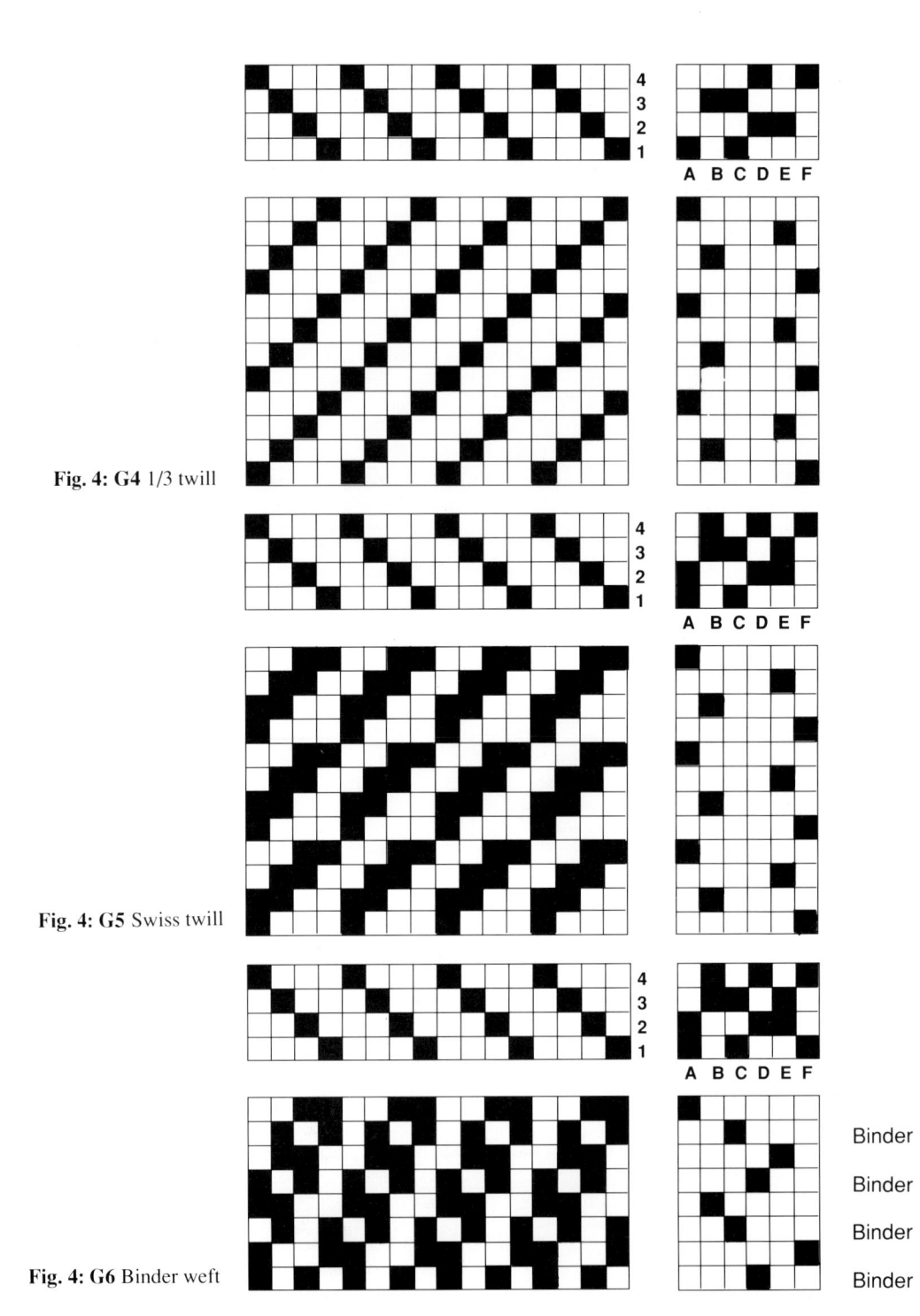

Fig. 4: G5 Swiss twill

Fig. 4: G6 Binder weft

A B C D E F

A B C D E F

A B C D E F

Binder
Binder
Binder
Binder

82 • THE ASHFORD BOOK OF WEAVING

Throwing the shuttles and beating

Try to develop a rhythm from the beginning. As the shaft positions are changed by depressing the treadles, without removing your hands from the beater or shuttle, it is possible to change sheds at any point in the beater movement.

A good ryhthm is as follows:

1. Throw the shuttle with the right hand from right to left.
2. Catch with the left hand.
3. Beat with the right hand in the centre of the beater.
4. As the beater touches the fell of the cloth (the last weft pick), move your foot to the next treadle and change sheds. This will clear the shed easily for the next weft pick. Reverse the hand movements for the next pick.

With some practice, these hand movements will give you an even beat. You can prevent mistakes by matching your shuttle and treadle movements. Make a habit of throwing your shuttle from the right when you are using your right foot, and throwing the shuttle from the left when using your left foot. Then, if you find yourself out of this sequence, you will know there is a mistake somewhere.

There are other methods of beating, when weaving different cloth structures. For example, when weaving a weft-face fabric, the shed is changed just before you beat. It is not usual to beat with a closed shed – where the shafts are all in the lower position – as this can cause friction on the warp ends.

SHUTTLES

Because floor looms are wider than most table looms, the distance the shuttle can be thrown has increased. This makes a stick shuttle clumsy to use, unless you are weaving a narrow width: it will not slide through the shed because the weft yarn rubs on the warp, and slows it down. Shuttles that can be thrown, such as ski and rug shuttles, can be used as these will slide across the shuttle race, and cover the full width with the wooden edges running smoothly across the warp.

Ski and rug shuttles will hold a quantity of thicker weft yarn, but the yarn must be unwound from the shuttle for the next weft pick. If your shuttle is not gilding smoothly through the shed, check the level of the lower warp layer. This lower layer should lie on the lower edge of the reed on the shuttle race. Even one warp end lying above this level, will impede the passage of the shuttle, and can cause the raised end to break. The level of the beater can be adjusted to keep the lower layer in the correct position on the shuttle race.

There are two other types of shuttles that are useful on a floor loom, particularly when weaving with a fine weft yarn. These are boat and end delivery shuttles. Both these shuttles are shaped to fit easily in your hand.

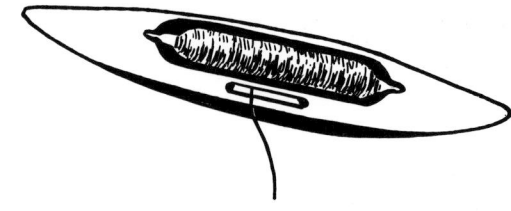

Fig. 4:H Boat shuttle

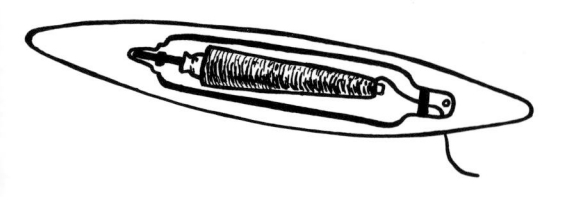

Fig. 4:I End delivery shuttle

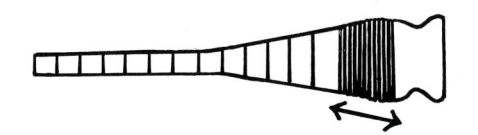

Fig. 4:J Winding a pirn

4:7 The Ashford bobbin winder

Boat shuttle
This shuttle has two parts: the shuttle itself and a separate bobbin or tube which holds the yarn. The shuttle is oblong and is shaped to slide smoothly through the shed. The ends are rounded and curved upwards. Inside the shuttle is a cavity, with a metal rod which holds the bobbin or tube carrying the yarn. The yarn winds off the bobbin through an opening in the shuttle side.

Traditionally the tubes or bobbins are wound with a small bunch at each end, and then the centre section is filled in by traversing the yarn up and down.

The bobbin will continue to rotate after the shuttle is thrown, and extra yarn either spills out or winds back on to the bobbin itself. Place your fingers on the bobbin to stop it rotating as soon as it leaves the shed. The yarn winds off a full bobbin at a different speed than off an empty one, and this can cause tension differences which in turn can cause uneven selvedges and may affect the beating. When the bobbin is nearly empty, the diameter decreases, the tension increases, and there is more pull on the yarn.

End-delivery shuttles
This shuttle also consists of a shuttle and a yarn holder, but it differs to the boat shuttle in that the yarn holder does not rotate, therefore there is no over-run of yarn and the yarn winds off at an even tension from both a full and an empty bobbin. The yarn holder, called a pirn, is shaped somewhat like a cone, with an elongated end. The pirn is wound by building up a cone shape at the thicker end, and then continuing this cone shape as the remainder of the pirn is filled. The yarn winds from the end of this pirn through a tension device at the end of the shuttle as the shuttle is thrown through the shed.

The speed with which the yarn is pulled from the pirn can be adjusted for the correct weft tension. If the yarn is taken from the shuttle straight from the pirn it will run off more quickly than yarn that is taken through two eyes at right angles to each other. There are various tension devices on end-delivery shuttles, so experiment by taking the yarn out through the various passages. When you can throw the shuttle leaving the yarn lying smoothly at the selvedge with no little loops, the tension is correct. As a general rule, if loops are left, the yarn is pulling out too quickly, and needs slowing down. If the weft is tugging and pulling in at the selvedges, the weft is pulling out too slowly, and needs easing up.

Winding bobbins
With all methods of winding, the yarn must be wound on at tension using some type of bobbin winder.

There is an excellent section on winding bobbins in *Handloom Weaving Technology* by Allen Fannin (see Bibliography, page 197).

5. THE EIGHT-SHAFT TABLE AND JACK LOOMS

WEAVING HAS BECOME more sophisticated in the last few years, and more weavers are turning to eight-shaft looms. These multi-shaft looms enable you to weave more complex weave structures than on a four-shaft loom. Elaborate patterns and designs can be woven and twills and block designs can be extended. As there are more shafts than on a four-shaft loom, the warp ends can be spread out between these extra shafts and this helps with a close-sett warp. More layers of fabric can be woven too. On a four-shaft loom two shafts can be used to weave one layer and the other two shafts for the other layer: only a plain weave structure is possible. With an eight-shaft loom, these two layers could be woven in twill, or four layers could be woven in plain weave.

There are various ways of tackling an eight-shaft loom. Many weavers learn the basic weaves on a four-shaft loom and when they have mastered that they move on to an eight-shaft loom. Other weavers tell me they have begun with an eight-shaft loom and learned the basic weaves on that loom from the very beginning.

In this chapter I will assume you have mastered the basics of four-shaft weaving. If you are an absolute beginner with an eight-shaft table loom, I suggest you follow Chapter Three and thread your loom as for a four-shaft loom and weave the sampler suggested on page 63. If you are a beginner with an eight-shaft jack loom, I suggest you follow the same course with Chapter Four. This will give you the basic knowledge needed to understand this section.

There are some differences beween using eight-shaft table and jack looms. A table loom has an independent shaft action, that is, each shaft can be lifted on its own. On a four-shaft loom, there are 14 possible combinations of the four shafts which form a shed. If all the shafts are up or down, there is no shed. On an eight-shaft loom there are 254 possible combinations. No weaver would want to use all these combinations in one piece of weaving, but on a table loom it is possible in theory.

On the Ashford eight-shaft jack loom, there are 10 treadles. These can be tied to any combinations of shafts, but only 10 possible combinations can be used in one piece of weaving, unless you want to re-attach the treadles to different shafts while you are weaving, which would be so slow as to be ludicrous. You could also tie only one shaft to one treadle, and this would give you greater variety, but your feet would have to cover several treadles at once, which may be awkward and cumbersome.

In the pattern drafts in this section, I will give both the treadling sequence for jack looms, and the lifting sequence for table looms. The lifting sequence will be to the right of the treadling sequence. Use whichever sequence is correct for your loom. The lifting sequence for table looms has been written with the left-hand handles attached

5:1 Ashford eight-shaft table loom

A Castle
B Beater
C Reed
D Ratchets
E Heddles
F Front roller
G Back roller
H Handles

to shafts 1, 3, 5, 7 on the left of the draft, and the right handles matching the right side of the draft with shafts 2, 4, 6, 8. With an eight-shaft table loom, it is easier to change all the handles on one side, then move to the other side. If you move from left to right haphazardly, you will become confused. If you need further help with pattern drafting, read Chapter Eight.

TABLE LOOM

This loom is the same size as the four-shaft loom. The castle contains the eight shafts, with the handles for lifting shafts 1, 3, 5, 7 on the left side, and the handles for shafts 2, 4, 6, 8 on the right. This enables you to lift all the right handles at once, then all the left handles, when weaving plain weave.

There are three sizes, 410mm (16in), 610mm (24in), and 810mm (32in).

JACK LOOM

There are two sizes, 1100mm (45in) and 970mm (38in) wide. The looms have 10 treadles. Two treadles are tied for plain weave with shafts 1, 3, 5, 7 on one treadle and shafts 2, 4, 6, 8, on the other. I suggest for this first piece of weaving that you tie the two right-hand treadles up for this plain weave. This will keep them out of the way when using the other eight treadles. Those eight treadles are usually tied up for the twill sequences. It is a good idea to have all the cords attached to every hole in the lamms, then the treadles can be changed from shaft to shaft easily. This does mean tying 72 ties to the lamms but this only takes about half an hour. When you are changing the cord to lamm tie-up, just slide the cord out of the slot when that shaft is to remain stationary, and slide the cord into the correct slot for the shaft that is to rise. The quick and easy change-over method on the Ashford loom makes this process simple.

There are two methods of altering the weaving sequence, that is the order in which the shafts are lifted. If you compare **Figs. 5:C** and **5:D** (p.91), you can see that the tie-up sequences in the top, right-hand corner are different. The treadling sequence, in the lower, right-hand section, is the same in both drafts. I feel this is an easier way to weave, as it only takes a few minutes to change the tie-up on your loom and your feet just follow the right to left movement whatever the draft. I use my left foot for treadles A B C D, and the right foot for treadles E F G H, when I am weaving twills. If you wear soft-soled shoes or treadle with bare feet, your feet can easily find the correct treadles by feel.

The other method is to change the treadling sequence for each piece of weaving, and keep basically the same tie-up. This is usually

5:2 Ashford eight-shaft jack loom

A Castle	I Warp beam
B Beater	J Cloth beam
C Reed	K Breast beam
D Ratchet lever	L Back beam
E Brake lever	M Heddles
F Treadles	N Spacer
G Parallel lamms	O Friction brake
H Jacks	

done with four-shaft drafts where there are fewer treadles. However, with the ten treadles on an eight-shaft loom, I find it more difficult to remember a frequently-changing treadle sequence.

In the following eight-shaft drafts I have used the former method, and you will be changing the tie-ups for each weave structure and, because this is a sampler, you will be changing the tie-ups more often than you would on normal weaving. When you have re-tied the treadles to the lamms for a new tie-up, check that the sequence is correct. Sit at the loom again, depress each treadle in turn, and check that the correct shafts are rising. It is frustrating to find too late that one treadle has a tie in the wrong place.

If you find changing the tie-ups tedious, or if you are not agile enough to get under the loom to change the tie-ups for each piece of weaving, I suggest you use the latter method.

It will help to put a sticker on each treadle with a letter on it to correspond with the treadle letters on the weaving drafts. Treadle A is the left-hand treadle, and treadles I and J will be the plain weave treadles on the right. This will help you to attach the correct treadles to the lamms.

DIFFERENTIAL RISE AND FALL

An eight-shaft loom should have the shaft heights adjusted for a level lower shed. The warp level at the breast and back beam is at a constant height. However, each shaft is at a slightly different point along this warp line. When a shaft is raised or lowered, it brings the warp ends on this shaft to a different level than the warp on another shaft. With four shafts the difference is not great, but with eight shafts the shed will be uneven because the shafts are so spread out. The level of the upper warp layer is not as important as the lower layer, as it is this lower layer that supports the thrown shuttle.

It is not usually necessary to adjust the shafts for differential rise and fall on the eight-shaft table loom. It is not as wide as the eight-shaft jack loom, and the shuttle is not thrown across the table loom shed in the same way as on the jack loom, because there is no shuttle race and the shed is smaller. Therefore, a slightly uneven lower shed will not hinder the shuttle as it would on a jack loom.

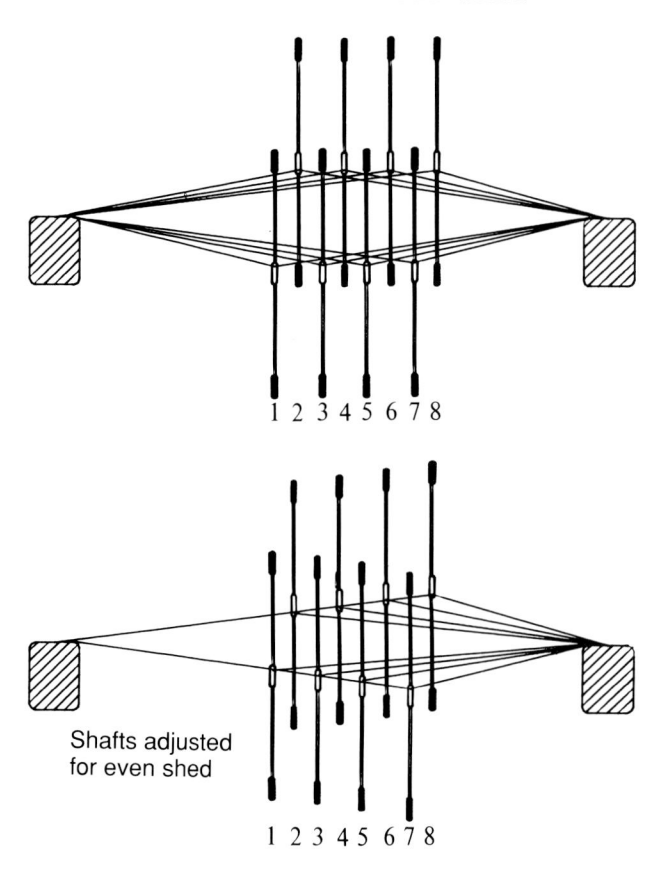

1 2 3 4 5 6 7 8

Shafts adjusted for even shed

1 2 3 4 5 6 7 8

Fig. 5:A Differential rise and fall

On an eight-shaft jack loom the shafts sit on rests attached to the loom sides. On the later models of the Ashford eight-shaft jack loom these rests are sloped down towards the back of the loom. This causes the back shafts to be slightly lower than the front shafts, and the lower warp layer will be level. If your loom is not adjusted for differential rise and fall, and you have problems throwing the shuttle across the warp width because of the uneven lower layer, I suggest you use ski shuttles: the curved ends on this shuttle seem to be high enough to glide across the warp without any problems.

WEAVING

We will begin learning how to use an eight-shaft loom by weaving a sampler. This sampler will demonstrate the basic eight-shaft weaves before you progress to the eight-shaft projects in Chapter Ten. This sampler is an introduction to eight-shaft weaving only, and I hope it will stimulate you to further study on this engrossing subject.

If you have a eight-shaft table loom, follow the instructions in Chapter Three, pages 49–63 on how to thread this loom. If you have an eight-shaft jack loom, follow the instructions in Chapter Four, pages 78–80. These chapters will also describe how the two types of looms work. The only difference is that you will thread the sampler on all eight shafts, as follows:

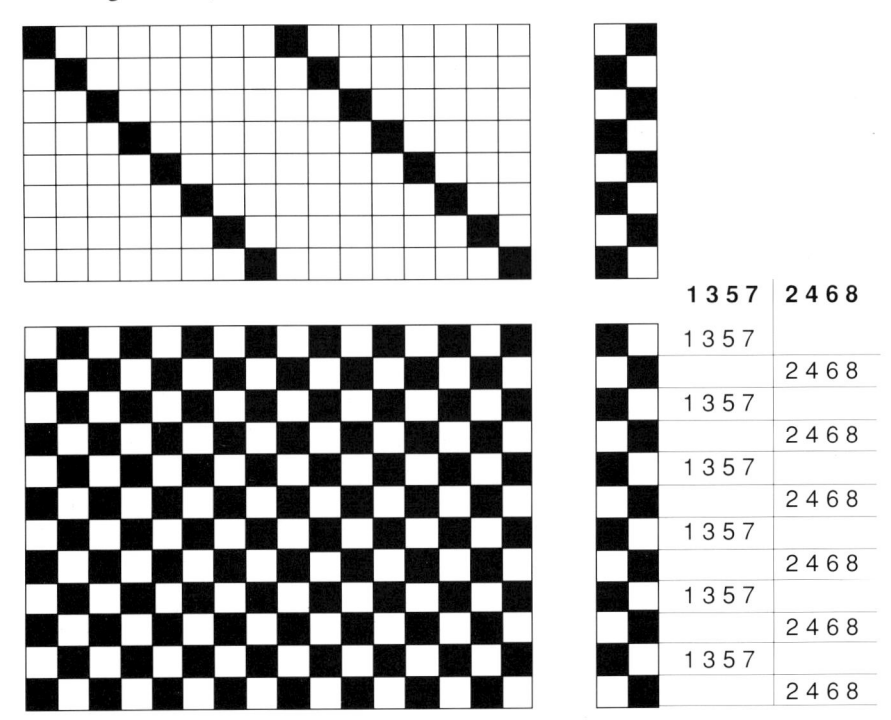

Weave a few cm(in) in plain weave, as in **Fig. 5:B**. This will make you familiar with all the shafts on your loom, and reading the drafts. Now for some twills.

Fig. 5:B Straight draw

TWILLS

The weft for the following twill weaves should be in a contrasting colour to show up the weave structure. On a four shaft loom, the twills are limited to 1/3, 3/1, 2/2 twills and combinations of these. With eight shafts we can weave these twills and more. A 2/2 twill has the weft thread going under 2 warp ends and over 2. To extend the twills, we can design a twill that goes under 2, over 1, under 2, and over 3. The total of these numbers adds up to the number of shafts needed for this twill; in this case 8. This extended twill can be written: $\frac{2 \quad 2}{1 \quad 3}$

Extended twill (1)

Extended twill (2)

The horizontal line represents the weft thread. The weaving draft for this twill is given in **Fig. 5:C**.

Remember, when reading the draw-downs on the pattern drafts (the lower left quadrant) the black squares are the warp ends on the fabric surface. For the jack loom, you will need to tie up the treadles to the lamms, following the tie-up section of the draft, the top right-hand section. Treadle A is tied to shafts 1, 2, 4, 5, and so on. Another extended twill is shown in **Fig. 5:D**. You will need to change the tie-up when weaving this draft.

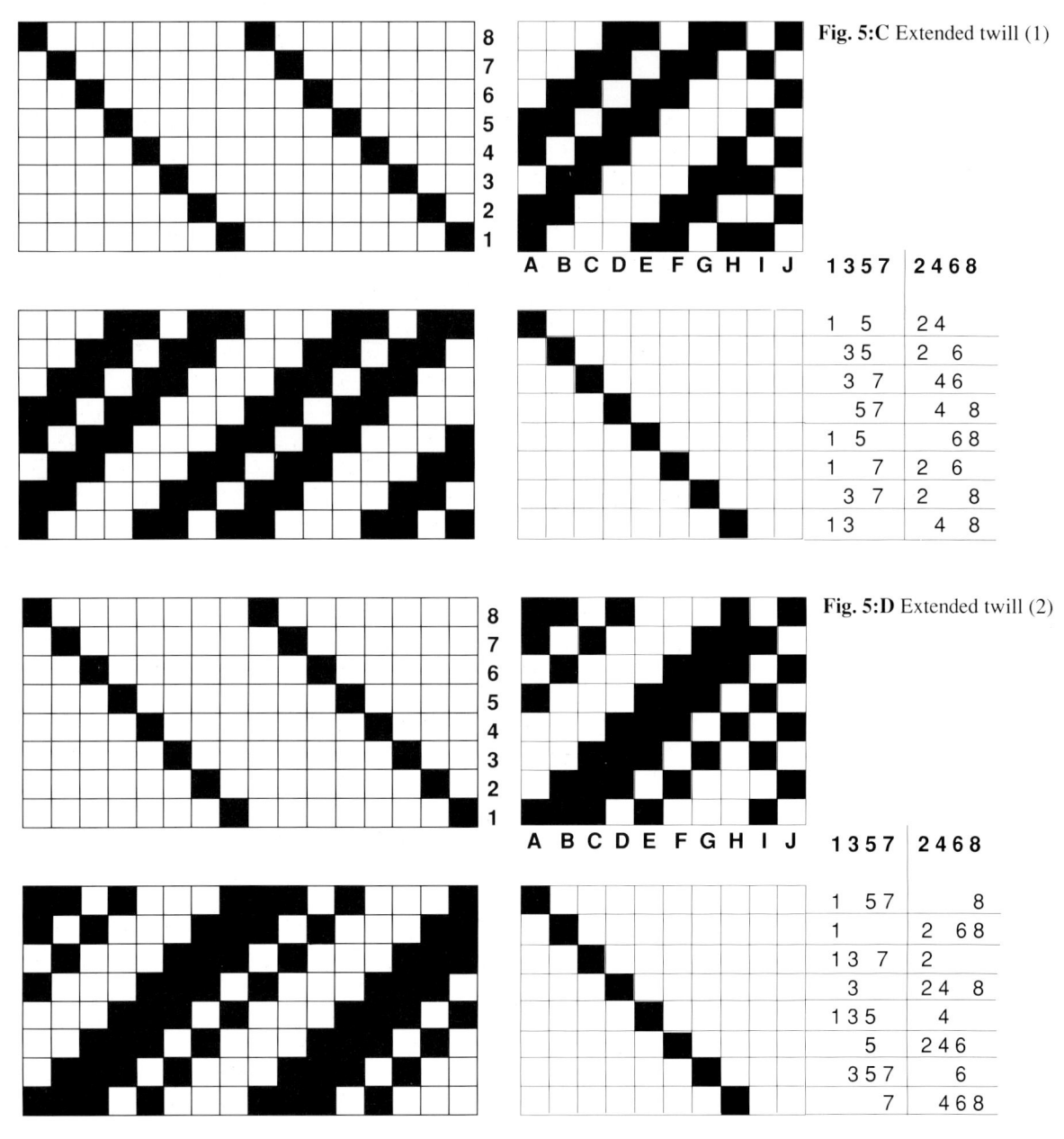

Fig. 5:C Extended twill (1)

1 3 5 7	2 4 6 8
1 5	2 4
3 5	2 6
3 7	4 6
5 7	4 8
1 5	6 8
1 7	2 6
3 7	2 8
1 3	4 8

Fig. 5:D Extended twill (2)

1 3 5 7	2 4 6 8
1 5 7	8
1	2 6 8
1 3 7	2
3	2 4 8
1 3 5	4
5	2 4 6
3 5 7	6
7	4 6 8

THE EIGHT-SHAFT TABLE AND JACK LOOMS • 91

There are many more twills that can be designed on eight shafts, and you can make up your own, or find them in books. *Looking at Twills* by Leslie Voiers, and *8, 12 . . . 20* by Kathryn Wertenberger are two excellent books.

The length of the float, the warp or weft threads that float or skip over the surface, is important. If it is too long it will catch, and also weaken the fabric. The length of the float depends on the sett of the yarn. If you have a yarn that is sett at 24 ends to 2.5cm (1in), then a thread that floats over 6 ends will only cover a distance of 4mm (0.25in), and this is acceptable. If the sett is 8 ends to 2.5cm (1in), then the float is three times longer. If you

Block twill

Reflected diagonals

are making a wall hanging, a float of that length is all right, but if it is for a length of skirting fabric it is not suitable as it will catch and perhaps break.

There are also point twills and broken and undulating twills which you can explore, but as these require re-threading the pattern in the heddles, we will not weave them on this sampler. The point twill threading is one of the most versatile threadings, as it can be used for weaving waffle weave, overshot patterns, and many others. Project Twelve is one example of an overshot pattern on four shafts.

With the straight draw, there are many other variations you can try on this sampler. Try some of the following weaving drafts.

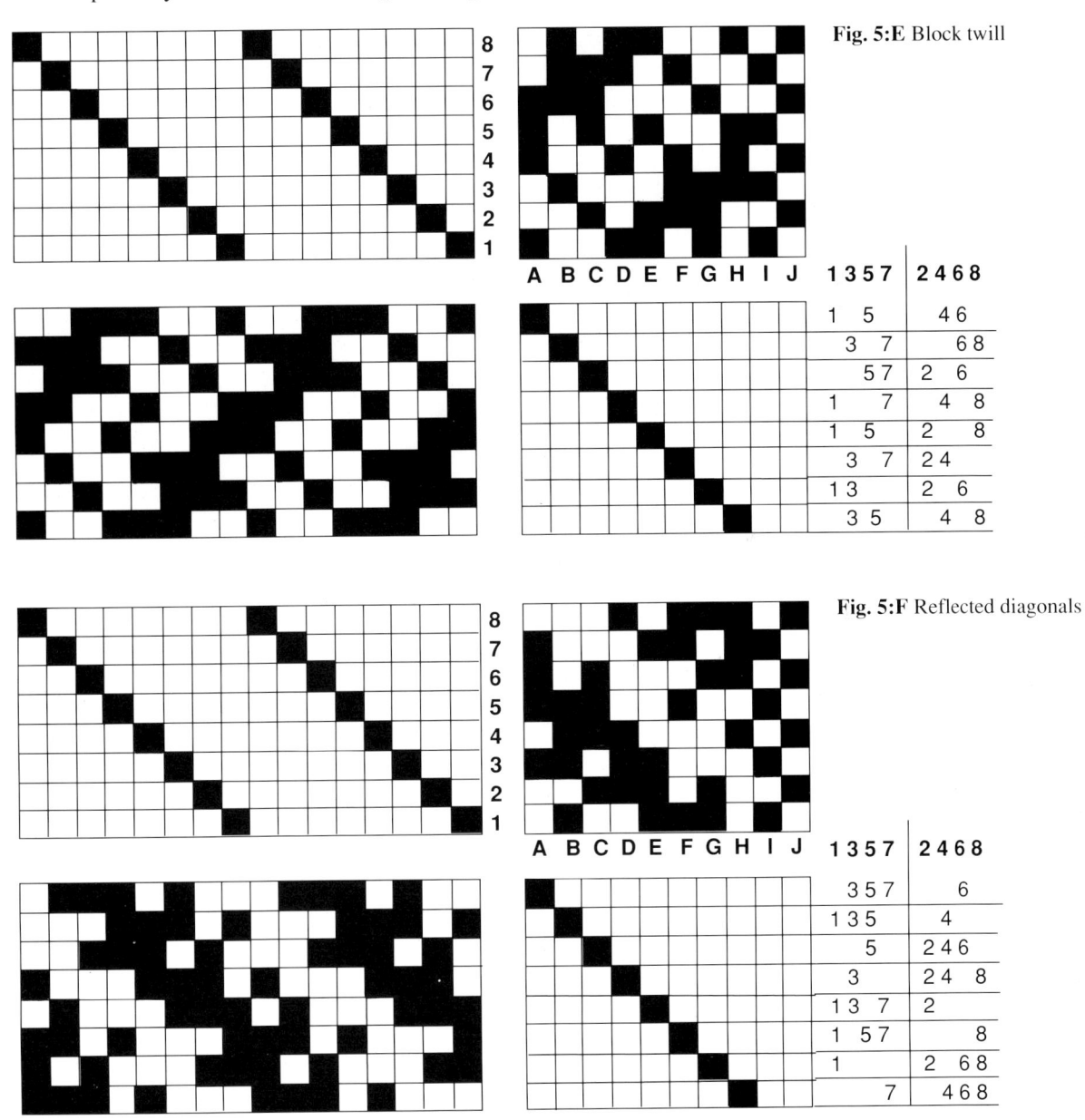

Fig. 5:E Block twill

1 3 5 7	2 4 6 8
1 5	4 6
3 7	6 8
5 7	2 6
1 7	4 8
1 5	2 8
3 7	2 4
1 3	2 6
3 5	4 8

Fig. 5:F Reflected diagonals

1 3 5 7	2 4 6 8
3 5 7	6
1 3 5	4
5	2 4 6
3	2 4 8
1 3 7	2
1 5 7	8
1	2 6 8
7	4 6 8

THE EIGHT-SHAFT TABLE AND JACK LOOMS • 93

Interrupted twill

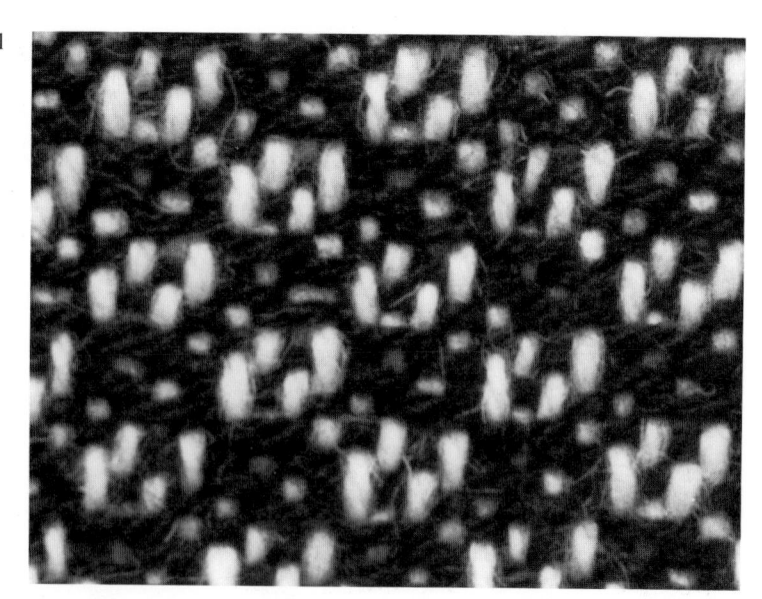

Wide zig-zag twill

OVERSHOT WEAVES

These are extended twills, but woven with a plain weave binder in between each twill pick. If you are not familiar with this weave, read the information in Chapter Three, pages 65–66. The binder weft is usually the same yarn as the warp yarn, and the twill pattern yarn is slightly thicker and softer. This binder weft does strengthen the fabric, and also elongates the design. The binder also enables each pattern or twill pick to be repeated without the previous pick undoing.

Fig. 5:G Interrupted twill

1 3 5 7	2 4 6 8
3	2 4 8
1	2 4 6
1 3 7	4
1 3 5	2
7	4 6 8
5	2 6 8
3 5 7	8
1 5 7	6

Fig. 5:H Wide zig-zag twill

1 3 5 7	2 4 6 8
1	2 4 6 8
1 3 5 7	2
3	2 4 6 8
1 3 5 7	4
3	2 4 6 8
1 3 5 7	2
1	2 4 6 8
1 3 5 7	8
7	2 4 6 8
1 3 5 7	6
5	2 4 6 8
1 3 5 7	6
7	2 4 6 8
1 3 5 7	8

THE EIGHT-SHAFT TABLE AND JACK LOOMS • 95

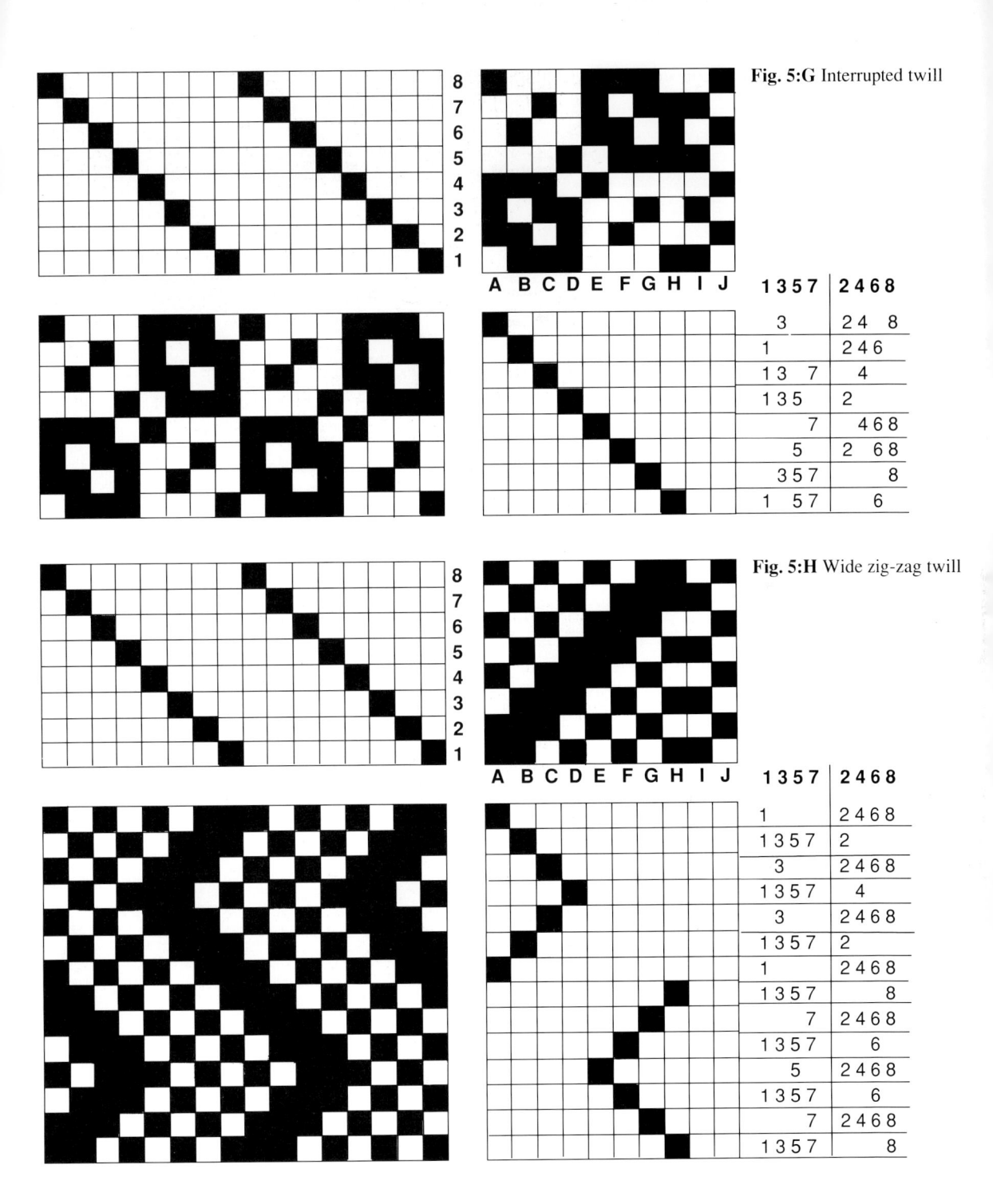

This gives unlimited scope to designing overshot patterns, which is one reason for their popularity.

As an example, take **Fig. 5:I** and add a binder in between each pattern pick. Weave this binder on the plain weave shafts of 1, 3, 5, 7 and 2, 4, 6, 8. On the jack loom, these are tied to treadles I and J. It will help you to remember which treadle to push for plain weave if you throw the shuttle from the left when depressing the left-hand treadle, and from the right when depressing the right-hand treadle. On a table loom use the same method with the handles, moving the right handles when the shuttle is thrown from the right side. Otherwise you can get into a muddle. Choose a contrasting colour and a thicker, softer yarn for the pattern weft.

Now try elongating the pattern in **Fig. 5:I**. Weave the second block three times, as in **Fig. 5:I1**.

Although the draft shows long floats, these are tied down by the plain weave binder and do not appear in the actual weaving. It makes the weaving drafts too long to show this plain weave, and it usually appears on the draft somewhere as an instruction. When I first began weaving I did not know about these binder wefts and the one book I had assumed I knew to put them in. I wove overshots, or at least they were supposed to be overshots, for a year before I found out what to do.

Try some of the drafts from **Figs. 5:E to H**, using a binder and repeating some of the treadling sequences as in **Fig. 5:I1**. You can also repeat one pick twice, the next pick three times, and so on, and the variety is endless. You can vary the colour by changing the weft colours. Try weaving **Fig. 5:I1** with pattern picks 5, 6, 7 (I am not counting the binder wefts) in black, picks 8, 9, 10 in navy blue, 11, 12, 13 in medium blue, and picks 14, 15, 16 in light blue.

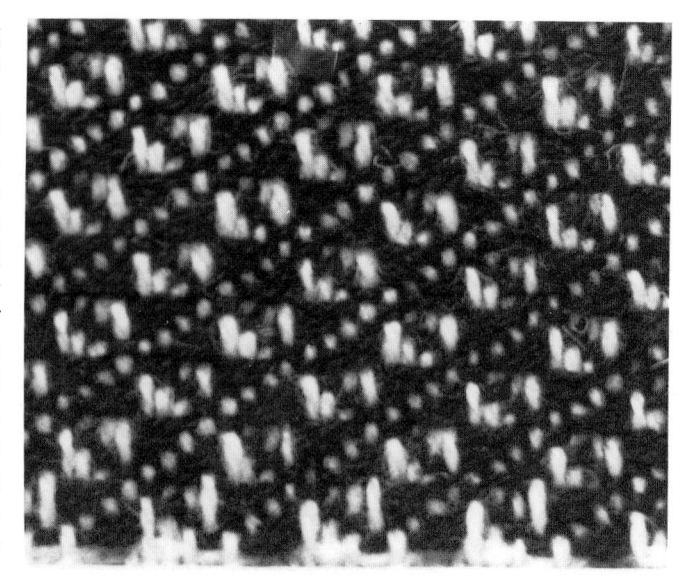

Spliced twill

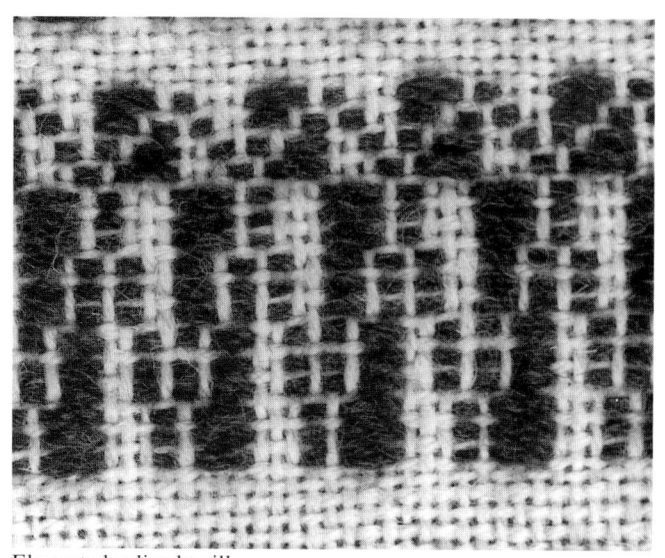

Elongated spliced twill

That will demonstrate how versatile this overshot weave can be. The treadling drafts are read from the top down.

DOUBLE WEAVE

It is possible to weave more than one layer at the same time. As I have said, on a four-shaft loom two shafts can weave one layer and the other two shafts can weave another layer, so only plain weave can be used. On an eight-shaft loom there are many more possibilities.

96 • THE ASHFORD BOOK OF WEAVING

Fig 5:I Spliced twill

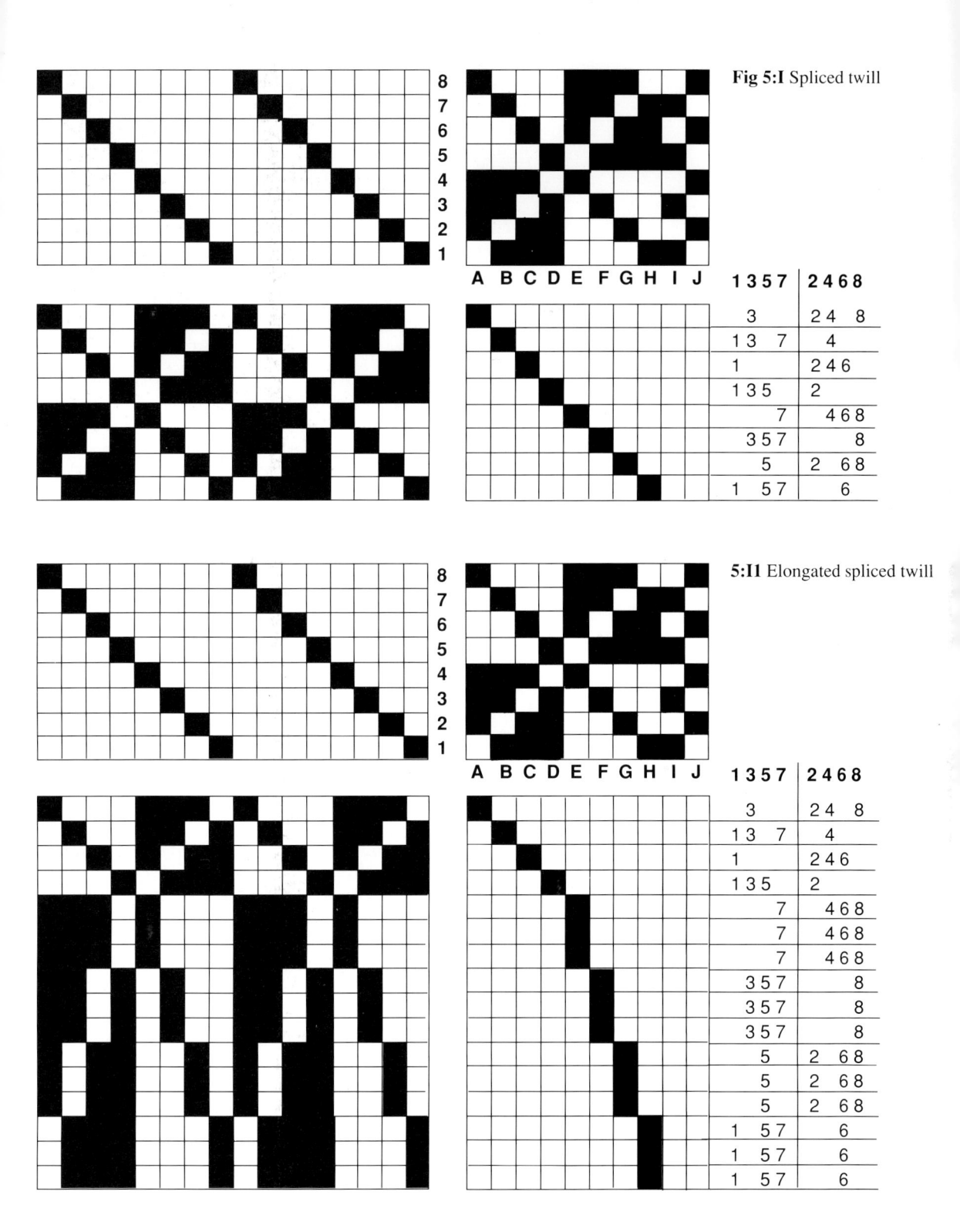

	1 3 5 7	2 4 6 8
	3	2 4 8
	1 3 7	4
	1	2 4 6
	1 3 5	2
	7	4 6 8
	3 5 7	8
	5	2 6 8
	1 5 7	6

5:II Elongated spliced twill

	1 3 5 7	2 4 6 8
	3	2 4 8
	1 3 7	4
	1	2 4 6
	1 3 5	2
	7	4 6 8
	7	4 6 8
	7	4 6 8
	3 5 7	8
	3 5 7	8
	3 5 7	8
	5	2 6 8
	5	2 6 8
	5	2 6 8
	1 5 7	6
	1 5 7	6
	1 5 7	6

THE EIGHT-SHAFT TABLE AND JACK LOOMS • 97

Twill double weave
The woven fabric is now separated into two layers, with half the number of warp ends in each layer. To compensate for this, while weaving this section of the sampler, double your weft thread. Normally, the warp would be sett twice as close.

Shafts 1, 3, 5, 7 are the upper layer, and shafts 2, 4, 6, 8 are the lower layer. Choose a light coloured weft for the upper layer, and a dark weft for the lower layer. Reading from the top of the treadling/lifting section of **Fig. 5:J**, you can see that the first pick lifts the upper shafts 1 and 3. The second pick is actually the first pick in the dark weft in the lower layer. To weave this lower layer, the upper

Twill double weave

Reverse double weave

layer must first be lifted out of the way. This is why shafts 1, 3, 5, 7 are raised as well as the lower layer shafts 2 and 4. On the floor loom this does make the treadles heavier when weaving the lower layer. The third pick is the second pick in the lower layer, the fourth pick the second in the upper layer, and so on.

Reverse double weave
To reverse the layers is simpler with a table loom, as shafts 1, 3, 5, 7 now become the lower layer. On the jack loom, the treadles must be re-tied **(Fig. 5:K)**.

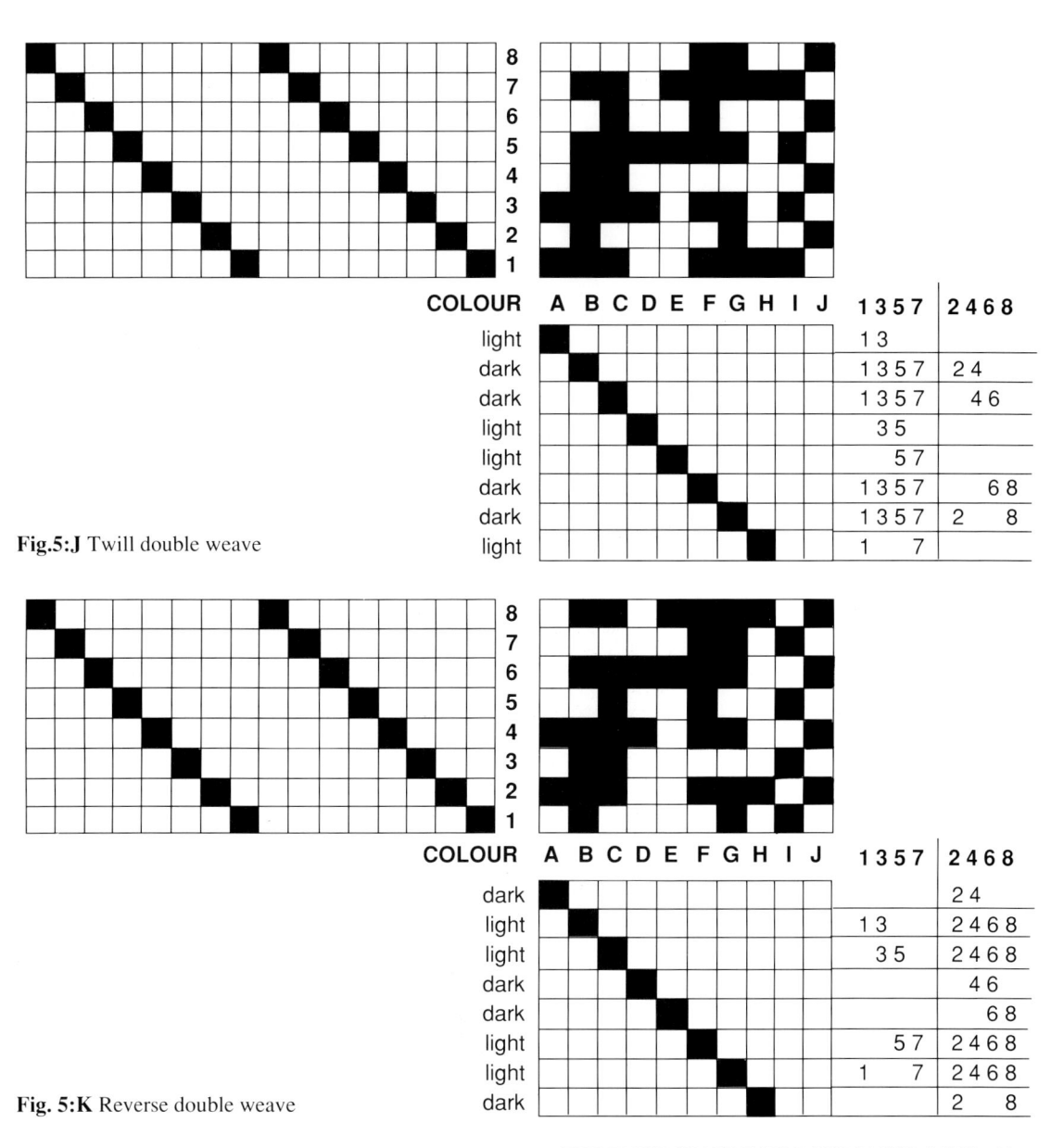

Fig.5:J Twill double weave

COLOUR	A	B	C	D	E	F	G	H	I	J	1 3 5 7	2 4 6 8
light	■										1 3	
dark		■									1 3 5 7	2 4
dark			■								1 3 5 7	4 6
light				■							3 5	
light					■						5 7	
dark						■					1 3 5 7	6 8
dark							■				1 3 5 7	2 8
light								■			1 7	

Fig. 5:K Reverse double weave

COLOUR	A	B	C	D	E	F	G	H	I	J	1 3 5 7	2 4 6 8
dark	■											2 4
light		■									1 3	2 4 6 8
light			■								3 5	2 4 6 8
dark				■								4 6
dark					■							6 8
light						■					5 7	2 4 6 8
light							■				1 7	2 4 6 8
dark								■				2 8

THE EIGHT-SHAFT TABLE AND JACK LOOMS

Stitched Double weave

The two layers do not have to be separate. By letting one warp end from the upper layer catch into the lower layer, and vice versa, the layers are joined together, to make a reversible fabric which has a different colour on each side. This is a useful technique for a floor rug.

Double weave (2)

The layers can be woven in different weave structures. In **Fig. 5:M**, the lower layer is woven in plain weave, and the upper layer in a twill. The twill layer will pull in more than the plain weave layer.

Stitched double weave

Double weave (2)

There are many more techniques based on the double weave theory. Four layers can be woven on eight shafts, each layer in plain weave. The layers can be joined at one side to weave a folded cloth, (see Project 20), or joined at both sides to form a tube.

SURFACE TEXTURE

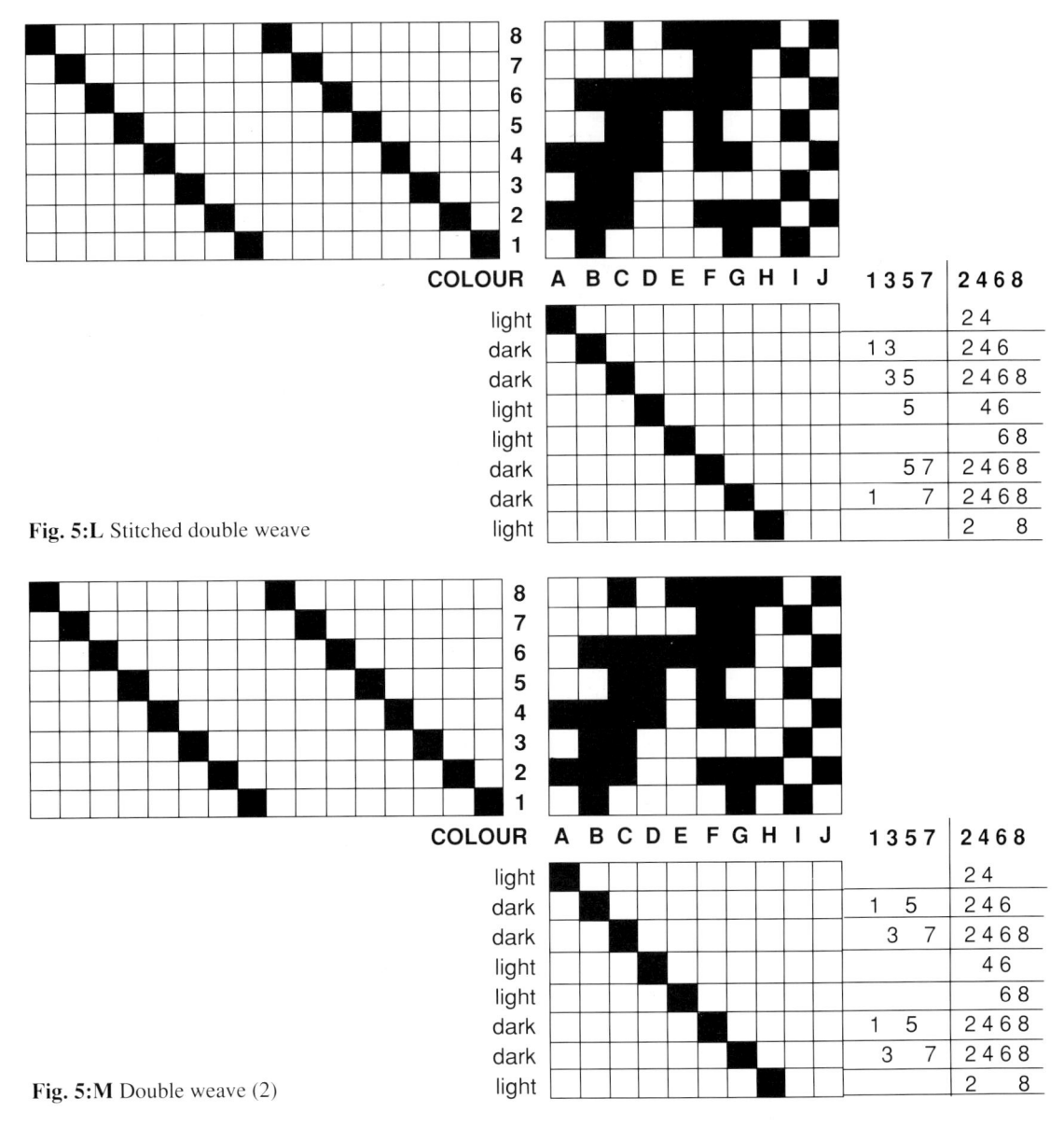

Brighton honeycomb (**Fig. 5:N**) is an interesting, textured weave, with warp and weft floats forming a cellular effect on the upper surface. The reverse side of this fabric has a flatter surface. The true structure of this cloth will show up when the weaving is removed from the loom, the tension relaxes, and the fabric is washed.

COLOUR	A	B	C	D	E	F	G	H	I	J	1 3 5 7	2 4 6 8
light												2 4
dark											1 3	2 4 6
dark											3 5	2 4 6 8
light											5	4 6
light												6 8
dark											5 7	2 4 6 8
dark											1 7	2 4 6 8
light											2	8

Fig. 5:L Stitched double weave

COLOUR	A	B	C	D	E	F	G	H	I	J	1 3 5 7	2 4 6 8
light												2 4
dark											1 5	2 4 6
dark											3 7	2 4 6 8
light												4 6
light												6 8
dark											1 5	2 4 6 8
dark											3 7	2 4 6 8
light											2	8

Fig. 5:M Double weave (2)

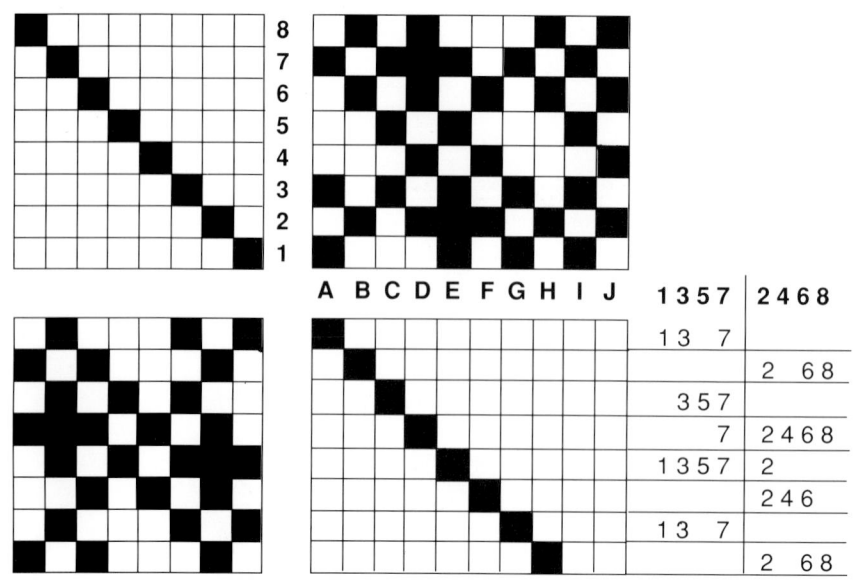

Fig. 5:N Brighton honeycomb

	1 3 5 7	2 4 6 8
	1 3 7	
		2 6 8
	3 5 7	
	7	2 4 6 8
	1 3 5 7	2
		2 4 6
	1 3 7	
		2 6 8

Brighton honeycomb

There are eight picks to a repeat in the treadling/lifting sequence. The last two picks are the same as the first two picks, but it is easier to weave on the jack loom if those last two picks are tied up to treadles G and H, and you weave the eight picks with eight treadles.

This sampler will introduce you to some of the possibilities of eight-shaft weaving. The scope of this loom is almost endless, and we have only just begun the exploration in this chapter. Lately more books have been written for multi-shaft looms, and the use of computer programmes in weaving has also made designing for eight shafts a quicker and easier process. Chapter Ten has some projects designed for eight shaft looms, or you may like to use some of the weaving drafts in this section, and design your own projects.

SECTION TWO
MATERIALS & TECHNIQUES

6. CHOOSING YOUR YARNS

THIS SECTION ON YARNS is intended as a reference section, one that you will refer back to as you weave rather than read straight through.

Choosing the correct yarn for a particular project is not easy. There are so many yarns available, with more coming on to the market all the time, that it can be confusing for the beginner. This section will cover the properties of each yarn, what the yarn is suitable for, and how it should be finished. If you are not sure how a yarn will stretch, shrink, or behave on the loom, I suggest you weave a small sample first. Wind a few strands around a small cardboard square to act as a warp, and weave under and over these with a darning needle. Before you cut the piece off the cardboard, mark its outline onto the card. Wash and dry the sample, and compare it with the marked outline to assess the shrinkage.

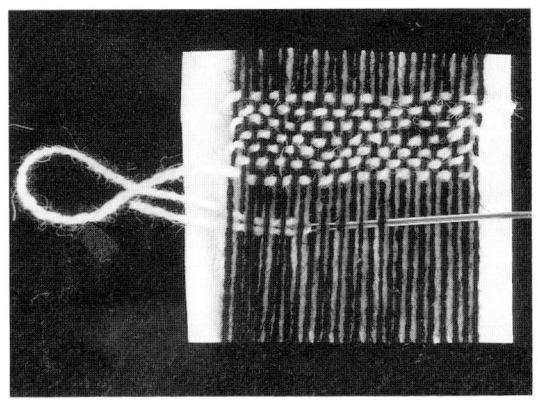

In Chapter Ten the yarns for each project have been chosen for you. The yarns can be changed, but if you are a beginner weaver you will find it easier to use the suggested type of yarn, until you have gained some experience of how yarns behave on and off the loom. A student in one of my classes used fine wool for a set of tablemats instead of fine cotton and the mats looked great until they had been washed a few times, when they shrank and became matted. The lesson learned was that most wool yarns do not stand constant washing in a washing machine. If you do want to change the yarn type, check that it has almost the same qualities as the original yarn. For example, a linen could have been substituted for the cotton in the tablemats without any problems.

Fibres can be divided into five groups: animal, vegetable, mineral, man-made and synthetic.

ANIMAL FIBRES

WOOL

This is one of the most popular fibres for the weaver, particularly in colder climates. Many weavers are also handspinners of wool and this adds to the range of wool yarns that can be produced. The properties of wool vary from sheep to sheep, from breed to breed, and from country to country.

The wool fibre, when seen under a microscope, has an outer cuticle of overlapping scales which play an important part in wool shrinkage. These scales point towards the tip of the fibre. The natural crimp of the wool gives it elasticity and resilience, which prevents the finished cloth from creasing and crushing. The crimp varies from breed to breed. Fine wools, such as Merino, have more crimp and elasticity than stronger breeds.

Properties

Wool takes up more moisture than any other fibre, and can absorb about one-third of its own weight of water without feeling damp. This absorption generates heat, which is the reason for the warmth of wool garments. Yet wool, although it absorbs water vapour readily, will not absorb rain quickly, and has excellent water-proofing qualities. It felts and mats readily and is easy to dye using acidic and basic dyes, but it is prone to insect attack and mildew. Wool yellows and weakens with exposure to boiling water, sunlight, chlorine bleaches and alkalis.

The burning test is a simple way to differentiate between wool and man-made fibres. Wool burns in but not out of the flame, and leaves a black, crushable bead.

Uses

Wool can be woven into all types of fabric, from heavy to lightweight.

Finishing

All wool fabrics need a particular type of finishing. Wool is a very elastic yarn, and if left unwashed, the fabric will look unsatisfactory because the warp and weft will remain separate. Correct finishing merges the warp and weft threads together and makes a strong, firm fabric. Do all mending, darning-in of ends, etc, before you wash the fabric.

The type of finishing will depend on the amount of wear the fabric will be subjected to, and the yarn type. There are two types of yarns made from wool: worsted and woollen.

Woollen spun yarn

Woollen yarn is a soft, fluffy yarn, with fibres that do not run parallel to each other. The fibres are not all the same length, it is not as strong as worsted-spun wool, and is usually more suitable for a weft rather than a warp yarn.. To strengthen this fabric, 'fulling' (also called 'milling') is necessary. This process slightly felts the yarn, causing it to expand and mesh together. Allow for a 15–20 per cent shrinkage rate in the finished piece. Dissolve soap flakes or powder in hot water. Soft water, rather then hard, makes a better bath for the fabric. Soak the fabric in the soapy water for about half an hour, remove it from the water and prepare another hot soapy bath. Immerse the fabric and knead it, but do not rub. It is the constant pressure of the warm soapy water through the fabric which does the fulling. Check frequently, and when the fabric is of the required firmness, rinse thoroughly in warm water.

This process can be done in a washing machine, as this will provide the agitation necessary to full the fabric, but check frequently to see how much the fabric has fulled. From two to eight minutes in the washing machine is usually sufficient for most pieces. If the finished fabric is not fulled enough, it can always be washed again, but do not over process the fabric because the fulling process is irreversible. A cold water rinse will complete the shrinking cycle.

Dry the fabric lying flat, or wind it around a roller to dry. If using a roller, unwind and re-roll the fabric from the opposite end each day, and stand the roller on alternate ends. Any wrinkles or creases left at this stage are permanent. While still slightly damp, press with a steam iron. Do not rub the iron over the fabric as you normally would, but press in one place, lift, press, and so on across the fabric. Commercial pressing is helpful for large pieces.

This is only an approximation of commercial fulling. In some places it is possible to have your handwoven fabric commercially fulled for you.

Worsted spun yarn

Worsted yarn is much smoother and stronger than woollen spun yarn because it is spun with the fibres parallel. Worsted has a harder feel than a woollen spun yarn, is harder-wearing, and is suitable for both a warp and weft. It can be used both plied and unplied.

Worsted yarn should not be allowed to relax and loose its parallel structure, so the fabric is 'crabbed'. This can be done at home by steam pressing the fabric with a damp cloth and heavy iron pressure, as soon as the fabric comes off the loom. Again, lift and press, and do not rub the iron over the cloth surface. Then wash the fabric in a hot, soapy bath. While washing, keep the fabric under tension by rolling it from one roller to another through the bath, and while rinsing. Dry under tension on a tube or roller. If the tension is not maintained, the fabric will crinkle permanently.

SILK

This fibre comes from the cocoon of the silkworm, which is fed on mulberry leaves. The cocoon is dropped into boiling water before the moth emerges, and the loosened silk is unwound. Several strands are twisted together to make a strong thread. Broken cocoons yield short lengths of silk which is spun into another grade. Wild silk, or tussah (tussore), comes from silkworms fed on oak and other trees, and is beige in colour.

Properties

Silk is a strong, smooth, inelastic, fibre with a high lustre. It dyes easily with the same dyes used for wool.

Uses

Silk is mainly used in fine fabrics, both as a warp and weft.

Finishing
Handwash in warm soapy water, dry flat, and press with a warm iron.

MOHAIR
This is the hair of the angora goat. The fibres have fewer scales, and these scales overlap less than wool.

Properties
Mohair is smooth to handle, and has a lustrous finish. It does not burn easily, is elastic, warm, and will felt, although not as much as wool. It is damaged by insects, heat, alkalis, and chlorine bleaches. Mohair is often used in combination with other fibres, such as wool, with which it has much in common. Mohair dyes well, and is very hard-wearing.

Uses
Mohair is ideal for durable fabrics such as upholstery and rugs, but is also suitable for most other fabrics.

CASHMERE
The goat of this breed, native to Kashmir, has a soft undercoat or down called 'pushum' which is spun into cashmere yarn.

Properties
Cashmere is a fine and costly fibre, with a very soft handle and drape. It is not hard-wearing, should be handled carefully, and is easily damaged by alkalis. Because of its high cost, it is often combined with wool. Cashmere is very warm.

Uses
Cashmere is usually used for shawls, stoles, scarves and other light-weight articles.

CAMEL HAIR
The camel's downy undercoat is used for weaving yarns because it is as fine and soft as Merino wool. The coarse outside hair is used in industry.

Properties
Camel hair is a very warm and comfortable fibre, and is used in its natural, tawny-brown colour.

Uses
This fibre is mainly used for coats and dressing gowns, but can be used in other fabrics.

LLAMA
The llama is a South American camel, with white, black, grey or fawn hair. The hair is slightly coarser than camel hair and is used in rugs and fabrics.

ALPACA
This comes from an animal closely related to the llama. The fibre is finer and has less lustre than mohair, and is used for fabrics.

ANGORA RABBIT
Angora rabbit hair is of two types. The coarse outer layer and the soft undercoat combine to give the yarn a characteristic appearance, with the stiff outer hairs protruding from the yarn.

Properties
Angora fibre absorbs water less readily than wool, felts very easily, and has a soft, luxurious handle. It is often combined with wool.

Uses
Angora yarn is eight times warmer than wool, and is used for light-weight garments such as stoles and scarves.

VEGETABLE FIBRES

COTTON
Cotton is the most common of the vegetable fibres, and has a natural twist. Mercerizing is a chemical treatment that adds strength and lustre to the fibre.

Properties
Cotton is stable under heat and tension, is absorbent and dyes well, but will weaken with constant exposure to light. Cotton shrinks up to 10 per cent, has little elasticity, is flammable and prone to mildew.

Uses
Cotton is suitable for both a warp and weft, and makes comfortable, hard-wearing fabrics. It can be used plied, and as singles.

Finishing
Wash in warm, soapy water, kneading the fabric until it is well soaped and wetted. Rinse in warm water and dry lying flat or around a roller. While still quite damp, press with a hot iron.

LINEN
This is another popular yarn for weavers. It is a bast fibre stripped from the stalk of the flax plant. The long fibres are spun into 'line', the broken fibres into 'tow'.

Properties
Linen is a strong fibre, with very little elasticity. It is not recommended as a warp for beginners, because this lack of elasticity can cause tension problems. Slacken the warp off after each weaving session, otherwise the threads will break. Linen is hard to dye and crinkles easily, yet linen fabric improves with age and wear. It is very lustrous, cool to touch, prone to mildew and is flammable.

Uses
Linen is used in fabrics and table linen, both as a warp and weft. Because of its lack of elasticity, it is better to use it unmixed with other fibres however Cottolin, a manufactured blend of cotton and linen, is an excellent yarn for weavers.

Finishing
Wash vigorously in warm, soapy water, rinse and steam press with a hot iron while the fabric is still wet. This gives linen its crisp, lustrous appearance. Linen crushes very easily, so do not iron the folds into the cloth, and store the fabric rolled around a cylinder, or over a coat hanger. Linen will wear at the folds if it is not stored properly.

JUTE
This is a rough, prickly fibre, used mainly in sculptural weaving.

Properties
Jute rots and disintegrates, so cannot be used for anything long-lasting. It dyes well, but the colours are not permanent, and it is difficult to bleach. Jute has little strength and elasticity.

MINERAL FIBRES

FIBREGLASS
This is a fibre spun from hot glass.

Properties
Fibreglass is slippery to use and difficult to dye, but it will not fade, wrinkle, stain or burn. It is strong, resistant to light, mildew, insects and chemicals, is non-absorbent and cleans easily. Fibreglass has a low resistance to abrasion, and does not bend well.

LUREX
This is a metallic yarn, which needs gentle washing and ironing, as it may break with creasing. It is made from aluminium foil which is coated with acetate or polyester film.

Uses
Lurex is commonly used in small quantities as a decorative thread in fabric.

MAN-MADE FIBRES

Cellulosic fibres are made from chemically treated wood or cotton pulp, and are of two types, viscose rayon and acetates.

RAYON
This fibre can be spun in two ways: (a) into a continuous filament yarn which resembles silk; (b) into a staple fibre yarn which looks like cotton.

Properties
Rayon is absorbent, flammable, inelastic, and prone to mildew. The fibre is not as stable as cotton, especially when wet, and rayon fabrics will not keep their shape as well as cotton. Cotton dyes are used.

Finishing
Take care to use mild soaps, warm water, and handle rayon fabrics gently, with no rubbing and stretching. (Trade names: Coloray, Dy-lok, Encel.)

ACETATE
This fibre can also be spun into continuous filament or staple fibre yarn.

Properties

Acetate absorbs less water than rayon, is stronger when wet, and burns less rapidly. It resists mildew, requires special dyes and produces static electricity. Acetate fabrics are crease-resistant and dry very quickly. This fibre is often blended with natural fibres. Finish with the same care as when washing nylon. (Trade names: Chromspun, Estron, Celanese.)

SYNTHETIC FIBRES

These are manufactured fibres with a chemical base. Trade names will be included in each group as, if each fibre can be placed in the correct group, the general properties can be determined. Otherwise, with so many new fibres coming onto the market, it is easy to become confused. For practical purposes, finishing and burning tests are the same for all synthetic fibres, and will be described at the end of the section. There are three main groups of synthetic fibres: nylon, polyesters, and acrylics.

NYLON

This is a petroleum product. Nylon yarn is elastic, very strong, and it resists abrasion. It is very stable and loses none of its strength when wet. It is often blended with other fibres. Basic and acidic dyes are used. Trade names include Celon, Caprolan, Enkalon, Perlon, Antron, Qiana, Crepeset.

POLYESTERS

Terylene is the main polyester fibre. It is strong, stable and very crease-resistant. It is resistant to sunlight but does have a tendency to pill, that is, tiny balls form on the cloth surface with wear. Both filament and staple yarns are made. If the staple yarn is crimped to form Crimplene, the wash and wear capabilities are improved. It is often used in blends with cotton fibre to make a more comfortable and absorbent fabric. Use disperse or special reactive dyes. Trade names: Dacron, Tetoron, Fortrel, Kodel, Vycron.

ACRYLICS

Orlon was the first acrylic and as the acrylics all have the same properties it will be used as an example. Orlon is very soft to handle, being lightweight and crease-resistant. Soft-twist yarns can cause pilling. Orlon is resistant to sunlight and is dyed with basic dyes. Acrylics such as Orlon are often blended with other fibres to give the yarn a soft, crease-resistant appearance. Trade names: Acrilan, Courtelle, Cashmilon, Exlan, Vonnel, Creslan, Dralon, Zefran, Beslan, Chinon, Wintuk, Sayelle.

Finishing of synthetic fabrics

Very little shrinkage takes place with these fibres: usually the only take-up will be in the release of tension when the piece is cut off the loom. Wash gently in mild soaps and warm water, taking care not to rub or stretch the fabric. Usually no pressing is needed as synthetic fibres are drip-dry, but if a light press is needed, use a warm iron. Ironing with a hot iron will stretch the fabric, and this is irreversible.

Static electricity

One problem that can be encountered when weaving with these synthetic fibres is the amount of static electricity they can generate. This causes the threads to cling together while you are threading the loom or weaving. The drier the air, the more electricity is generated, so one way around this problem is to spray a fine water vapour over the fibres.

Burning test

All synthetic fibres melt and shrink from the flame, leaving a hard, uncrushable bead.

BLENDED YARNS

There are two types of blended yarns: those that are blended before spinning, and those blended in the fabric itself. The former group are mixtures, such as Viyella, which is a blend of wool and cotton spun together. Most yarns state the percentage of each fibre on the packaging, e.g. 65% Dacron, 35% cotton. Until you have gained some experience, it is difficult to know how these blends will react on the loom, or when finishing or dyeing. A small woven sample may be the only answer. When dyeing one fibre may take up the dye and the other reject it, which gives interesting but unplanned results. Dyeing a small sample skein first will quickly show any problems. If you know the percentage of each fibre in the finished yarn, you can plan accordingly. For example, a yarn with 90% nylon, and 10% cotton will react very much like an ordinary nylon yarn, with little shrinkage, as there is so much nylon in the blend.

The other type of blending is when you mix two different fibres on the loom. If you weave with a warp yarn of one fibre, and a weft of another, there are very few problems, as the tension on the warp differs markedly from the weft tension while weaving. An example of this is Linsey-woolsey, which has a linen warp and a worsted wool weft. However, a fabric which has different warp fibres can cause problems. A warp with alternate stripes of wool and acrylic is one example, as the wool shrinks and is more elastic than acrylic. When washed the finished fabric will crinkle. The same thing happens with a mixture of acrylic and wool in the weft, but not to such a marked degree, as the weft is not under tension. This type of blending is only for experienced weavers desiring a crepe effect, not for beginners. If you are not sure whether the yarn you have bought is acrylic or wool, the burning test, described on page 105, will differentiate.

SELECTING WARP AND WEFT YARNS

WARP YARNS

These need to be stronger than weft yarns, as they will be under tension on the loom. A plied yarn, of two or more strands twisted together, is stronger than a single yarn of one strand. A smooth warp yarn is preferable, as a slub yarn will catch in the reed or the heddles. Some friction occurs with the movement of the heddle so rub your finger-nail up and down the yarn to see if it frays easily. If so, it is not suitable for a warp. Test the strength of a warp yarn by pulling the yarn over your thumbnail. If it snaps at the first pressure, it is not strong enough for a warp. If a fluffy yarn is used as a warp, sett it further apart, to prevent the strands sticking to each other, and closing the shed.

WEFT YARNS

Almost any yarn can be used as the weft, as these yarns do not need to be as smooth or as strong.

Consider the possibilities of using other materials such as leather strips, raffia, bamboo, rags, as weft yarns to add interest to the woven surface.

YARN DESIGN

Beside practical concerns, another aspect to consider is the texture and appearance of the yarns you weave with. Texture and weaving techniques should be considered together. A highly textured yarn is one which reflects light and shade and if it is used in conjunction with a technique which also reflects light and shade, the effect can be too much and the yarn will obliterate the technique or vice versa. One example of this would be using a very shiny slub yarn to weave an overshot pattern as on page 162. This shiny slub yarn would be shown to its best advantage with a plain, balanced weave. A good rule to follow is 'the fancier the yarn, the plainer the weave'.

Look at the yarn before you begin to weave, and use a technique which enhances the inherent qualities of that yarn. A boucle yarn will look best when lightly beaten, thus letting the structure of the yarn show in the finished weaving.

YARN COUNTS

There are so many different ways of measuring yarns that it is often difficult to know the length of a given weight of yarn. The ply number only tells us how many strands are plied together, and nothing about the thickness of the yarns themselves. However, an international system called 'Tex' is being introduced which will solve this problem. It is a metric system in which yarns are described by the weight in grams of 1000 metres. A size 100 yarn (R 100 Tex) is spun with 1000 metres weighing 100g. A size 200 yarn (R 200 Tex) is spun with 1000 metres weighing 200 g. A low number indicates a fine yarn, a high number a thick yarn. This is the final size of the yarn regardless of the ply. The ply number is added at the end. 200 Tex/2 means that 2 single yarns were plied, and the combined yarn weighs 200g per 1000 metres.

7. DESIGNING WOVEN PROJECTS

IN CHAPTER TEN I have given you detailed information on weaving specific projects. It is necessary for beginner weavers to have this information because it is difficult to plan projects when you do not have enough experience to visualize how a certain technique will look when it is woven. Once you have built up some basic knowledge, it is possible to plan your own projects. Copying a project out of a book is the same as using a recipe book, and most people have to learn to cook from a recipe book at first. However, there comes a time when this is not enough and we want to make up our own recipes. This section is to help you do just that.

One of the most difficult decisions to make is where to start designing a specific project. There are so many related factors to take into account: the colour, shape, yarn, pattern and finishing, all of which can be confusing. Often we just pick up a yarn and start threading the loom, and hope inspiration will come during the weaving process. Sometimes it does, but more often we make an expensive mistake. Making mistakes is all part of weaving, and we learn much by them, but too many failures will take the fun out of weaving and cause us to lose confidence in our ability and to become hesitant and unadventurous.

In this chapter I will describe a method of designing projects that I use with my students which will give you a clear-cut planning system. I hope you will alter it to suit your particular needs. All projects have a set of built-in guidelines because the end use of the project determines how it is made. For example, a scarf would not usually be 20 metres long and 5m wide, unless you have a giant in the family. If Aunt Mary asks you to weave a scarf, you know it will probably be about 150cm (5 feet) long, and 15-30cm (6 - 12 in) wide. The scarf will be made in something soft to touch, and will drape well. If Aunt Mary has not got a coat she wishes it to match, the scarf can be woven in a neutral colour of white or cream. A pattern will not be woven into the centre of the scarf, as that part sits at the back of the neck when worn, and will not be seen. The pattern would be best at each end of the scarf, or down the middle end to end.

Note how I have been able to design this scarf almost completely from the end use of the project, and it makes planning so much easier.

There will always be exceptions to this way of planning (Aunt Mary may be a very tall woman who needs a scarf 200cm (80ins) long) but it does give you that starting point and a system of slotting into the project all the relevant factors.

I will give you some general guidelines for specific projects to show you how the planning is done. When I am teaching this method of designing, I cut pictures out of home decorating magazines and ask the students to design certain projects to fit the illustrated room. Fashion illustrations in magazines are also useful. It is very good practice to design this way and easier for a beginner to weave projects with a specific purpose, that is, for a certain room or person, so try this method yourself. When weaving for exhibitions or for sale to shops, the guidelines cannot be specific and this will be discussed briefly later in the chapter.

Under each of the following headings – size, yarn, washing, pattern, colour, technique, and finishing – list all the relevant details for your particular project, as I have done below. The headings will change from project to project but the information collected will enable you to design that article as an entity. Design and colour aspects of a piece of weaving should not be separate, they are as much a part of it as the size or function. When we separate colour or design decisions from the planning process they become difficult, and the end result is a confused and unsatisfactory piece.

CUSHIONS

Size

Most cushions, to use on chairs, couches etc., are 40-50cm (15-20in) square. Floor cushions can be any shape or size. If you are making cushions for a particular room, decide whether round, triangular, rectangular or square cushions would match the room and furniture shape.

Yarn

Cushions need to be flexible and comfortable, so wool is often the best yarn.

Washing

If woven in a light colour, cushions need to be washable. This means the woven cover should be removable, with some sort of fastening. The fastening can be a zip, velcro, or an envelope or overlapping type of cover. The inner cushion may also be washable, if the correct filling is used.

Pattern

Look at the cushion shape. The woven pattern will need to fit into this shape. A square cushion could have any of the designs opposite, all of which emphasize the square outline.

Look at the room you are making the cushions for. What are the predominant shapes and patterns in this room? Can you echo the shape of the fireplace, for example? Does the curtain pattern suggest a pattern? An article with a familiar feel to it, that fits in with other pieces in the room, will be in harmony with its surroundings.

Colour

Do you want the cushion to blend in with its surroundings? If so, choose a colour that matches the main room colour. Do you want the cushion to stand out, and provide an accent? Choose a colour that is present in the room in very small quantities. The curtains may be basically green but with a hint of gold. Choose this gold colour for the cushions. You could also choose a colour that is seen through the windows.

Technique

If you have a very textured yarn in a bright colour, choose a plain weave. A good guideline is that the brighter the colour and the more textured the yarn, the plainer the weave structure should be. Otherwise, the cushion can look busy and overdone as all the elements fight to dominate. A textured yarn is often lost in a weft-face weave as it is packed down tightly and the yarn structure disappears. A plain, balanced weave will show a textured yarn to its best advantage.

Fig. 7:A Designs for a square cushion

Finishing

Because a cushion is usually made in one long piece and then folded over, it will have two selvedge sides, one fold, and one end where the fringe is the end finish. When sewn together, these different edges will not look the same. This is the reason why most cushions look best with a braid or fringe around all four sides. Chapter Nine describes some suggested finishes.

SCARVES

Size

The most common size is 120–150cm (4–5 feet) long, and 15–25cm (6–10in) wide for a woman's scarf. A man's scarf is usually slightly longer and wider.

Yarn

Choose a yarn that is soft to touch, as a scarf is worn next to the skin It can be wool, cotton, silk, etc, but rub the yarn against your face to test for feel.

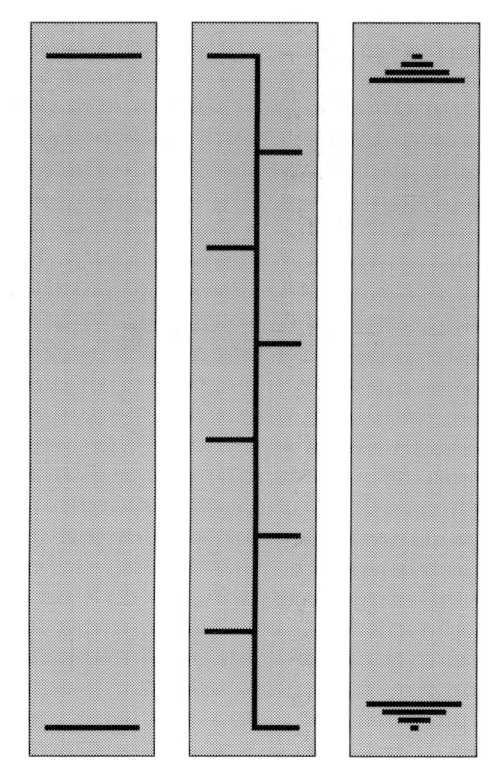

Fig. 7:B Scarf designs

Washing
A scarf should be able to be washed, therefore the colour must be fast.

Pattern
Look at the scarf outline as this will suggest suitable patterns.

A light lacy scarf will suit some of the lace weaves such as Leno and Brooks Bouquet. A man's scarf, which may be more firm, can be woven in checks and plaids

Colour
If the scarf is for a particular outfit, choose a colour that either blends in with the main colour, or makes a strong contrast. One hint: if you can not match the colour of your outfit exactly, go several shades deeper or into lighter tints. A colour that is a fraction off can be annoying.

Neutral colours such as pale grey or cream are always safe. A bright white scarf is not always kind to an older person's skin colour and cream is more flattering. A scarf is always worn near the face, which means that as we talk to a person, the scarf will dominate. Tone the colours and design, down, rather than up. A scarf worn as a sash around the waist can be much brighter.

Tie-dyed, or random-dyed scarves always seem to be effective. If using bought, random-dyed wool, the colour changes are very seldom absolutely random, and the scarf may end up in stripes of different colours. Breaking the yarn every now and then will break up these stripes, but you may not want all the joins.

Technique
A scarf must drape well and be comfortable to wear. A balanced, plain weave scarf should be woven with a gentle, light, beat. A twill weave will drape very well, and the weave structure adds bulk to the fabric.

Finishing
A scarf usually looks better with a fringe as a hem will prevent the scarf from hanging well. The fringe should be in proportion to the scarf length: a 152cm (5 ft) scarf would look best with a fringe of 7–8cm (3 in) at each end, for instance. Fancy, knotted fringes can enhance a plain scarf.

TABLEMATS

Size
A good size for a tablemat is a finished length, that is after washing and shrinkage, of 36cm (14 in), with a 2.5cm (1in) fringe at each end, and a width of 28–30cm (11–12in). I weave most tablemats to 40cm (16in) on the loom, and thread the loom 33cm (13in) wide. This seems to give me the above measurements after washing. If you are weaving mats for a particular dinner set or table, the plate, or table size should be taken into account. I personally like to have enough mat around the plate to put the cutlery on.

Yarn
Tablemats do need frequent washing, at least in our house! Cotton and linen mats seem to stand up to this washing better then most other yarns. If you are using wool, choose a hard-wearing wool such as rug or carpet wool. The mat should have a reasonably flat surface on which to put plates,

cultery, etc, so a very bumpy yarn may cause problems, as you will spill your wine glass or coffee cup.

Washing
Tablemats should be washable and colour fast.

Pattern
End borders are most commonly used on tablemats because a centre pattern will be hidden under the plate. A flat pattern like Leno, that is built into the weaving not raised up from it, is best as again this avoids spillage problems. Choose a design that suits the tablemat size.

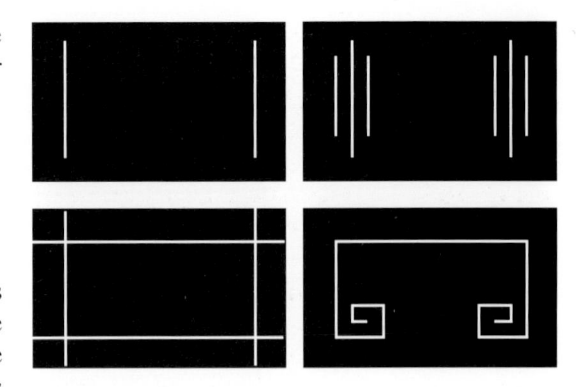

Fig. 7:C Designs for tablemats

Colour
If you are matching a set of mats with a dinner set, you can co-ordinate the two. The mat can be the same colour as the plate, in which case the two will blend and be indistinguishable, or a contrasting colour can be used to make the plates stand out from their surroundings. The table colour does matter too. A brown mat on a brown, wooden table will merge together. If you have a small table, and do not want it to look cluttered, this is one solution. Cream tablemats on a wooden surface are a traditional combination that always looks good.

Technique
Weft-face mats will take a long time to dry, so if the mats will require frequent washing, a plain balanced weave background is best. Beat firmly, as a strong fabric will wear well.

Finishing
If a fringe is left, keep this reasonably short, about 2.5cm (1 in) as this will not get raggedy with the frequent washing. Hemming is used on many tablemats, particularly the finer linen or cotton mats. Thicker wool mats will not hem well, as the edge is bulky. Hemstitched ends look good on most mats.

UPHOLSTERY FABRIC

Size
Measure the piece of furniture to be covered, and be very generous with the shrinkage allowance. If you are weaving a large amount of fabric, it is a good idea to weave a small sample first to make sure all the details are correct before starting the larger piece. This sample can be measured, washed, and then measured again, to find the correct shrinkage allowance.

Yarn
A hard-wearing yarn is necessary, and one that will bend around corners without strain It must not be scratchy or itchy to sit on. Wool is a common yarn, and is also reasonably resistant to fire. Some of the synthetic blends have proved to be very inflammable, and also give off dangerous fumes when on fire. Check on this property carefully.

Washing
Give the fabric a very vigorous washing after it comes off the loom, to ensure a firm, close, hard-wearing fabric. The fabric will probably not be washed again, once it has been made into the chair covering.

Pattern
Choose a pattern without long floats – long threads on the surface of the weave – which can catch and pull with wear and spoil the appearance of the fabric. A small, overall pattern, or a textured yarn will be effective.

Colour
Choose a colour that will not fade, as sunlight is a

real enemy of upholstery fabric. Put some yarn in a matchbox, with half the yarn in the box, and half out, and expose it to bright sunlight on a window sill for some days or weeks, to test for fading. Any coverings for chairs or couches will be a major area of colour in a room and a large expanse of bright colour may be hard to live with. Muted and mixed colours are often restful. Go around furnishing shops and look at the coverings they use for ideas, or look in interior decorating magazines. Because of the difficulty in removing coverings, a very light colour that will soil easily, may be difficult to keep clean.

CURTAINS

Size

Again be generous with shrinkage allowance and always weave more than you think you will need. A sample can be woven as described under upholstery fabric.

Yarn

Curtains hang with most of the strain on the warp, so choose a strong warp that will not stretch and sag. The weft yarn does not take much strain but curtains seem to hang best with the same warp and weft. Wool or cotton are two common yarns for curtains. If wool is used, remember it yellows with exposure to sunlight, and should be lined with strong sun-resistant material.

Washing

Curtains need to be washable but since they will only be washed perhaps once a year this is not a major factor.

Pattern

Border patterns on curtains are effective in some rooms, and a weaver can make original curtains that could not easily be made from manufactured cloth. Check that the border pattern will look as good when the curtain is pulled back at the side of the windows as it does when the curtains are covering the windows. This is a factor often forgotten in designing curtains. A border pattern will appear to add weight to the lower, bordered edge, so lighten the colour of the border to counteract this tendency.

Colour

Again, curtains take up a large area, so tone down the colours or else they will overwhelm everything in the room. Bright, primary colours, that is blue, yellow, or red, with no added colours to soften them, can be too strong and should be used with care. If you look outside at the natural colours of the plants, flowers and trees, you will very rarely see these primary colours. Most natural colours are mixtures of two or more colours. A rose may be yellowy-gold, with a touch of red bordering the petals. A garden is a great place to use as inspiration for our colour schemes.

Technique

A plain, balanced weave will make a fabric that will drape well, an important quality in curtains. Beat carefully, as uneven beating will show up as streaks when the light falls through the curtain

Finishing

Neat finishing and sewing are important. If you think your sewing may not be neat enough, get the curtains professionally made: you have spent so much time on weaving, that it would be a pity to spoil all that effort in the final stage. Let the curtains hang for a few days before doing the final hemming, as this will let the fabric find its own level.

CLOTHING FABRIC

It is very satisfying for a weaver to wear a garment made up from fabric woven by him/herself, and many beginner weavers make clothing fabric their first project. It does take some expeience to weave a sound cloth that can be cut into without fraying, and the finishing of the cloth is as important as the weaving. Chapter Six describes how to finish fabrics, according to the type of yarn. The beginner weaver may be best to start with a jacket, such as that in Project Nine, which requires no cutting, or Project Seven, which has very little cutting.

Jacket fabric can also be slightly heavier and more open than skirt or dress fabric, and is somewhat easier for the beginner weaver.

Size

Be generous with the shrinkage allowance. A small sample can be woven first, as described earlier.

Yarn

This depends on the climate and the availablity of yarn. Wool is probably easier for the beginner, as it is more elastic than cotton or silk. As with curtains, fabric woven with the same warp and weft yarn seems to hang well. Do not mix wool and acrylic yarns, as the wool shrinks more than the acrylic, and the fabric will crinkle when washed.

Washing

All fabric should be washed after weaving. See the instructions in Chapter Six for your particular yarn type. After this initial wash, the fabric can be washed or dry-cleaned.

Pattern

Remember that any pattern on fabric worn on the body will move as the wearer moves and as it shapes to the contours of the body. A pattern that looks good when lying flat on the loom may therefore look 'busy' once it has been made into a garment. Understate the pattern rather than overstate it for this reason. Do not choose a pattern with long floats as they will catch, and the fabric will look untidy. Border patterns can be very effective, and will make your garment unique.

Colour

To avoid the 'busy' look mentioned above, choose a background colour that is lighter than the pattern colour. A white background with a contrasting colour such as dark blue will make the pattern stand out much more. A pale blue background would tone down the contrast. Again, large areas of primary colour can be overwhelming.

Technique

A plain, balanced weave construction will drape well. A weft-face cloth is not suitable. Textured yarns can be used to great effect when weaving clothing fabric and even small amounts can be very exciting.

Finishing

If your sewing skills are not up to standard, ask a dressmaker to make up the fabric. The sewing finish is very important with all garments, and can spoil a beautiful piece of fabric.

Joining Fabric Pieces

Knee rugs, shawls, and tablecloths can be woven on any of the Ashford looms, but if the loom is only 610mm (24in) wide they will have to be woven in sections and joined. When joining pieces, try to make the join part of the design. Four quarters joined together can look better than joining a piece straight up the centre. Plan the method of joining before you begin weaving. If the fabric to be joined is woven in a very plain yarn and weave structure, the join will be very noticeable. A textured yarn, woven with a pattern, will make the join less visible. A pattern that carries over from one section to another, will help link the sections together.

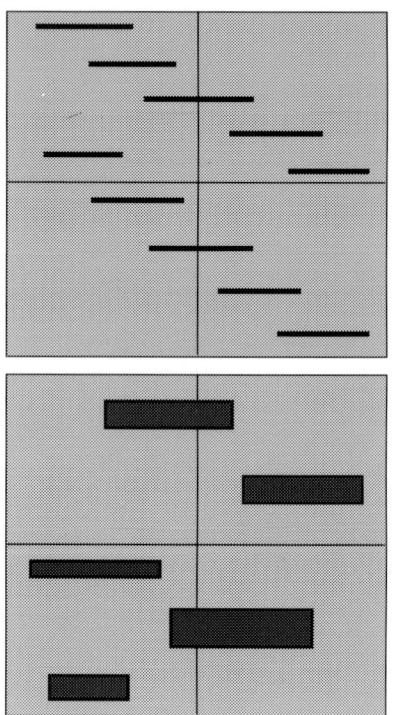

Fig. 7:D Designs that link sections together

Shawls and knee rugs should be light, softly draping, and soft to the touch. Tablecloths should be firmly beaten, and able to withstand many washings.

WALL HANGINGS

Size

These can be any size.

Yarn
Any type of yarn can be used from tree bark to cellophane strips.

Washing
May or may not be washed.

Already the difficulties of designing woven wall hangings are apparent: there are **no** guidelines. Wall hangings are usually decorative, and have no other function. This freedom seems to be the reason we see so many unsatisfactory wall hangings. The beginner would be best to weave his/her first hanging for a specific place because then the decisions about size, yarn, etc, are easier to make. Use the shapes and designs in the room for inspiration. An archway may suggest a curved design, a brick wall could suggest a squared design. If the hanging is to stand out from the wall colour, choose a contrasting colour which will also make the hanging appear dominant. A hanging that blends in with the wall colour will appear smaller and will merge with the background.

With hangings I find it better to let one of four factors dominate. These factors are yarn, colour, design and technique. For example, if the yarn is very textured and exciting, I let that feature dominate. If I use very bright colours, I use plain yarns. If I try to use bright colours, textured yarns and an intricate design, the hanging looks busy and confused.

The finishing and method used to hang the piece are also important, and should fit in with the overall design. A heavy wooden batten may look good on a large, dark, solid piece of weaving, but would be wrong on a light transparent hanging.

WEAVING FOR EXHIBITIONS AND SHOPS

Most weavers weave articles for specific people or places before they begin to sell their work. During the weaving of these specific pieces, you gather information on what works best. For example, I learned quickly that cream tablemats were always popular. Part of this knowledge I gained through my own weaving, and comments from friends and relations, but I also learnt much from looking in shops and galleries.

When you want to sell your work, it pays to do some homework first. Ask a shop or gallery for help if they are the approachable sort. Shops in particular want articles that will sell quickly, and they may tell you that tie-dyed scarves are all the fashion this year. It is depressing to weave 20 white scarves, only to be told when you take them into a shop that they do not want them.

The advantage that handweavers have over the weaving manufacturer is our ability to change quickly. We can adjust immediately to a swing in fashion colours and styles. Make the most of this fact. You can offer to weave a range of scarves to complement jackets and other stock in the shop.

Presentation of your woven articles is all important. Have them labelled, with after-care instructions, and neatly packaged. A portfolio of your work will show the buyers the range of your weaving, and it looks professional.

Exhibitions are another thing again If possible visit the gallery before you start weaving. See how big the gallery is and what provision it has for hanging woven pieces. If the wall colour will not suit your particular piece, then you can ask for it to be hung against a different background. Exhibitions are a great opportunity to try out those pieces that have been waiting in your head to be woven, but you have not found the right wall space, room, or person for that particular design. However, it is as well to realize that unless someone visiting that exhibition has that right wall space, or room which will suit your hanging, it may remain unsold.

Weaving for exhibitions will help get your name known, however, and orders can follow. They also give you a standard to measure yourself against, as you can see your work against that of others.

8. PATTERN DRAFTING

A PATTERN DRAFT is a set of instructions for threading the loom, and weaving a pattern. It is necessary to understand how patterns are drafted before we can use the many thousands of patterns that are available as a resource. Weaving is an ancient craft, and a vast store of material is accessible to weavers.

Basically, these drafts are just a type of weaving 'shorthand'. Unfortunately there is no standard method of setting out these drafts, and every book will differ in some aspect. However, if you understand the basics of pattern drafting, it can be seen that drafts have much in common. Whenever you choose a weaving draft from a book, and you are not familiar with the drafting method, read the relevant chapter in the book first to discover how the drafts are written. For example, Swedish drafts are written with shaft 1 at the back of the loom, and this can complicate matters if you do not know that.

The use of computer programmes for writing drafts has changed pattern drafting in the last few years. The basic concepts are still the same, but the process has become much quicker. The speed of computer drafting means that in a few moments a weaver can generate patterns that would have taken hours using pencil and graph paper. This should stimulate weavers to experiment with patterns, and will extend their knowledge of weave structure and analysis. To use computer weaving programmes, only basic computer skills are necessary, and these can be learnt at many schools and colleges. I have used a computer programme to write all the drafts in this book.

PATTERN DRAFT

A pattern draft is divided into four quadrants: the threading draft, tie-up, treadling (or lifting section), and the draw-down.

Threading Draft

This is also called the draft notation, and is the top, left quadrant of the pattern draft. It is read from right to left, with shaft 1 at the lower edge of the draft, as

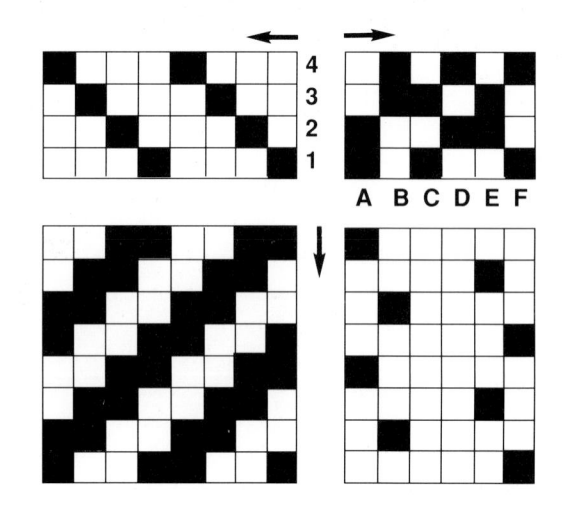

Fig. 8:A Pattern draft

indicated by the shaft numbers to the right of the threading draft itself. A filled square means that a warp end is entered on that shaft in the order given. If one repeat of the pattern is short, I will give two or three repeats of the pattern. When you reach the left-hand side, return to the right and continue threading until the warp ends are all threaded.

With some weave patterns, such as plain weave (also called a straight draw), it does not matter which shaft you finish on; with others, you must finish at the end of a repeat. In the projects in Chapter Ten, I will indicate this.

Sometimes the pattern drafts will be threaded as units, with the number of times a unit is to be repeated shown on the draft to save space (**Fig. 8:B**). If the pattern needs more ends threaded on to one shaft than the others, this will also be indicated in the instructions, as it can be infuriating to suddenly run out of heddles. It is a good idea to count and note the number of heddles on each shaft on your loom, and to mark the centre heddle on each shaft.

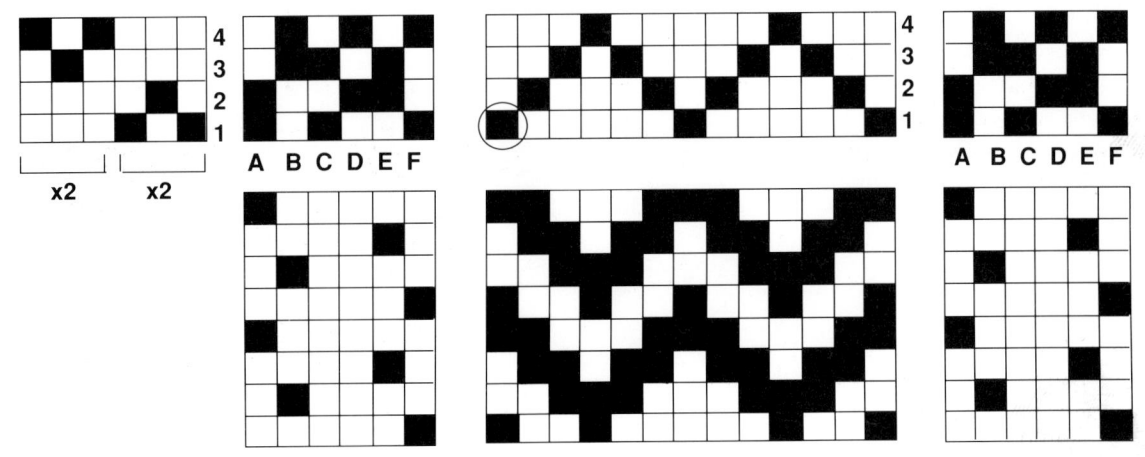

Fig. 8:B Repeating units

Fig. 8:C Point twill.

In the point twill threading with two repeats in **Fig. 8:C**, it can be seen that the last thread, on shaft 1, is only repeated at the very end of the sequence, at the left selvedge. If it is added in at the end of each repeat, we would have two adjacent ends on shaft 1, which is not correct. I will circle this added end to indicate this. This pattern, with six ends to one repeat, is one where the total number of warp ends should be divisble by six to make the pattern balance. Then add one extra warp end, for the circled end on the left.

Tie-up Quadrant
This is the top, right-hand quadrant of the draft and it shows which shafts are tied to which treadles. This section is not necessary for table looms, which have each shaft directly attached to a handle on the top of the loom. When weaving on the Ashford jack looms, the treadles are tied, via the lamms, to certain shafts. Each treadle on the tie-up draft is named. In **Fig. 8:A** you can see that treadle A is tied to shafts 1 and 2, treadle B to shafts 3 and 4, and so on. It would help to label the treadles on your loom to match the draft lettering.

The tie-up draft is read from left to right. Plain weave and twill are two of the most common weave structures:the centre two treadles are tied up for plain weave and the outside four for twill.

There are many different tie-ups and every weaver has his/her favourite one. For more information about tie-ups read page 75, Chapter Four and pages 86–88 in Chapter Five.

The tie-ups change with the pattern being woven, so always check this part of the quadrant before you begin weaving, to see if the tie-up has changed from the one you have been using. It does pay to make the tie-ups so the treadling is as simple as possible. If you are weaving with 10 picks to 2.5cm (1in), you will be depressing the treadles 10 times for that distance, and if you have to keep looking at your feet, or you lose your way among the treadles, it can be irritating.

Treadling Quadrant
This is sometimes called the lifting plan and is the lower, right-hand section of the draft. This quadrant indicates which shafts are raised in each pick.

ASHFORD JACK LOOM

The treadling instructions are in graph form, directly underneath the tie-up quadrant, and the named treadles. In **Fig. 8:A**, note that the first pick, read from the top down, indicates that you depress treadle A, which lifts shafts 1 and 2. For the second pick, depress treadle E to lift shafts 2 and 3. Pick 3 raises shafts 3 and 4, and pick 4 raises 1 and 4. This is called 'walking the treadles' and uses your left and right feet alternately, as in walking. This method of treadling is less tiring than others, and if used in conjunction with shuttle throwing; that is, the left foot is used when the shuttle is thrown from the left and vice versa, you will make fewer mistakes.

MATERIALS AND TECHNIQUES • 119

ASHFORD TABLE LOOMS

Four-shaft
The shafts are numbered at the top, and the I under a shaft means that this shaft is to be raised (**Fig. 8:D**).

Eight-shaft
With eight handles to move, four on each side of the loom, the draft (**Fig. 8:E**) is easier to read if it is divided into the same sections, with shafts 1, 3, 5, 7, on the left, and shafts 2, 4, 6, 8, on the right. Read the numbers from the top down, and lift the shafts indicated in each row. It is quicker to move all the handles on one side, and then move to the other side.

In some projects which can be woven on both the table and the jack loom, both types of lifting drafts will be given.

Draw-down
This quadrant is also called a draft development, weave notation, or the design quadrant, and is a diagram of the warp and weft interaction. A filled square represents a warp end crossing over a weft thread, (shafts up), and a blank square represents a weft crossing over a warp end. (shafts down).

This quadrant is useful in seeing the structural development of the fabric, even although it may not look like the finished weaving. It also shows the floats where the weft or warp float over several threads, and this can be useful, as long floats may not be suitable.

On some double weave drafts, with two layers, the draw-down quadrant is not shown, as it would be confusing. After you have woven a draft shown in this book, compare your weaving with the draw-down. With experience, the relation between the diagram and the actual cloth becomes clear, and soon you can just look at a draw-down and visualize the finished cloth. This ability will help you to choose suitable patterns from this and other books.

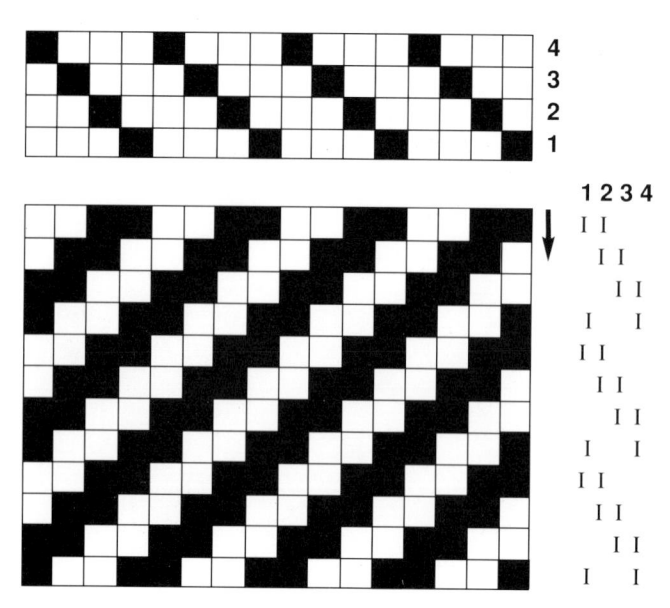

Fig. 8:D Four-shaft table loom draft

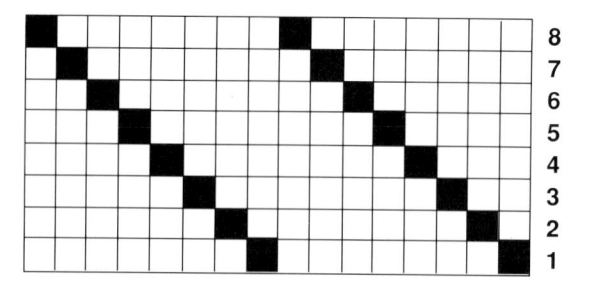

Fig. 8:E Eight-shaft table loom draft

9. FINISHING

THE FINISHING of a woven article is as important as the weaving of it. When I first began weaving, I was so impatient to get a piece woven that I gave very little thought to how I was going to finish it off. Usually I would take it off the loom and then work out ways of finishing it. Sometimes this was fine, but sometimes I would have a disaster on my hands with not enough for a hem or not enough warp for a fringe.

The finishing is an integral part of the piece and should be planned from the beginning. With the projects in Chapter Ten, I have done all the thinking for you and the finishing has been planned along with the weaving. However, when you begin to plan your own projects, you will find this section on finishing useful as a resource to refer back to when necessary. In this chapter I have included some knitted finishes, along with the more traditional edgings, as these finishes give shape to a woven article, and it is often difficult to buy matching braids.

WARP FINISHING

There are various ways to strengthen the warp where it emerges from the weft, to prevent fraying. This finishing should be done as soon as the piece comes off the loom, **before** washing, as it is surprising how quickly the weaving comes undone.

Decide on the finishing method before you begin to weave, to allow the correct amount of warp. For example, a knotted fringe takes up more warp than a hemstitched fringe. Also, many finishes are easier to do on the loom, while the piece is under tension.

Choose a finishing technique which is appropriate for the design of the article and the end use, so that the finishing becomes part of the design of the whole piece. A plain piece may be enhanced by a fancy fringe, as in Project Eight, whereas a brightly patterned piece may be better without a fringe at all. Remember that a fancy fringe will become the focus of attention, and could draw the eye away from the article itself.

Because the warp ends are left at the end of most pieces of weaving, this does not mean that they must be the fringe. With a widely-spaced warp, as in weft-face weaving, the fringe may be too sparse and the wrong colour. In this case the fringe should be hemmed in, the warp ends darned in, or an extra fringe added with rya knots (see Project Thirteen).

Hemstitching
This is done on the loom. Use a matching thread, usually a piece of the weft, and a tapestry needle. Leave a suitable amount of weft (three times the width is sufficient) over from the first pick. Right-handed weavers will find it much easier to start hemstitching at the right side, left-handed weavers from the left side. Weave about 2.5cm (1 in) then begin hemstitching. This is a very firm finish, as the stitching is done around both the warp and the weft, and is probably the most common finish used by weavers. It is particularly suitable for slippery yarns. (See **Fig. 9:A** over.)

Blanket stitch
This is a decorative finish done on the loom and often used to bind jacket edges (**Fig. 9:B**). It is not as firm as hemstitching, and is more suitable for woollen fabrics which do not fray easily.

Warp ends darned in
This is done after the weaving is removed from the loom. The warp ends are knotted together, two by two, and then darned back into the body of the weaving for about 2.5cm (1 in). Leave at least 8–10cm (3–4 in) of warp when cutting the weaving off the loom, or you will have difficulty threading the needle. After darning the ends in, cut them off close to the weaving on the wrong side (**Fig. 9:C**).

Hemming
This is done off the loom. Secure the warp ends by hemstitching, or blanket stitch before you turn the edge under and stitch it into place. This finish is only suitable for fine fabrics, as hemming thick fabrics will leave a bulky edge.

Overhand knot
This is a bulky knot, done after the weaving is

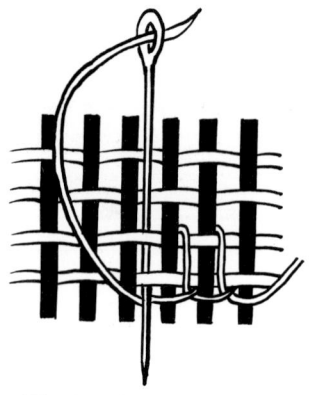

Fig. 9:A Blanket stitch

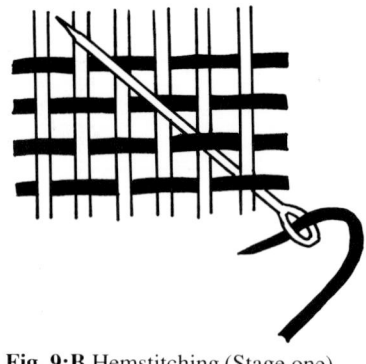

Fig. 9:B Hemstitching (Stage one)

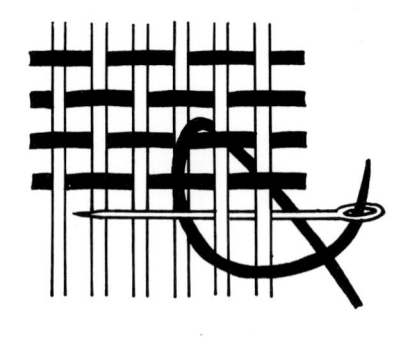

(Stage two)

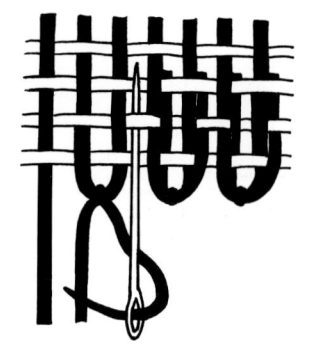

Fig. 9:C Warp ends darned in

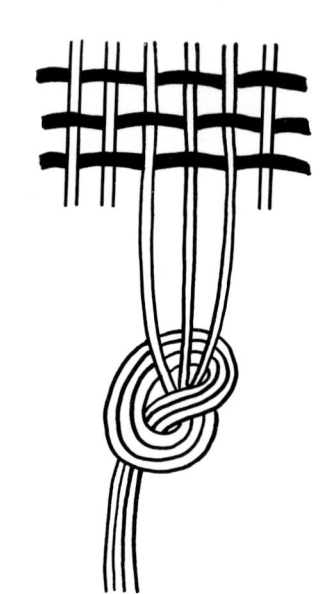

Fig. 9:D Overhand knot

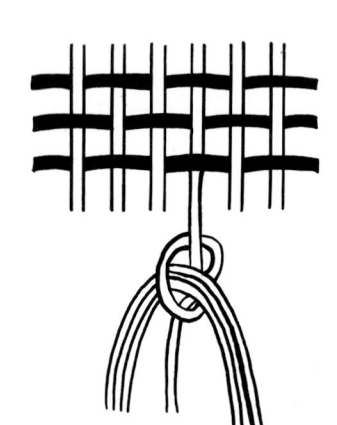

Fig. 9:E Extra threads added to overhand knot

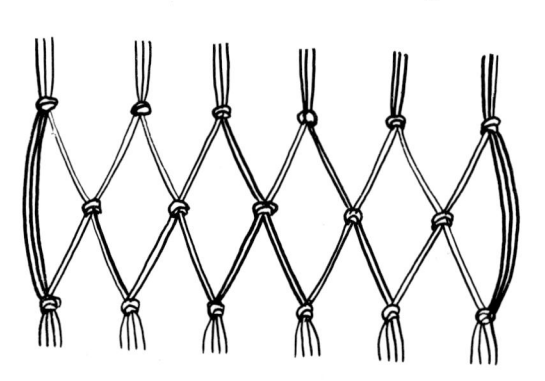

Fig. 9:F Triple knotted fringe

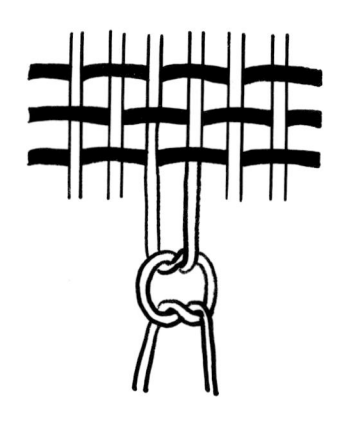

Fig. 9:G Reef knot

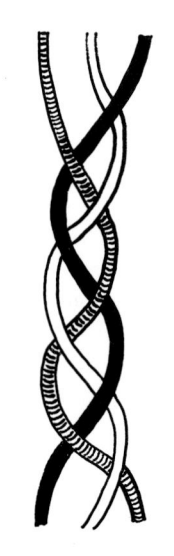

Fig. 9:H Plaited fringe

removed from the loom and is not suitable for table linen or other articles which require a flat finish. It is a quick finish, but take care that not too many strands are gathered in one knot, as this causes the fabric to buckle. Slip the knot up close to the woven edge (**Fig. 9:D**).

Extra strands can be added to make the fringe thicker (**Fig. 9:E**), and an interesting fringe is made by halving groups of overhand knots, and then re-knotting. (**Fig. 9:F**)

Reef knot
This fringe is also done after the weaving is removed from the loom. It will hang badly until the article is washed, and is a slow finish, and therefore not suitable for articles with a great number of warp ends to tie, as in a set of six table mats. (**Fig. 9:G**)

Plaited fringe
This is a very hard-wearing fringe done off the loom. Finish with an overhand knot. It is used a lot for rug fringes. (**Fig.9:H**)

Twisted fringe
This is done off the loom and is particularly suited for woollen articles. Twist each separate end in the direction of the warp twist. Take two or more of these twisted ends and join them, twisting in the opposite direction. Finish with an overhand knot. If the woollen article is then washed, and dried (and it must be absolutely dry) the overhand knot can be cut off and the fringe will not come undone. This is because the ends have felted together slightly in the washing process. (**Fig. 9:I**)

Philippine edge
This makes an attractive border (**Fig. 9:J**).

Added fringe
This finish leaves a fringe in the same colour as the weft, and is particularly suitable for weft-face fabric. It is done off the loom. Knot and darn the existing ends back into the cloth, as in **Fig. 9:C**, but do not cut short. Add the fringe with a snitch knot (see **Fig. 10:1** where the chaining technique begins with a snitch knot) using a crochet hook. The fringe should be attached to the weft, as this is

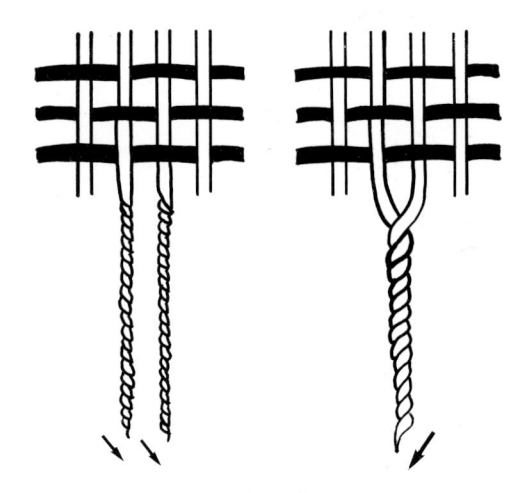

Fig. 9:I Twisted fringe

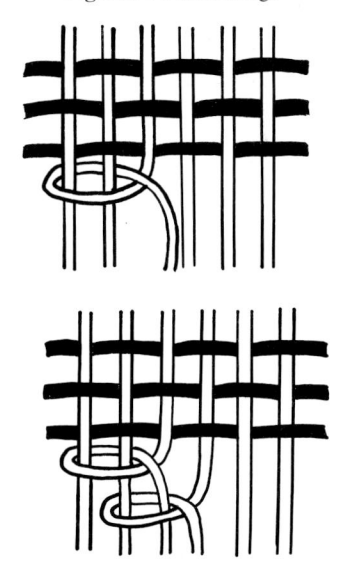

Fig. 9:J Philippine edge

firmer than the darned-in warp ends. Once the complete fringe is knotted, cut short the darned-in ends. If these ends are cut short earlier, they have a tendency to pull out while you are knotting.

Fringes on all four sides
Allow 6–8 extra warp ends while planning and winding the warp. These extra ends are wound on as usual but are threaded through a heddle, or a slot in the rigid heddle, some distance apart from the rest of the warp. The space left will be equivalent to the fringe length.

MATERIALS AND TECHNIQUES • 123

When weaving, the weft will form the selvedge fringe, as the shuttle carrying the weft goes around these extra ends at the extreme left and right of the weaving. If these selvedge edges are to be stitched, this should be done before the weaving is wound on to the front roller. After the weaving is removed from the loom, cut the weft close to the outside warp ends to make the fringe. If a looped fringe is required do not cut the weft, but pull out the extra warp ends. If the fringes are to be knotted, remove the weaving from the loom, cut the weft and knot.

To hold the edges of the weaving firmly in place, it may be necessary to take every fifth and sixth pick to the edges of the main body of the weaving only. This is necessary for slippery yarns, and it makes the weft fringe less dense but more secure.

Braids and edging strips

It is sometimes difficult to buy suitable braids and strips to finish off a garment or article. The following braids or edgings can be made in the same yarns as the body of the garment, and this can add much to the appearance of the finished article.

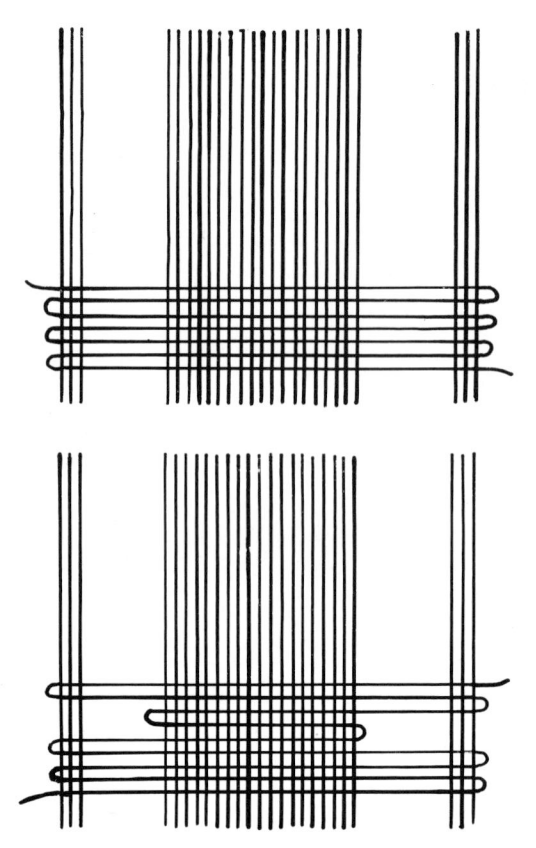

Fig. 9:K Fringes on all four sides

Knitted fringe

Cast on 8 sts, using 5mm needles. The equivalent in English needles is size 6, the American equivalent is size 7. Work every row as follows: wool round needle purlwise, purl 2 together, continue to end.

Work until the piece is the desired length, then cast off 2 sts. Unravel the remaining work down the length of the knitting. The fringing may be cut or left as loops. These directions give you a 14cm (5.5 in) fringe, including a 2.5cm (1 in) heading. The number of cast-on stitches can vary – 6 sts gives an 8cm (3 in) fringe, for example. The heading can be made deeper by casting off 4 sts instead of 2 at the end. Work in even numbers throughout. This fringe is ideal for cushions as well as garments.

9:I Knitted fringe

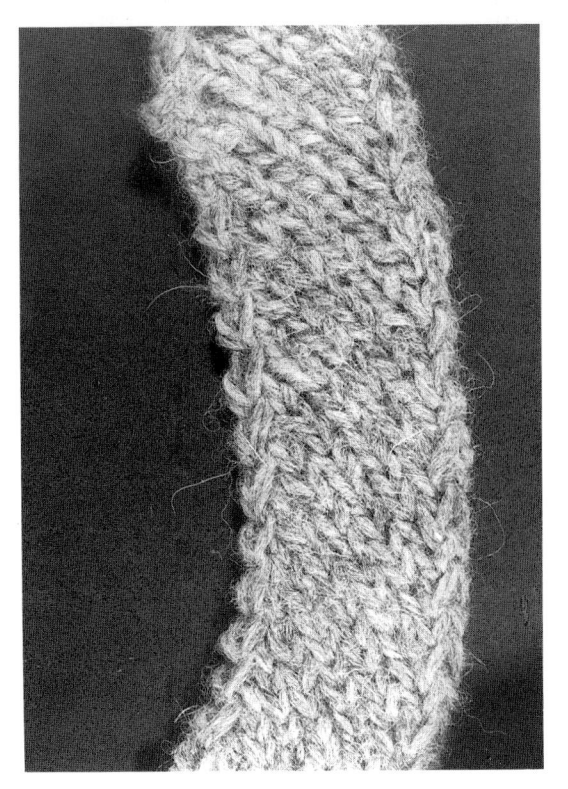

9:2 Knitting a bias edging

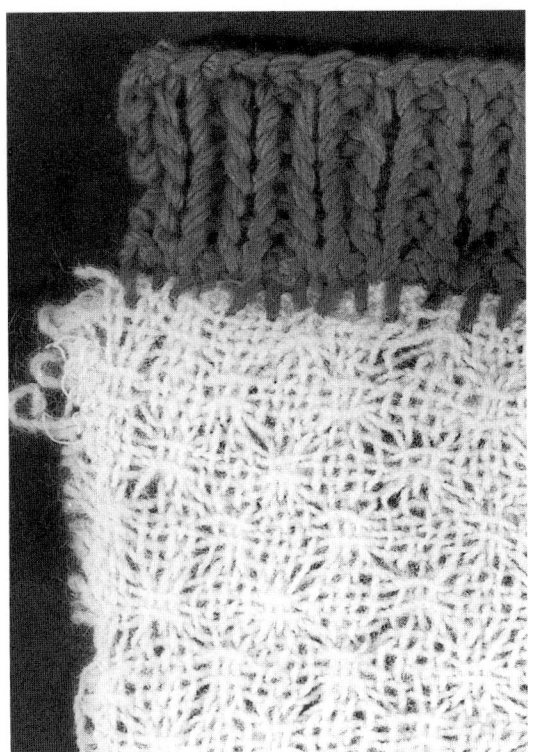

9:3 Knitting directly onto a garment

Knitting a bias edging
Cast on 6 to 8 sts.
1st row – plain.
2nd row – purl.
3rd row – plain, increase by knitting the first stitch, then pick up and knit the loop directly below the second stitch. Decrease in the last stitch by knitting two together.
4th row – purl.
Repeat the 3rd and 4th rows until the edging is the required length, and cast off.

Handsew the bias edging onto the garment where required, with right sides together. Fold the edging in half, and sew the other side to the wrong side of the garment.

Knitting directly on to a garment
Handwoven garments can be tailored to give shape and form to the garment by attaching knitted ribbings to the cuffs, collars and front openings. These ribbings will gather in the loose edges, making the garments warmer as well as close fitting. These ribbings can be attached to both selvedge or cut ends.

Firstly the edge must be firmly sewn. Hemstitch the edge if it is not a selvedge. If you wish to attach a ribbing to a cut edge, zig-zag the edge firmly by machine with a matching thread. Cut the pieces close to the machine stitching. If the edge is hemstitched, make sure the hemstitching is firm and fine, and then cut the edge close in. If you feel the hemstitching may pull out, machine zig-zagging may be necessary.

If the knitting is attached directly to the fabric, it will pull out so the next step is to make a firm row of stitches to anchor the knitting to. There are two ways of doing this. If you can crochet, make this edge by using a row of double crochet along the edge to anchor the knitting to.

For those who cannot crochet, use the following Peruvian needle stitch, in a matching yarn. Make a cross stitch to begin with, *then slide the needle under the X at its centre point. Be careful not to catch up the fabric. Go around and under the edge

MATERIALS AND TECHNIQUES • 125

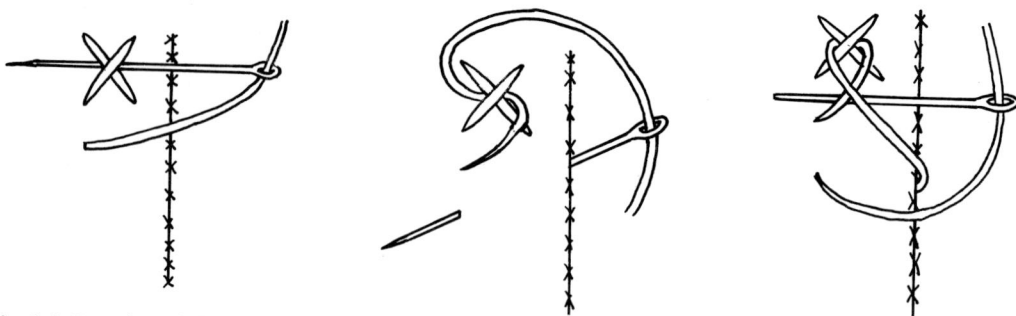

Fig. 9:L Peruvian stitch

of the fabric, and bring the needle through the fabric at point A. This will complete the second cross.* Slide the needle under this cross and so on, repeating from * to *. After you have done a few stitches you will notice that the edge is rolling under and a tidy firm edge is provided, with a chain-like row of stitches forming along the edge.

These are the stitches which will be picked up with the knitting needles. Again use a matching yarn (in the photographs I have used contrasting yarns and large stitches to show the stitching). Pick up and knit the ribbing in knit 1, purl 1, or whatever ribbing you wish.

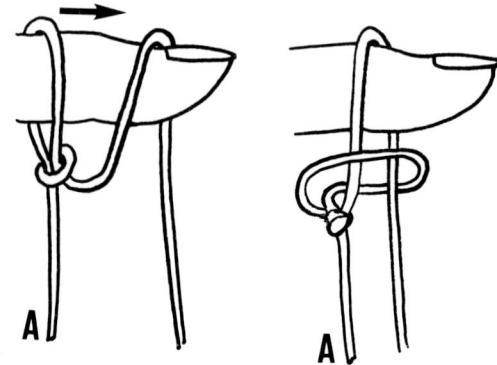

Fig. 9:M Finger crochet

Twisted braid

Take several strands of yarn and attach one end to a fixed point, such as a chair leg. Make a loop at the other end, put a pencil in the loop, and twist the strands until they kink and curl. Halve the twisted strands and let them twist back on themselves. The secret of this braid is to make sure the strands are very tightly twisted.

Finger crochet

This makes an excellent braid for cushions and bags. Use about ten strands of 2-ply wool for a strong braid. The flat side of the braid is sewn to the article, with the slightly rounded side to the outside. Tighten the braid by pulling on end A after each chain.

SECTION THREE
WEAVING PROJECTS

10. WEAVING PROJECTS

THE WEAVING PROJECTS described in the following pages have been carefully thought out to give you experience in some of the basic weaves. The first projects are simple, and are suitable for beginner weavers, and the projects will increase in complexity as you work your way through them.

I have covered as wide a range as possible of the articles that most weavers want to weave, in my classes anyway. For example, most beginners want to weave a cushion fairly early on in their weaving life, so a cushion project is number three.

The instructions not only cover how to thread the loom and weave the article, but also how to finish it: something which seems to be a neglected part in many books – the finishing of a piece can make or break it.

The weight of each finished project is given and, by adding extra for loom wastage, the amount of yarn needed for each project can be worked out.

A major problem with all weaving books that give project details is that it is not always possible to buy the exact yarn given in the instructions. You may find the sett, the number of threads per cm (in), for your local yarns may be different. To help overcome this, where possible I have also given the length per weight figures for each yarn, and this should help you choose a matching type of yarn. Photographs over the page show all the yarns used in the projects, and this will help you in identifying the yarn size, so that you can match it with your local yarns.

If your yarn is thinner than the yarn specified, and you sett it at the same sett as the yarn used in the project, the fabric will be loose and sleazy. The way to overcome this problem is to find the 'Weave Structure' line in each project. It will say 'Plain balanced weave' or whatever. Now turn to Chapter Three, page 49. Under the heading 'Calculating Sett', you will find how to measure your own yarn to reach the correct sett for each weave structure.

In the project instructions, under the heading 'Sley' you will see how to thread for that particular sett. For example, to thread five warp ends to 2.5cm (1in) on an 8-dent reed you will find:

/*/*/ /*/*/ /*/ /

This means that you thread the first two dents (spaces in the reed), miss the next, thread the next two, miss the next, thread one, miss one, and repeat this across the warp width. The / represents the metal spacers in the reed, and the * represents a warp end.

When I weave projects such as these, I usually weave more than one article on the same warp. For example, I will weave six to ten knee rugs at once to save time and materials, as a sort of production run. I vary each article, to prevent boredom and to make each piece as original as I can. However, for beginners, short warps are easier to handle, and will give the variety necessary when learning. So the following projects usually have only one or two articles on each warp. I have written out the instructions to make it easy for you to extend these warp lengths.

Look at the first project, weaving two scarves. Under the heading 'Length' you will find the total length of each scarf. Under this I have noted the number of scarves to be woven, then added the loom wastage to give the total warp length. If, for example, you want to weave four scarves instead of two, just multiply the number of scarves by four instead of two, add the loom wastage, which remains the same, and you have the total warp length.

The projects for this section were woven by my students and weaving friends – in fact in all cases the weavers fit into both those catagories. Some of the weavers have had little experience, some with only six or eight lessons before they tested my instructions and wove the projects. So if they can do it, so can you!

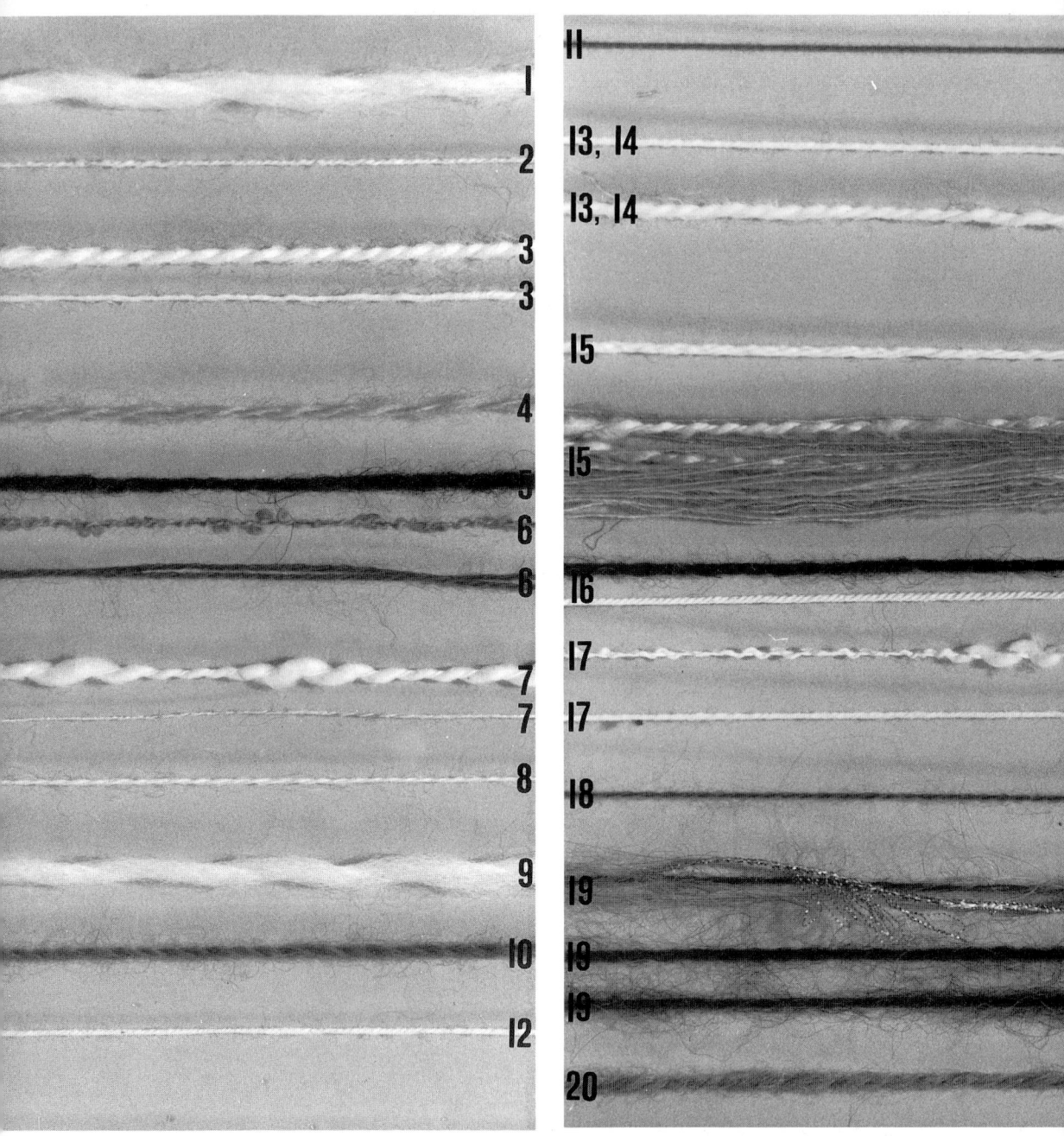

10:A Yarns used in the weaving projects. (Numbers indicate project number.) These are shown at their actual size: laying your yarn over the photographs will help you to check that it is as close as possible to the original.

130 • THE ASHFORD BOOK OF WEAVING

PROJECT ONE: TWO SCARVES

These can be woven on a rigid heddle loom, a four-shaft table loom, and a four-shaft jack loom. Any width loom is suitable.

Warp: White wool, Hanna yarn, 500 tex. 2000m/kg (994yd/lb)
Weft: Same as warp
Pattern yarn: Blue Hanna yarn, 500 tex
Sett: 5 ends per 2.5cm (1in)
Width:
- finished article: 20cm (8in)
- add draw-in: 5cm (2in) (There is a high shrinkage rate in this yarn.)
- total warp width: 25cm (10in)

Length:
- finished scarf: 135cm (53in)
- warp take-up: 15cm (6in)
- fringe allowance: 15cm (6in)
- total length of scarf: 165cm (65in)
- number of scarves: 2 x 165cm (65in) = 330cm (130in)
- loom wastage: 61cm (24in)
- total length of warp: 391cm (13 feet)

Total number of warp ends: 50
Weave structure: Plain balanced weave
Threading: Straight draw, 1,2,3,4
Sley: For an 8-dent reed, thread /*/*/ /*/*/ /*/ /
Selvedge: Sley two outside ends in one dent.
Extra equipment needed: Plastic clip clothes peg
Weight: Each scarf weighs 100gm (3.6 oz)

Warping

For a table or jack loom, wind the warp with two crosses (see page 69) because this yarn is fluffy and will stick together. On a rigid heddle loom, wind on in the normal manner.

FIRST SCARF

Weaving

Weave a heading. Leave a gap of about 2.5cm (1in), then weave 5cm (2in) in plain weave (1 and 3, 2 and 4), with the white Hanna yarn. Count the number of weft picks in this 5cm (2in). For a correct balanced weave, there should be ten picks in this section. Do not worry if the weaving looks very open at this stage; it will close up when washed. Adjust your beating pressure if the number of picks is not correct. The pressure should be very light.

Hemstitch the beginning of the scarf, around a group of three ends.

Fig. 10:1 Chaining

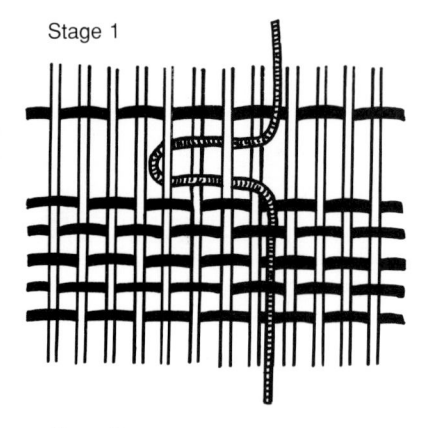

Stage 1

Stage 2

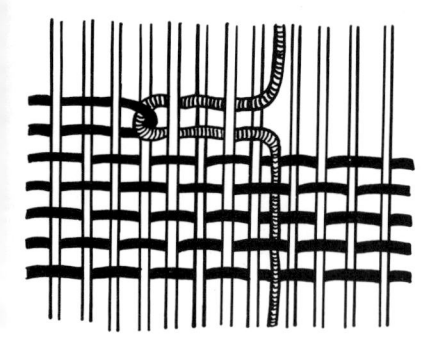

Fig. 10:2 Linked weft

Chained border
Take the blue Hanna yarn, and break off about 150cm (5 feet). In a closed shed, beginning on the left, make a snitch knot around the outside warp end with the doubled blue yarn. Chain around groups of five warp ends, as illustrated (**Fig. 10:1**) until you reach the right side of the weaving. Leave the chains very loose, and then the warp will not be distorted. Break off the blue yarn, leaving a tail of about 2.5cm (1in) to tuck into the next shed.

Continue in plain weave for 140cm (55in), measuring from the chaining, then weave another border in the chaining technique. Weave a further 5cm (2in) in plain weave and hemstitch the end as for the beginning of the scarf. Leave a gap of 15cm (6in) between this and the next scarf.

SECOND SCARF

For this scarf we will use a linked weft technique. Take a cone of the blue Hanna yarn or, if it is not in a cone, wind off a small ball of yarn. We will need about 3m (3yds). Go to the back of the loom, place the ball or cone on the floor, lined up with the centre of the scarf. Take one end of the yarn over the back of the loom, and through a central heddle eye. If the loom is a table or jack loom, take the central heddle, and thread the blue yarn in the same eye as a white warp end, and then through the matching dent in the reed. If on a rigid heddle loom, thread the pattern end through a central slot.

Place a pin in the centre of the weaving at the very end of the first scarf, and attach the pattern end to the pin with a figure of eight. Go to the back of the loom, and atttach the plastic clothes peg to the pattern end just before it reaches the floor. This clip will weight the end sufficiently so that it is the same tension as the rest of the warp. (The only problem I ever have with this extra warp end is that my cats think I have put it there just for them to play with.) When the clothes peg reaches over the back of the loom, just clip it further down near the floor again

Weave about 8cm (3in) in plain weave, with the pattern warp end behaving just like the end it is partnered with. Hemstitch the ends as before.

In the next shed, take the shuttle through to the extra warp end and link the weft around this added warp end, then return to the same side. Pull the weft and the attached warp end into the required position, about 2.5cm (1in) from the selvedge, and beat. The warp now becomes part of the weft. Put the background weft back into the **same** shed through to the opposite selvedge and beat again. (**Fig. 10:2**). Continue weaving and add this linked weft at intervals of about 20cm (8in), but alternating the sides from which the linked weft is pulled to.

Weave until the second scarf is 1.5m (60in) in its complete length, then hemstitch the ends as before and cut the scarves off the loom, leaving a fringe of 8cm (3in) at the end. Check for and mend any broken threads. Wash the scarves in warm soapy water, rinse well, and dry. Press when still slightly damp. You will notice that the scarves shrink to fill in the gaps left in the loose weaving, and a soft, fluffy surface is left. Because the Hanna yarn has a nylon binder to hold the unspun wool in place, the yarn is strong enough for both the warp and weft.

1. Scarf woven in linked weft by Helene Gourlay.

Variations
If you have a four- or eight-shaft loom, these scarves can be woven in a 2/2 twill, but sett the yarn at six ends per 2.5cm (1in) instead of five. This will make the scarves slightly bulkier and softer.

WEAVING PROJECTS • 133

PROJECT TWO: SIX TABLEMATS

These can be woven on a rigid heddle loom, a four-shaft table loom, and a four-shaft jack loom. Any width loom is suitable.

Warp: Marks Cottolin, 60% cotton, 40% linen, Nel 22/2, 6,400m/kg (3180yds/lb)
Weft: Same as warp
Sett: 16 ends per 2.5cm (1in)
Width:
    finished article: 30cm (12in)
    add 10% draw-in: 3cm (1in)
    total warp width: 33cm (13in)
Length:
    each finished mat: 36cm (14in)
    warp take-up: 5cm (2in)
    fringe allowance: 5cm (2in)
    total length of each mat: 46cm (18in)
    number of tablemats: 6 x 46cm(18in) = 276cm (109in)
      loom wastage: 61cm (24in)
    total length of warp: 337cm (11 feet)
Total number of warp ends: 208
Weave structure: Plain balanced weave
Threading: Straight draw, 1, 2, 3, 4
Sley: In an 8-dent reed, sley two ends in each dent.
Selvedge: Sley four outside warp ends in one dent.
Extra equipment needed: A pick-up stick, or spare stick shuttle
Weight : 150gm (5 oz)

Weaving
Weave a heading. Place a narrow stick across to separate the heading from the weaving proper. Weave 5cm (2in) in plain weave (1 and 3, 2 and 4). Hemstitch the end of the mat, using a length of the weft yarn left hanging out from the first pick. Hemstitch around a group of four ends. Count the number of weft picks in this 5cm (2in). If you are weaving a correct balanced weave, there should be 32 weft picks. If there are more or fewer, then change the pressure of your beating.

Leno Border
Begin by weaving a narrow border on the right side of the weaving. Weave nine picks on the first eight warp ends only (counting both the upper and lower warp layer), beating this narrow section with the same pressure as the first 5cm (2in). Do not change the position of the shafts after the last weft pick, which leaves the shuttle on the inside of the border.

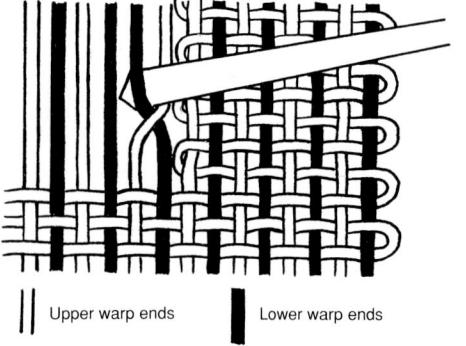

|| Upper warp ends   ■ Lower warp ends

Fig. 10:3 Leno

134 • THE ASHFORD BOOK OF WEAVING

Examine the first two warp ends next to the border, that is one lower and one upper end. If the lower end is to the right of the upper, cross it to the left as it is brought to the surface. If the lower end is to the left, it is crossed to the right. In **Fig. 10:3** the lower warp end was to the right, therefore it crosses to the left. If these ends are not crossed in the opposite direction, the characteristic twist is lost. Use a pick-up stick, or a spare shuttle to pick up the lower ends.

Continue across the weft, picking up all the lower warp ends and sliding them down the stick or shuttle. When you have only eight ends left on the left side, check that all the ends are correctly twisted. Turn the stick or shuttle on its edge, and insert the shuttle through this newly created shed.

Beat the weft into place with the stick, lying flat once more, and remove it. Take the weft out through the border ends to the selvedge. It is important that this is all done without changing sheds, in other words, the shed remains the same from one selvedge to the other. Weave the opposite border in the same manner as the first, for nine picks, using the shuttle or your fingers to beat the weft into place, as the beater cannot be used. The weft will enter the open area from the upper edge of the border and emerge from the lower.

When the left border is complete, the next complete pick, from left to right, will return the ends to their normal, untwisted position.

Weave 28cm (11in) in plain weave, measuring from the upper border of the Leno pattern, then repeat the Leno pattern. Weave 5cm (2in) of plain weave, then hemstitch the end of the mat, again with a length of the weft. Place a 2.5cm (1in) wide stick or ruler across the next shed, change sheds, and place another stick across. This will ensure a 5cm (2in) gap, which will form the mat fringes.

Weave six tablemats in the same manner. Cut the weaving off the loom, leaving a 2.5cm (1in) fringe on the last mat. Cut the mats apart, leaving a 2.5cm (1in) fringe on the end of each mat. Check for any mistakes or skipped threads, and mend these. Trim off any loose ends, from the hemstitching, or whatever, wash the mats in warm water in a washing machine, and press when still slightly damp.

Variations

You can twist two or three ends together instead of one. Do not twist more than this, or the warp ends become distorted.

A similar pattern, Brooks bouquet (**Fig. 10:4**) can be woven instead of the Leno border. This pattern does not need a pick-up stick. The shuttle itself wraps bundles of the upper warp layer. The shuttle goes under three upper warp ends, and back around these three, then continues on under the next group of three; that is you take the shuttle under six and back over three each time.

Fig. 10:4 Brooks bouquet

2. Tablemat woven by Mary Hastie (see page 134).

3. Cushions woven by Lynda Russell.

PROJECT THREE: TWO CUSHIONS

This project can be woven on a rigid heddle loom, a four-shaft table loom, and a four-shaft jack loom. The width of the loom needed for this project is no less than 610mm (24in).

Warp: White 2-ply rug wool. 1430m/kg(710yds/lb)
Weft background: White singles wool. 3125m/kg (1553yds/lb)
Weft pattern: White carded fleece wool, and a few locks of dyed or coloured fleece.
Sett: 5 ends per 2.5cm (1in)
Width:
    finished article: 43cm (17in)
    add draw-in: 3cm (1in)
    total warp width: 46cm (18in)
Length:
    each finished cushion: 86cm (34in)
    warp take-up: 5cm (2in)
    total length for cushion: 91cm (36in)
    number of cushions: 2 x 91cm (36in) =182cm (72in)
    loom wastage: 91cm (36in) (includes warp between cushions)
    total length of warp: 273cm (9 feet)
Total number of warp ends: 90
Weave structure: Plain weave. Because there is such a great difference in the size of the pattern weft, the carded wool, and the warp, this is not a balanced weave.
Threading: Straight draw, 1, 2, 3, 4
Sley: In an 8-dent reed, sley /*/*/ /*/*/ /*/ /
Weight: Each cushion cover weighs 430g(15oz).

Weaving
Weave a heading. Place a narrow stick across the warp to separate the heading from the weaving proper. Weave the edge of the cushion

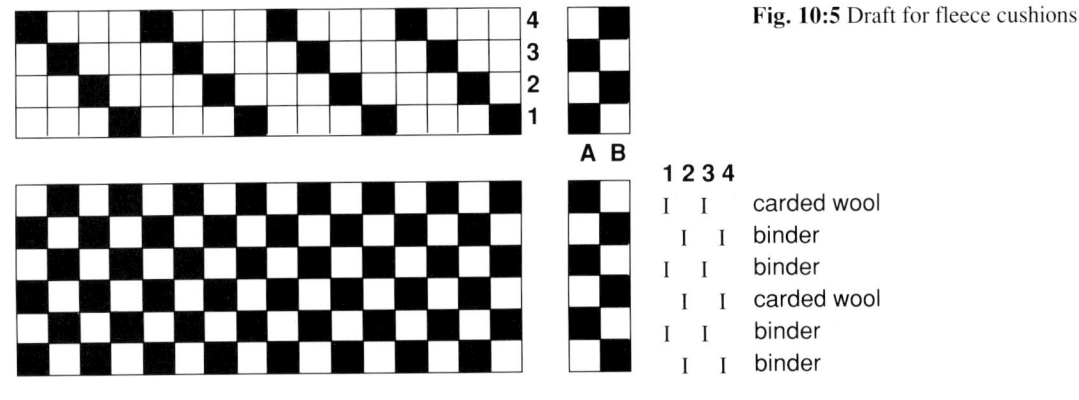

Fig. 10:5 Draft for fleece cushions

1 2 3 4	
I I	carded wool
I I	binder
I I	binder
I I	carded wool
I I	binder
I I	binder

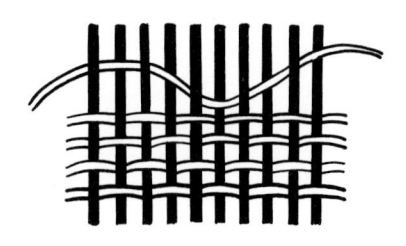

Fig. 10:6 Bubbling the weft

in the white singles wool in plain weave (1 and 3, 2 and 4), leaving a tail of three times the width for hemstitching the end. Weave 10 picks in this singles, bubbling the weft across the warp to form a firm weft-face edging (**Fig. 10:6**).

Place the weft through the shed at an angle, as in **Fig. 2:F**, then bubble it, beginning at the fixed edge.

When weaving a weft-face fabric, place the weft through, bubble it, then change sheds before you beat. This spreads out the weft bubbles, and distributes the weft evenly across the whole width. The weft should cover all the warp ends. Hemstitch this end, going around two warp ends in a group.

Take the carded fleece wool, break off about 2m (6 ft), and split the carded wool lengthwise. It may take some experimenting to gauge the correct amount of carded wool in each pick. Remember that it packs down in the weft, and the amount you put in determines the thickness of the cushion.

Take the carded wool and put it through the next shed, still in plain weave. Leave a tail of about 2cm (1in) hanging out the edge to tuck into the next shed. Use your fingers, not a shuttle, for placing this weft pick. Change sheds, weave one pick in the singles as a binder weft, change sheds again, and weave another binder pick. Into the next shed place the next carded wool pick. This is the basic weave technique for these cushions.

Weave for 13cm (5in) in this manner. The edges will have little loops where the carded wool is taken up the side. This adds to the character of the cushions, so try to keep these loops even. For the central 20cm (8in) of the cushion, add the dyed fleece locks at random, every third or fourth fleece pick. When placing these locks, weave one pick with the carded fleece, beat but do not change sheds, then lie the lock into the same shed in the required position. Beat, and then change sheds. This is an inlay (sometimes called 'laid-in') technique.

When the central 20cm (8in) is woven, weave 13cm (5in) to match the first plain section. This is one side of the cushion. Tie a piece of contrasting yarn to the selvedge to mark this central point, then weave the other half of the cushion, with the same measurements. There are no fringes on these cushions. Different coloured fleece locks can be used for the other side if wished.

When the first cushion is woven, with a total length of 91cm (36in), weave 10 picks in the singles to finish the end, bubbling it as before, and hemstitch the end. Leave a gap of 15cm (6in) between the first and the second cushion, which is woven in the same manner as the first.

When both cushions are woven, cut the weaving from the loom, and check for and mend any skipped or broken threads. Hand wash the cushions in warm soapy water, rinse, and spin the excess water out in the spin cycle of the washing machine. Do not use the washing machine for the initial wash, or the tumbler dyer, as this will cause felting. Dry lying flat in the sun. Press, and sew up the side seams by hand as follows.

Fold the cushion in half, with the loops of carded wool matching at each selvedge. Using the singles, binder yarn, sew the cushions together at each binder weft point. Machine stitch the hemstitched ends with a zig-zag stitch, or overlock the hem for added strength, place the cushion insert into the cushion cover, and sew the open end together. This can be done with a zip closure, or velcro, or it can be hand sewn.

Variations

Many materials can be added instead of the fleece locks as a surface pattern. I like the dyed fleece locks because of the colour variation in the locks, as the dye is absorbed to a greater depth at the tip of the lock. The main thing to remember is that the surface texture of these cushions woven with carded wool is quite striking, and should not be overwhelmed with too much detail. Leather, raffia, short pieces of silk rovings, or short pieces of rough, handspun yarns, are only some of the pattern materials that can be added.

This carded wool weaving technique can be used to make table mats also. Use the same materials as for the cushions, but follow the instructions for length and width of the mats, as given in Project Two.

PROJECT 4: KNEE RUG IN HANDSPUN WOOL

In New Zealand, this article is called a 'knee rug'; in other countries it is called a 'throw' or an afghan. Whatever it is called, it is a soft, cuddly wrap for knees, shoulders, etc. It took me 15 hours to spin the wool for this project, and only three hours to weave it. However, by spinning my own yarn, I finished with a unique knee rug, and there is as much satisfaction in the spinning as in the weaving of it.

This project can be woven on a four-shaft jack loom. The width of the loom needed for this project is no less than 970mm (38in).

Warp: Handspun wool, spun from a commercially carded blue/green mixture. Fleece type Romney/Dorset. The fleece was spun with a short forward draft to make a 2-ply yarn, with 15 wraps per 2.5cm (1in). 2500/kg (1243yds/lb)
Weft: Same as warp
Sett: 10 ends per 2.5cm (1in)
Width:
    finished article: 92cm (36in)
    add draw-in: 5cm (2in)
    total warp width: 97cm (38in)

Length:

finished rug:	150cm (59in)
warp take-up:	18cm (7in)
fringe allowance:	16cm (6in)
total length of knee rug:	184cm (72in)
loom wastage:	61cm (24in)
total length of warp:	245cm (96in)

Total number of warp ends: 380
Weave structure: Balanced 2/2 twill
Weave draft: See **Fig. 10:7**.
Selvedge: Thread the outside four ends on each side 1, 3, 2, 4. instead of the usual 1,2,3,4. Make sure the selvedge sequence does not allow two adjacent ends on the same shaft. For example, if you finish with an end on shaft 4, you follow the selvedge sequence above; if you finish on shaft 1, you thread the selvedge 4, 2, 3, 1, and so on. This will give a firm edge.

These outside four warp ends are to be sleyed double; that is, two in one dent, instead of singly, on both selvedges.
Sley: In a 10-dent reed, sley one end in each dent.
Weight: 482g (1lb 1oz)

Weaving

The beauty of this yarn is in its colour, with the random streaks of blue and green. To enhance this colour, I used a 2/2 twill weave, which gave a surface texture of diagonal lines which did not obscure the colour and texture of the handspun yarn.

Weave a heading, then weave a few centimetres (ins) in 2/2 twill, following the treadling sequence in **Fig. 10:7**. Stop and count the weft picks in 2.5cm (1in). There should be 10. If not, undo what you have woven, and change the pressure of your beating. When the beating is the correct 10 picks to 2.5cm (1in), the diagonal line of the twill should rise at a 45 degree angle.

Hemstitch the beginning, around four warp ends in one group, then continue weaving, marking every half metre (or 1 foot), until you have woven 168cm (66in). Hemstitch this end to match the

Fig. 10:7 2/2 twill

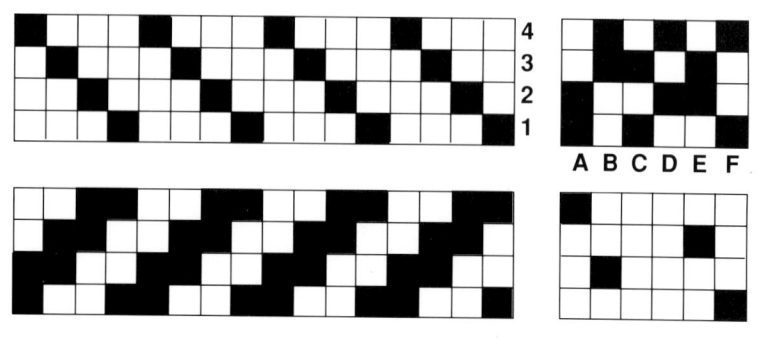

4. Knee rug spun and woven by Anne Field

beginning of the knee rug, and cut the weaving from the loom, leaving an 8cm (3in) fringe at each end.

Check for skipped threads, and mend any mistakes. Wash the knee rug in warm, soapy water and rinse well. A fabric softener may be added to the last rinse. Spin out the excess water in the spin cycle of the washing machine and dry in the sun. Do not dry in an automatic drier, as this may cause excess shrinkage. Press while slightly damp.

PROJECT FIVE: UPHOLSTERY FABRIC

This fabric is designed with a randomly striped warp. It can be woven on a rigid heddle loom, a four-shaft table loom and a four-shaft jack loom. The loom width should be not less than 610mm (24in).

Warp: 2-ply rug wool, in seven colours. 1430m/kg (710yds/lb)
Colour A   black
              B   dark brown
              C   light brown
              D   dark red
              E   medium red
              F   orange/red
              G   orange

Weft: 2-ply rug wool, in colour E
Sett: 8 ends per 2.5cm (1in)
Width:
          finished article: 51cm (20in)
          add draw-in: 5cm (2in)
          total warp width: 56cm (22in)
Length:
          finished fabric: 219cm (86in)
          warp take-up: 25cm (10in)
          total length of fabric: 244cm (96in)
          loom wastage: 61cm (24in)
          total length of warp: 305cm (10 feet)
Total number of warp ends: 176
Weave structure: Balanced plain weave
Threading: Straight draw 1, 2, 3, 4
Sley: In an 8-dent reed, sley one in each dent.
Selvedge: Double sley the outside two ends.
Weight: 700gm (25oz)

Warping

The design of this fabric is in the warp stripes. Winding the warp will be slow, but the actual weaving is very quick. Lay out the seven colours listed above, in order from dark to light. You can of course choose seven other colours, but try to have them graduating from dark to light. You could choose an autumn sequence of browns, reds, oranges and yellows, or a purple, blue, green sequence. Name the colours A – G as above, with A the darkest colour.

The warp width of my fabric is 56cm(22in). Halve this number, to get 28cm (11in). Then divide this half warp into segments, with the first segment 8cm (3in) wide, and four other segments of 5cm (2in) wide. The first segment is larger than the others because this

1 3 ins 8cm	2 2 ins 5cm	3 2 ins 5cm	4 2 ins 5cm	5 2 ins 5cm
ABC	BCD	CDE	DEF	EFG

Fig. 10:8 Colour sequence

part of the fabric will be wrapped under the seat and much of it will not be seen. Usually it is possible to divide the half into equal segments.

Take colours A, B, and C. Wind the first segment, 8cm (3in), in these three colours. Pick up the colours at random, but do not wind more than two adjacent ends in one colour (for example, the first eight ends might be: 2 black, 1 dark brown, 1 black, 2 light brown, 1 dark brown, 1 black). Tie the threads together to join on a new colour, at either end of the warp, using an overhand knot as illustrated in Chapter Nine, page 122.

Tie this first group of eight with your counting tie, and then wind two more groups of eight, using the same colours, A, B, and C. There will be lots of joins, but these will not matter.

Take colour A away, add colour D, and wind two groups with these three colours. Continue in this fashion, taking away the darkest colour and adding a lighter colour, for the remaining segments, until half the warp, 28cm (11in), is wound. The colour sequence could be described in diagrammatic form as in **Fig. 10:8**.

Take this first half of the warp off the warping board or mill, and wind the second half in the same manner. The colour sequences remain random, but the colour balance will be the same in each half. When putting the warp onto the loom, the dark edges go to the outside.

The knots where the warp was joined will usually pull through the heddles and reed when threading; if not, undo the knots.

Weaving

Weave a heading. Place a stick across to separate the heading from the weaving proper. Weave 5 – 8 cm (2 – 3 in) in plain weave (1 and 3, 2 and 4), using colour E. Beat this weaving firmly, as this is to be a strong, upholstery fabric. Count the number of weft picks to 2.5cm (1in), and you should have eight to ten picks. If not, change your beating. Hemstitch the ends, going around three warp ends at once. Weave the complete fabric length of 244cm (96in), marking every 30cm (12in), until you have reached the end.

5. Upholstery fabric in random, striped warp designed and woven by Anne Field

Hemstitch the end to match the beginning, cut the weaving off the loom, and wash in hot, soapy water. Rinse in cold water. This temperature change will slightly shrink the fabric, and make it solid enough for upholstery fabric. Spin in the spin cycle of the washing machine to take out the excess water, and hang out to dry. Press while still damp.

The chair shown in the illustration was simple enough to cover, as the chair seat lifted out. I measured out the amount of fabric needed for each chair seat, machine-stitched each piece to strengthen the edges, and then cut the fabric. I stapled the fabric onto the chair backing myself, stretching it firmly as I did so. A professional upholsterer may be necessary for more complicated chairs.

I keep away from very light colours when weaving upholstery fabric, because of the difficulty in cleaning. It is not possible to remove the fabric to wash it, so an upholstery cleaner, such as one of the spray-on types, is used instead.

PROJECT SIX: SURFACE WEAVE FABRIC

This project is a four-shaft pattern and it can be woven on the four-shaft jack loom. The loom should not be less than 970cm (38in) wide. There is enough fabric for a jacket – 4m (13 feet), which should be adequate for most jacket patterns.

Warp: Dark blue wool, two strands of fine 2-ply used as one thread.
.1 strand = 10,000m/kg(4970yds/lb)
Weft background: same as warp.
Weft surface pattern: Bouclé yarn, 95% wool, 5% nylon. 5000m/kg (2485yds/lb)
Sett: 8 ends per 2.5cm (1 in).
Width:
    finished article: 87cm (34in)
    add draw-in: 10cm (4in)
    total warp width: 97cm (38in)
Length:
    finished fabric: 4m (13 feet)
    warp take-up: 50cm (20in)
    total length of fabric: 4.5m (14 feet 8in)

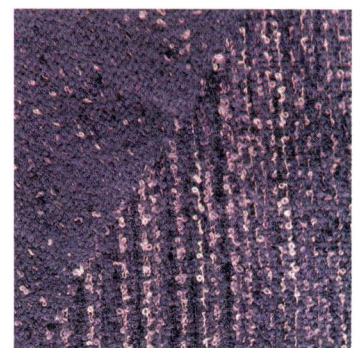

6. Surface weave fabric woven by Helene Gourlay.

WEAVING PROJECTS • 145

loom wastage: 61cm (24in)
total length of warp: 5.10m (rounded up to 17 feet)

Total number of warp ends: 304 ends

Weave structure: Plain balanced weave for the background fabric

Threading: Straight draw (see **Fig. 10.9**)

Sley: With an 8-dent reed, sley one end to each dent.

Selvedge: Put four ends in the outside dent on each side.

Weight: 1kg (2.2lbs)

Warping: Wind the warp with two crosses (see page 70) as this yarn will stick together and cause problems if it is wound on over two cross sticks.

Weaving

Weave a heading. Leave a small gap, then begin weaving, following the treadling draft on **Fig. 10:9**. Hemstitch or blanket stitch the edge to prevent it unravelling during washing. If you have a boat or end delivery shuttle, use this for the background weft, as this will speed up the weaving process. For the novelty yarn, use the ski shuttle.

After you have woven a few cm (in), check that you are weaving with an even beat, and with eight background picks to 2.5cm (1in). Mark every 0.5 metres (or 2 feet), and weave for 4.5m (14 feet 8in). Hemstitch or blanket stitch the end and cut the weaving from the loom, leaving about 5cm (2in) as a fringe, again to prevent unravelling during washing.

Check the fabric carefully for any skipped threads or mistakes, and mend any you find. Wash the fabric in warm, soapy water, kneading it for a short time to cause the background layer to mesh together to form a strong cloth. Rinse in warm water, and dry lying flat or around a roller. If using a roller, rewind the fabric and reverse it each day. Make sure the fabric is smooth so it will dry without any wrinkles. Press while still slightly damp, on the wrong side of the fabric, or have the fabric length commercially pressed.

If the fabric has been woven correctly with eight background picks to 2.5cm (1in), and washed with sufficient thoroughness to full the wool background, the fabric can be treated as normal, store-bought fabric and cut and sewn as usual.

Fig. 10:9 Surface weave

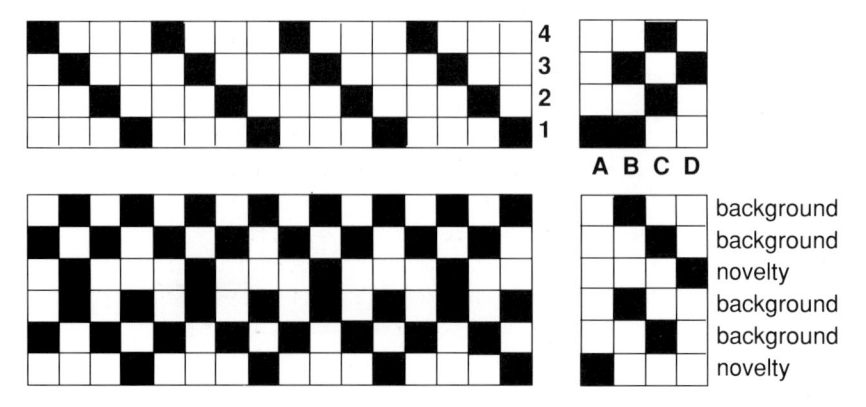

146 • THE ASHFORD BOOK OF WEAVING

PROJECT SEVEN: COTTON JACKET

This project can be woven on a four-shaft jack loom, or the four-shaft table loom. The loom should not be less than 610mm (24in) wide.

Warp: Fine, shiny, synthetic yarn. A fine mercerised cotton would probably be suitable too. 14,285m/kg (7100yds/lb).
Weft: Handspun cotton sliver spun around a cotton core, then plied with white sewing cotton. 2703m/kg (1344yds/lb). If you are not a spinner, an equivalent yarn is Patons 'Cottontop', 100% pure cotton, shade 100.
Sett: 18 ends per 2.5cm (1in) (see Sley below)
Width:
finished article:	52cm (20.5in)
add draw-in:	9cm (3.5in)
total warp width:	61cm (24in)

Length:
finished fabric:	3.10m (122in)
warp take-up:	10cm (4in)
total length of fabric:	3.20m (126in)
loom wastage:	61cm (24in)
total length of warp:	3.81m (150in)

Total number of warp ends: 432
Weave structure: Distorted warp. (Sett as for a balanced, plain weave)
Threading: Straight draw
Sley: If you have an 8-dent reed, I suggest you sett the warp at 20 ends per 2.5cm, instead of 18, and sley two in each second dent, and three in the alternate dents. If you have a 9-dent reed, sley two in each dent.
Selvedge: Put four ends in the outside dent on each side.
Weight: Total weight of garment is 500gms (17.6 ozs)

Weaving

Weave a heading. Leave a small gap, then begin weaving, following the draft in **Fig. 10:10**. Weave 12-14 picks per 2.5cm (1in). Hemstitch or blanket stitch the ends to prevent unravelling during washing. A ski or rug shuttle can be used for the weft.

As the warp is much thinner than the weft, the weaving is quick. The warp is a synthetic thread, and will not shrink much during washing, but the cotton weft will cause the width to shrink, so keep this in mind when you beat. Usually when you beat woven fabric, it looks slightly sleazy on the loom, but it shrinks and firms up when it is taken off the loom and washed. This fabric will not change much in length, but the distorted warp effect will show up with washing, and the relaxing of the warp tension.

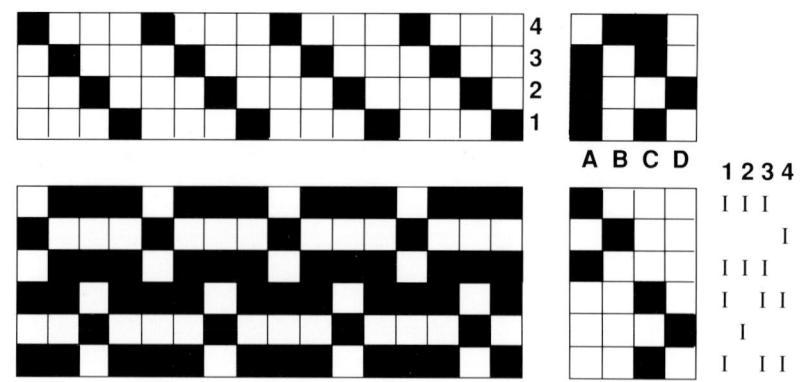

Fig. 10:10 Distorted warp

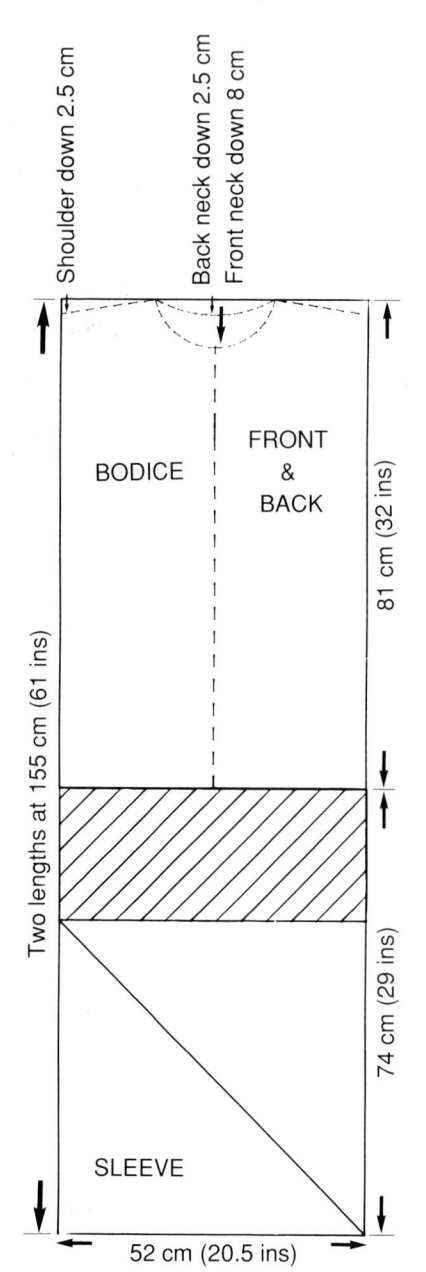

Weave for 3.2m (126in), marking each half metre or foot, to keep track of the length woven. Finish the end to match the beginning, and cut the weaving off the loom, leaving about 5cm (2.5in) to prevent unravelling. Check the fabric for skipped threads or mistakes, and mend these.

Wash the fabric in warm, soapy water, rinse in warm water, and dry lying flat. Press while still slightly damp.

Making up the jacket

There is a right and wrong side to this fabric. On the right side, the warp distortion will be apparent, so watch this when making up the jacket.

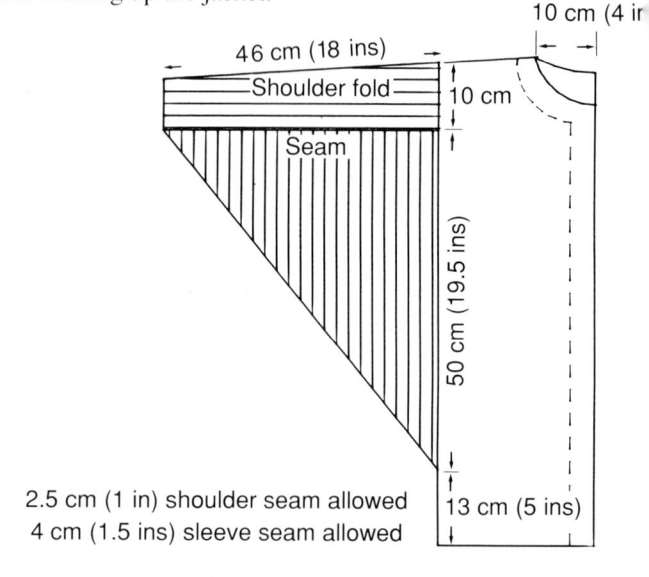

2.5 cm (1 in) shoulder seam allowed
4 cm (1.5 ins) sleeve seam allowed

Hem as required. Wrist stay stitched, trimmed, bound, turned in and top stitched.

Fig. 10:11 Making up

7. Jacket woven and designed by Fran Regan

The back has no centre seam. This jacket was not lined, but has facings around the neck and front edge of unbleached calico, backed with an iron-on vilene. The seams were overlocked, and bound with nylon chiffon for extra strength. The seams, apart from the shoulder seams, were all overstitched. A generous hem of 6cm (2.5in) on the lower jacket edge, adds weight to the jacket hem.

The cuff is narrow, so check that your hand can fit comfortably through. If not, trim the cuff back 2.5cm (1in).

PROJECT EIGHT: STOLE

This stole can be woven on a rigid heddle loom, a four-shaft table loom, and a four-shaft jack loom. The width of the loom should be no less than 56cm (22in).

Warp: Fine white 2-ply wool, 10,000m/kg (4970yds/lb).
Weft: Same as warp
Sett: 16 ends per 2.5cm (1in)
Width:
finished article:	51cm (20in)
add draw-in:	5cm (2in)
total warp width:	56cm (22in)

Length:
finished stole:	205cm (81in)
warp take-up:	20cm (8in)
fringe allowance:	30cm (12in) (Some of the fringe will be in the loom wastage.)
total length of warp:	255cm (101in)
loom wastage:	61cm (24in)
total length of warp:	316cm (125in)

Total number of warp ends: 352
Weave structure: Balanced plain weave
Threading: Straight draw, 1, 2, 3, 4
Sley: With an 8-dent reed, sley two ends per dent.
Selvedge: Thread four ends in the outside dents.
Weight: 200gm (7 ozs)
Warping: Wind the warp with two crosses, as described on page 69, to prevent the yarn sticking together.

Weaving

Weave a heading. Without leaving a gap, weave 2.5cm (1in) of balanced plain weave, using some of the warp yarn. Measure the exact width of the weft yarn on the last two picks across the warp by marking with a felt pen the weft yarn as it bends around the selvedge ends.

The measurement we need is the width of the weft yarn as it goes across the warp and back again. It is best to do a several picks before this measurement is taken, as the width should be constant by then.

Undo all the weft picks except the heading. Take the marked weft, and secure it around two strong pegs, with the marks just meeting over one of the pegs. This ensures that we will wind a hank of yarn, ready for dyeing, the same width as the warp on the loom. The pegs should be strong, to prevent movement while winding. I use my warping mill for this, as I can adjust the cross pegs to the corrrect length, but a warping board, or two pegs clamped to a table will do.

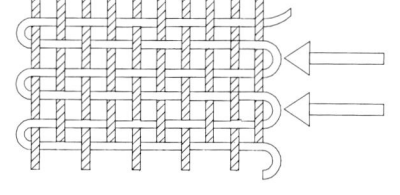

Fig. 10:12 Measuring the weft

Wind two hanks of yarn around the pegs, using the same yarn as the warp. There will be some build-up on the pegs, although I try to keep this to a minimum, as I want fractional changes in the hank size. If the weft is wound altogether in one hank, the build-up will cause the hank to vary too much in size. I wind 100 turns, then push this amount to the base of the pegs, wind the next 100 and so on.

To make sure the correct amount is wound, count the lengths as you wind. For a balanced weave, there will be 16 picks to 2.5cm (1in), so we will need 16 x 89 = 1424 turns. As one turn around both pegs equals two weft picks, halve this number to 712, and just count every time you go around the top peg. I always add a bit extra for luck, so I wind about 400 turns in each hank.

Dyeing the weft
I have a preference at the moment for cold water dyes, and for this project I used Earth Palette dyes, for silk and wool. The supplier is listed on page 196. The hanks are dip-dyed, that is I dipped part of the hanks into the dye. I do both hanks at once to guarantee that the same amount of each hank is dyed. Approximately half the hank is dyed, then I dip the very end of the dyed portion into another dye bath of a deeper colour. Follow the instructions that come with the dye for mixing and fixing the dyes. With the Earth Palette dyes, the hanks are wrapped in plastic and kept at 20 C (68 F) for 24 hours.

Weaving the stole
This is the fun part, as you can now see what sort of pattern the dyed weft makes. Because the hank was measured to the warp width, the pattern will form a repeat after a few cms (ins) have been woven.

As you can see by the photograph, the weft will gradually move across the warp. Where the movement is slow, with larger bands of weft colour, the weft hank was closest to the warp size. Where the movement is faster, the hank was a different size to the warp width. With absolutely accurate measuring, which is not possible with my equipment, the weft hanks could be dyed to the exact warp size, but I prefer the movement and the size change of the bands.

Make sure your beating is even, with 16 picks to 2.5cm, as this is important. The first stole I made in this technique, I beat too heavily, and ran out of weft, which was most frustrating. Hemstitch the ends, matching the yarn for hemstitching with the appropriate weft colour. Weave for 226cm (89in), hemstitch this end, then cut the weaving from the loom, leaving 30cm (12in) at each end for the fringe. Check for any mistakes or skipped threads, and mend these. Wash the stole in warm soapy water, and rinse well. A water softener can be added to the last rinse. Dry lying flat, then press with a damp cloth while slighly damp.

I finished the fringe with triple knots, as shown in Chapter Nine, page 122. This gave added interest to the stole ends, which are very noticeable on this type of woven fabric.

8. Stole designed and woven by Anne Field
(See page 150)

9. Cocoon jacket woven and designed by Anne Field
(See page 154)

PROJECT NINE: COCOON JACKET

This project can be woven on a four-shaft table loom, or the four-shaft jack loom. The loom should not be less than 710mm (28in) wide.

Warp: Wool, Hanna yarn, 500 tex, in mid-grey, blue, light grey and white. 2000m/kg (994yds/lb) This is a delicate yarn, and it can break, so check there are no rough edges on your shuttles. I keep some sandpaper handy when weaving with Hanna yarn, and smooth down my shuttles now and then. Even a broken fingernail can damage the yarn.
Weft: Same as warp, white
Sett: 6 ends per 2.5cm (1in)
Width:

finished article:	56cm (22in)
add draw-in:	15cm (6in)
total warp width:	71cm (28in)

Length: Two lengths are sewn together to make one shawl jacket.

length of finished jacket:	107cm (42in)
warp take-up:	10cm (4in)
fringe allowance:	15cm (6in)
total length:	132cm (52in) x 2 = 264cm (104in)
loom wastage:	61cm (24in)
total length of warp:	325cm (128in)

Total number of warp ends: 168
Weave structure: Balanced 2/2 twill
Threading: Straight draw, 1, 2, 3, 4
Sley: In an 8-dent reed, sley /*/*/*/ /*/*/*/ /
Selvedge: Thread the selvedge the same as that for Project Four
Weight: 425gms (15ozs)

Warping

For this striped warp, I wound 10cm (4in) of the blue and mid-grey colours alternately. To break up the stripes, every 6th end was white in the mid-grey stripes, and light grey in the blue stripes. Both outside stripes were blue, as I felt this would add interest to the centre back and make the join less noticeable.

Make the warp with two crosses, as described on page 69, as Hanna yarn is too soft and fluffy to be passed through cross sticks.

Weaving

Weave a heading. Leave a 2.5cm (1in) gap, then weave a few cms (ins) in 2/2 twill, following the draft **Fig. 10:7** (page 140). Count the number of weft picks to ensure you are weaving a balanced twill, with 6 picks to 2.5cm (1in). When weaving with Hanna yarn, there must be enough space for the yarn to puff up when washed, so the weaving will look open and sleazy on the loom. A very light beat is essential.

Hemstitch the end around three warp ends, using the weft yarn, and continue weaving until the piece measures 117cm (46in), marking every 30cm (12in). This measurement should be accurate, as the two pieces are to be sewn together later. Hemstitch the end of the first piece, leave a 15cm (6in) gap, and weave the second piece to match.

Cut both pieces off the loom, leaving an 8cm (3in) fringe at the end of each piece. Check for mistakes and skipped threads, and mend these. Wash the pieces in warm soapy water, rinse in warm water, and spin in the spin cycle of the washing machine to remove excess water. Dry lying flat or over towels on the clothesline. Never dry in a tumble or spin drier, as this will cause excessive shrinkage and matting. Press while slightly damp.

Making up
To make up the jacket, lie both pieces flat, with the centre seams butted together. With the white Hanna yarn, sew the two edges together on the wrong side, catching one weft pick to the opposing weft pick. Leave 25cms (10in) open at one end.

Fold the sewn piece over, and join the sleeve edges for 25cm (10in), using the same joining stitch as used on the centre seam. Turn the jacket to the right side and, using the light grey yarn, run a stitch up the centre back seam, going over two and under two threads, to match the light grey stripe that runs up the blue stripes. Do the same on the armhole seams.

The back neck edge needs some reinforcing, as it takes the strain while wearing the garment. I sew my label here, with strong machine stitching to give the extra strength required. Press the seams again after making up.

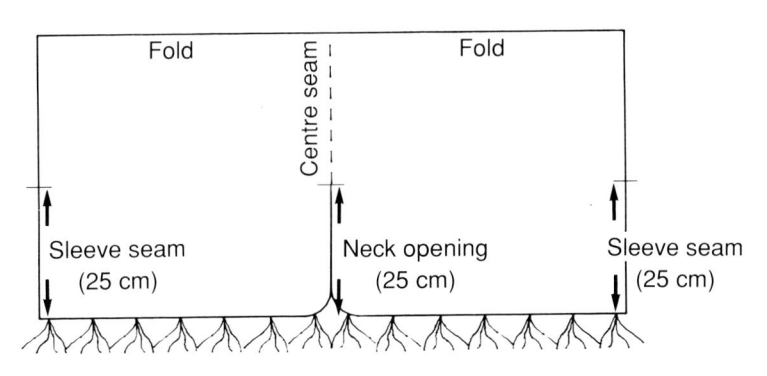

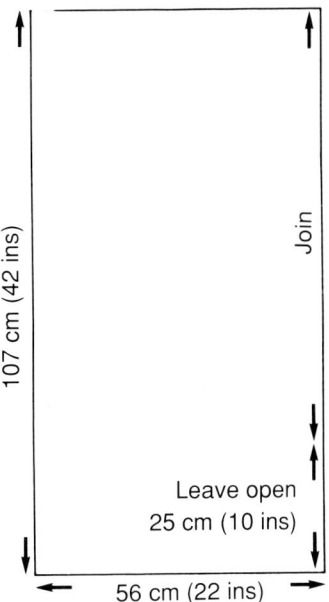

Fig. 10:13 Making up

PROJECT TEN: CROSSOVER SHAWL

This project can be woven on a rigid heddle loom, a four-shaft table loom, or a four-shaft jack loom. The width of the loom should be no less than 810mm for this project, however, if you have a 610mm loom, the shawl can be woven to that width, but it will be 2.5cm (1in) narrower than the one described in this project.

Warp: 2-ply wool 3448m/kg (1714yds/lb)
Weft: Same as the warp.
Quantities: For the warp and the weft combined, you will need 75gms (2.6oz) in the wine/red colour, 75gms (2.6oz) in the spray-dyed colour, (originally white), and 350gms (12.6oz) in the purple colour. See the instructions for winding the warp on how to dye the wool.
Sett: 10 ends per 2.5cm (1in)
Width:
finished article:	61cm (24in)
add draw-in:	3cm (1in)
total warp width:	64cm (25in)

Length:
length of each piece to crossover point:	97cm (38in)
warp take-up:	3cm (1in)
fringe allowance:	15cm (6in)
total length of each piece to crossover point:	115cm (45in)
crossover section:	64cm (25in)
loom wastage:	61cm (24in)

total length of warp:
    As part of the warp becomes the weft, as in **Fig. 10:14**, the calculations are difficult to do in the normal manner. Put on a warp of 4.5m (14.5 feet) in length, and 64cm (25in) wide, and take my word that it will be correct!

Total number of warp ends: 250 ends
Weave structure: Calculate the sett as if you were going to weave a balanced twill weave. The weave structure is actually plain weave, but the only section that is a balanced plain weave is the crossover section. The rest of the weaving has slightly more warp than weft, as this lets the long ends drape well. A twill sett will give you the correct sett.
Threading: Straight draw, 1, 2, 3, 4
Sley: Use a 10-dent reed, and sley one in each dent. If you have an 8-dent reed, I suggest you use a slightly thicker yarn and sett it at eight ends per 2.5cm (1in)
Selvedge: Do not thread the ends any closer at the selvedge.
Weight: 320gms (11.5oz)

10. Crossover shawl designed and woven by Ria Van Lith.

Warping

Wind the first 8cm(3in) in purple, and the next 8cms (3in) in wine red. The centre 32cms (13in) is wound with every second end in the purple, and every other end in the spray-dyed wool. This section of the warp can be wound with the two ends at once, as described on page 70. This dyed wool was made by winding the white wool into a hank, then different colours were sprayed on to the hank. Repeat the 8cms (3in) of wine red, and the 8cms (3in) of purple, to complete the warp width. A striped warp gives an effective focal point in the crossover section.

Weaving

Weave a heading. With a plain weave, that is lifting shafts 1 and 3, and 2 and 4 alternately, weave with eight picks per 2.5cm (1in), which is slightly less than for a balanced weave, in the purple weft. The hem will be knotted when the weaving is removed from the loom, so leave enough warp for the knots.

Weave for 1m (39in). Do not knot or stitch this end, but pull through and measure off another metre (39in) and cut the weaving and the 1m (39in) of unwoven warp off the loom. Slacken the warp

WEAVING PROJECTS • 157

off before you cut the weaving, otherwise you will lose the warp through the reed and heddles. Handle this piece carefully, and leave the heading intact to prevent the ends from unravelling. Lay it aside.

Re-tie the warp to the front stick, and weave another heading, then weave for a metre (39in) as before, finishing with shafts 2 and 4 lifted. Leave a piece of weft hanging out at the left side, to be used for the re-inforcing stitching. Make sure these measurements are accurate, otherwise you will have one section of the shawl longer than the other.

Take the first piece, and hang it over a support, to the left of the loom, at right-angles to the fell of the cloth, and at the same level as the weaving on the loom. As a support you can use a piece of furniture, such as a chair back, or part of a warping board. The first piece of weaving can also be supported by your left arm, as you weave, but it **must** be supported. The unwoven warp of the first piece should lie parallel to the breast beam of the loom.

The last weft pick of the supported piece is left hanging out from the selvedge nearest to the front of the loom, ready to be darned in as a re-inforcing stitch at the join Take the first length of unwoven warp from the supported piece, lift shafts 1 and 3, and place this length through the warp at right angles to the warp length on the loom, from left to right. The warp end can be threaded on to a large wooden needle or it can be put through one end of a shuttle, or placed by hand. Make sure the two woven areas of each piece meet. Beat this pick into place.

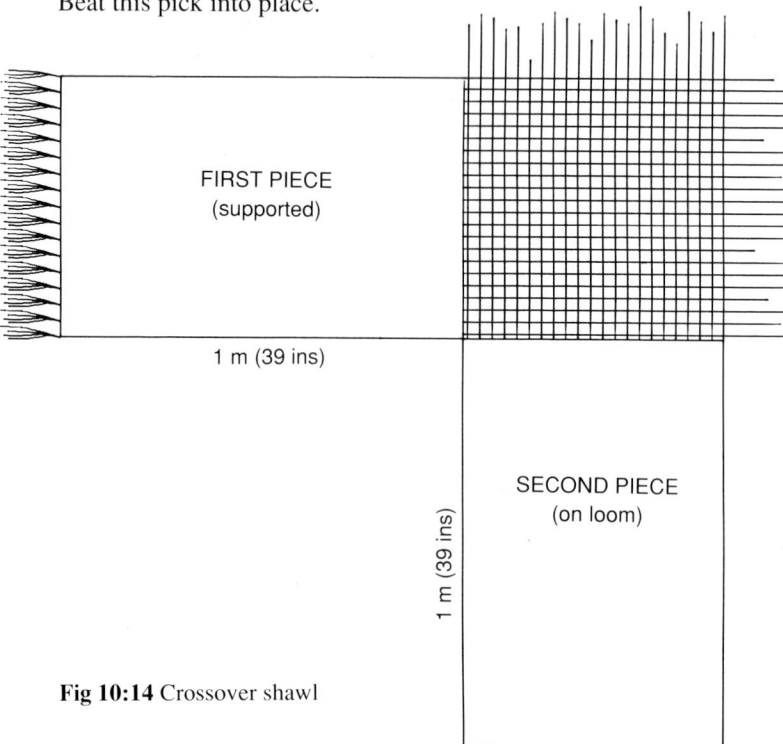

FIRST PIECE
(supported)

1 m (39 ins)

SECOND PIECE
(on loom)

1 m (39 ins)

Fig 10:14 Crossover shawl

64 cm (25 ins)

The first few picks are important, and care must be taken to see the two sections do not slide away from each other. The join must be neat and close. Change sheds, and place the next pick through and beat. This section of the shawl should be beaten slightly heavier than the other sections at 10 picks per 2.5cm (1in), to form a balanced weave, as this gives some weight to the crossed section, and it hangs well.

When you have woven four picks, knot them at the extreme right, using an overhand knot, to prevent the picks from pulling out. This weaving-in does get easier as you proceed.

Continue until all the ends are woven in and knotted, then cut the second piece of weaving from the loom, and knot the ends, again in groups of four, leaving a fringe. The point where the two sections meet should be reinforced with a few darning stitches, using the two lengths of left-over weft.

Undo the heading and knot the beginning of the first piece of weaving, in groups of four. Check for any mistakes and skipped threads, and mend these. Wash the shawl in warm soapy water, and dry lying flat. Press while still damp.

Variations

There are many colour variations that can be tried, and the colour combinations at the crossover section can be quite dramatic. When you are wearing this garment, you will find all your weaving friends walking around you in puzzlement, trying to work out how you made it!

PROJECT ELEVEN: INKLE LOOM BRACES

This project is woven on an inkle loom.

Warp: DMC No. 5 Perle embroidery cotton, 4348m/kg (2161yds/lb) Colours 930, 931, 758, 355, 356.
Weft: Same as warp, in blue (930).
Amount of thread:
    4 hanks of dark blue, colour 930 (1)
    2 hanks of light blue, colour 931 (2)
    2 hanks of dark rust, colour 355 (3)
    2 hanks of medium rust, colour 356 (4)
    1 hanks of light rust, colour 758 (5)
Width of finished article: 2.5cm (1in)
Length:
    length of each braid: 1.5m(61in)
    number of braids: 2 (each one has a separate warp)
    The warp is taken around pegs 1, 2, 3, 4, and 5, for this length. See page 13.
Total number of warp ends: 59
Weave structure: Warp-face
Weight: Each braid weighs 21.5g (0.8oz)

Warping the loom
Warp the loom, following **Fig. 10:15** for placement of the colours.

Weaving
Use the dark blue for the weft, as this matches the outside warp colour. Follow the weaving instructions in Chapter 1, and weave two braids exactly the same.

Making up
There are various ways of making up these braces. You can buy kits which contain all the necessary clips to attach to the braid, or you can buy the pieces separately.

Fig. 10:15 Threading graph for inkle loom braces

3	3	2	2	1	5	3	1	1	4	3	4	1	1	1	Unleashed
	2	3	3	2	1	5	3	1	1	4	5	4	1	1	1	Leashed

CENTRE   ← BEGIN HERE

1	1	1	4	3	4	1	1	3	5	1	2	2	3	Unleashed
1	1	1	4	5	4	1	1	3	5	1	2	3	3	2	Leashed

END   ← (CONT.)

1 Dark blue   **2** Light blue   **3** Dark rust   **4** Medium rust   **5** Light rust

11. Inkle loom braces designed and woven by Ann Clay

WEAVING PROJECTS • 161

PROJECT TWELVE: OVERSHOT RUNNER

This project can be woven on a four-shaft table loom, or a four-shaft jack loom. The width of the loom should be no less than 54cm (21in).

Warp: Beige, Marks Cottolin, 60% cotton, 40% linen, Nel 22/2. 6.400m/kg (3180yds/lb).
Weft: Beige, same as warp for background; blue, same as warp but doubled for the pattern weft.
Sett: 24 ends per 2.5cm (1in)
Width:
    finished article: 46cm (18in)
    add draw-in: 7cm (3in)
    total warp width: 53cm (21in)
Length:
    length of one runner: 71cm (28in)
    warp take-up: 5cm (2in)
    total length of runner: 76cm (30in)
    number of runners: 4 x 76cm (30in) = 304cm(120in)
    loom wastage: 61cm(24in)
    total length of warp: 365cm(144in)
Total number of warp ends: 502 + 4 (floating selv) = 506
Weave structure: Overshot, but sett as for a plain balanced weave.
Warping: Wind the warp with a cross at both ends, in two sections.

Threading
Thread the heddles in the groups as marked on the draft, check that each group is correct, then tie an overhand knot in the checked group. If taken step-by-step, this type of threading is not difficult. Check that you have enough heddles on your loom. (See **Fig. 10:16**)

Reading from the right of the draft, thread the warp ends in the following order (left column first):

Floating selvedge 2	Block VI once (6)
Selvedge ends 4	Block II once (22)
Block I threaded twice (32 ends)	Block III once (30)
Block II once (22)	Block IV once (36)
Block III once (30)	Block III once (30)
Block IV once (36)	Block II once (22)
Block III once (30)	Block I twice (32)
Block II once (22)	Selvedge 4
Block V six times (24 x 6 = 144)	Floating selvedge 2

This totals 502 ends (plus 4 for the floating selvedge)

Sley: With an 8-dent reed, sley three ends in each dent.

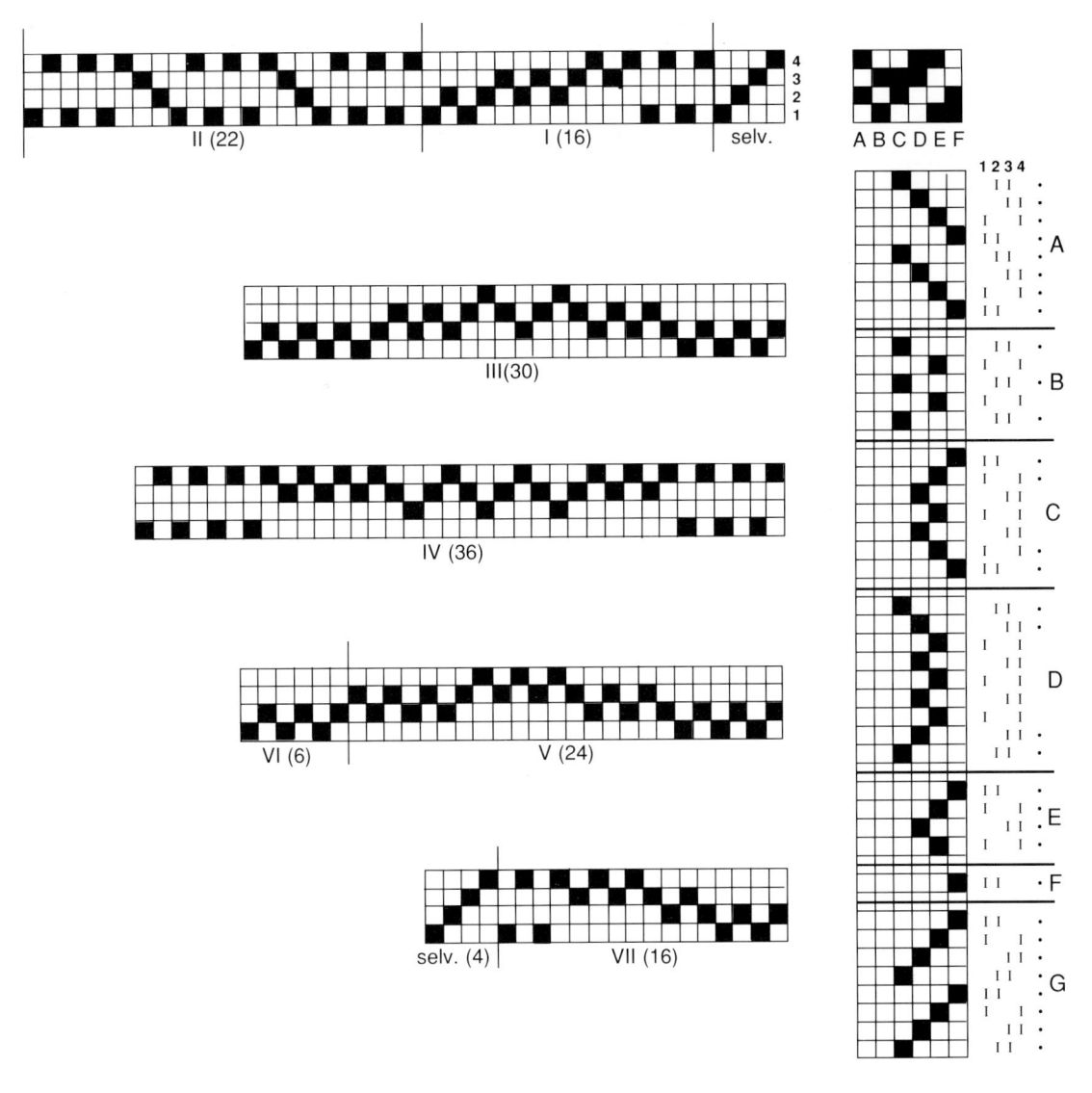

• weave this pick 3 times

Selvedge: Use a floating selvedge. Two ends on each side are not threaded in the heddles, but only through the reed. When weaving, the shuttles are taken under the floating ends when entering the shed, and over when leaving the shed.

Weight: Each runner weighs 80gms (2.8oz)

Fig. 10:16 Norse kitchen draft. This pattern was adapted from a draft on page 186, *A Handweaver's Pattern Book* by Marguerite P. Davison.

Weaving

Weave a heading. Weave 2.5cm (1in) in plain weave, using the beige background colour, directly onto this heading. Plain weave is woven on treadles A and B, lifting shafts 2 and 4, 1 and 3. This plain weave is continued as every alternate pick in between the pattern

WEAVING PROJECTS • 163

12. Overshot runner woven by Ann Clay

picks, but it is not shown on the draft. See page 65 for a description of using binder wefts.

Fill a second shuttle with the blue Cottolin doubled, and weave the blocks in the following order. Picks with "•" to the right of the draft are woven 3 times, (with the plain weave in between each pick).

Block A once. (24 pattern picks)
Block B once. (11 pattern picks)
Block C once. (15 pattern picks)
Block D once. (17 pattern picks)
Block C once. (15 pattern picks)
Block B once. (11 pattern picks)
Block E 12 times (144 pattern picks)
Block F once. (3 pattern picks)
Block B once. (11 pattern picks)
Block C once. (15 pattern picks)
Block D once. (17 pattern picks)
Block C once. (15 pattern picks)
Block B once. (11 pattern picks)
Block G once. (24 pattern picks)

Weave 2.5cm (1in) of plain weave in the beige to complete the runner. Place 2 sticks across the warp to separate this runner from the next, leaving a gap of about 5cm (2in). Weave the other three runners in the same manner.

Cut the weaving from the loom, check for any mistakes or skipped threads, and mend these. Remove the heading yarn, which had kept the beginning of the weaving from unravelling, and, on the sewing machine, hem under 1cm at the end of each runner. Wash the runners in warm, soapy water, dry lying flat, and press while still slightly damp.

PROJECT THIRTEEN: WEFT-FACE HANGING

This project can be woven on a four-shaft table or jack loom. The width of the loom needed for this project is no less than 610mm (24in).

Warp: Strong cotton 2000m/kg (994yds/lb).
Weft: 2-ply rug wool, 1430m/kg (710yds/lb), in seven colours. One colour (beige) is the background colour, and the other six are for the pattern weft.
Sett: 6 ends per 2.5cm (1in)
Width:
    finished article: 51cm (20in)
    add draw-in: 5cm (2in)
    total warp width: 56cm (22in)
Length:
    length of finished hanging: 92cm (36in)
    warp take-up: 2cm (1in)
    total length of hanging: 94cm (37in)
    loom wastage: 61cm (24in)
    total length of warp: 155cm (61in)
Total number of warp ends: *130 + 4 (floating selvedge) = 134. As there are 10 ends to a pattern repeat, this figure *, should be divisible by 10.
Weave structure: Weft-face weave
Threading: Queens Cord (see **Fig. 10:18** over page). This weave structure requires a floating selvedge to make a firm and tidy edge. Take the two outside ends on each side, and thread them through the reed, in one dent, but not through the heddle.
Sley: With an 8-dent reed, sley /*/*/*/ /*/*/*/ /
Selvedge: Floating selvedge, as described above
Weight: The hanging weighs 380g(13oz)

Weaving
Weave a heading. Place a narrow stick across the warp width, as this will give a firm edge to beat against. Weave for 4cm (1.5in), in the background colour, following Section 1 of the draft. For the floating selvedge ends, take the weft over these ends when entering the shed and under these ends, on the opposite side, when leaving the shed.
  Remove the stick, hemstitch the ends, then weave a row of long rya knots across the full width of the warp (**Fig. 10:17**). These knots will

Colours A–F

13. Weft-face hanging woven by Ngaio Donnell

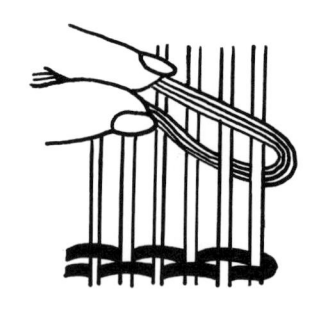

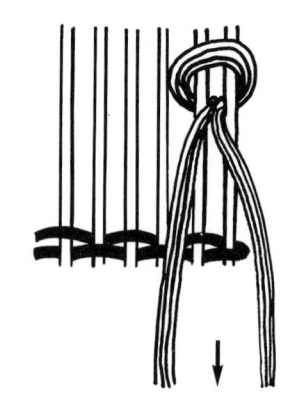

Fig. 10:17 Rya knots

Fig. 10:18 Queen's cord draft

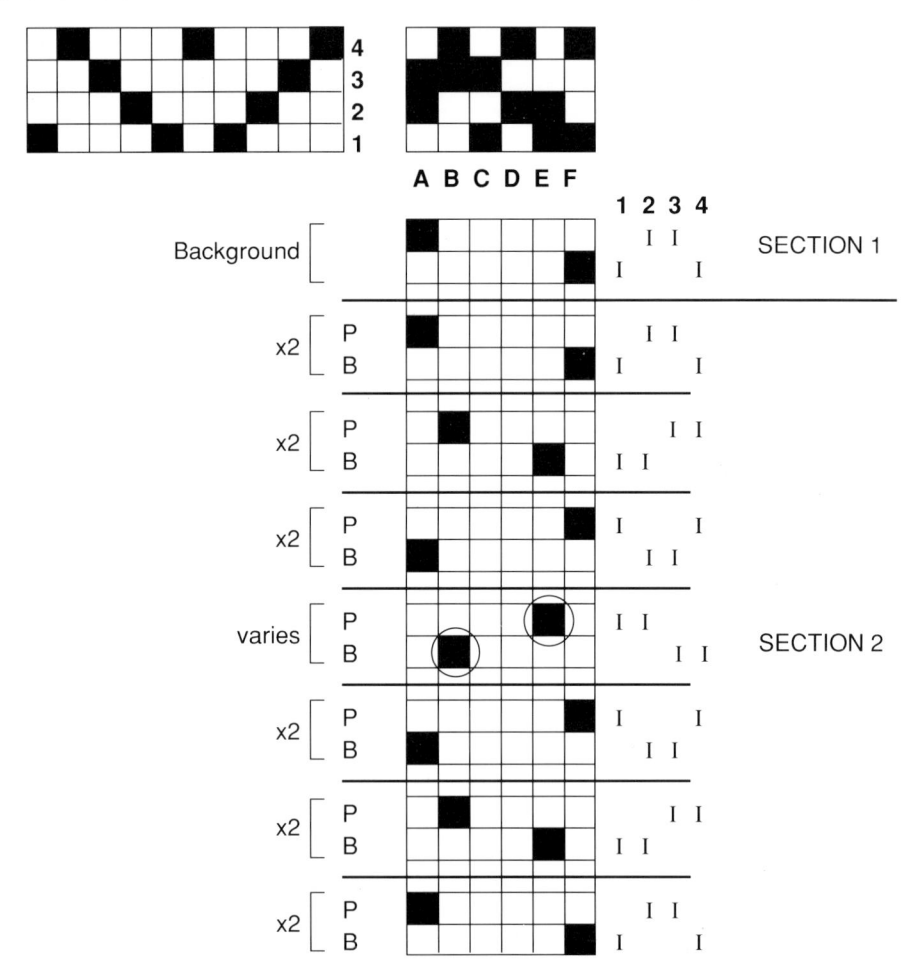

P = pattern weft
B = background weft

166 • THE ASHFORD BOOK OF WEAVING

form the fringe on the finished hanging. The lengths needed for the fringe will be approximately 38cm (15in).

The easiest way to make the fringe ends is to wind the wool around a book, about 18cm (7in) in width, then cut the wool down the opening edge of the book. The knots will be in the background colour.

To weave the row of knots, first close the shed. Take four strands of the cut yarn, and place them over two warp ends, as in **Fig. 10:17**, holding the tips of the strands in one hand. Put the thumb and forefinger of the other hand through the two warp ends, grasp the tips and pull them to the surface. Give a firm tug in the direction of the arrow, to tighten the knot. Knot each pair of warp ends across the warp width.

Weave for 2.5cm (1in) in the background weft as before, following Section I, then begin the pattern.

Boundweave on opposites
Take colour A, wind it onto a second shuttle, and weave Section II of the draft, with the background colour on the other shuttle ('B' on **Fig. 10:18**). Colours A–F are marked 'P' on the draft. As Colour A makes the largest pattern, the circled picks are woven for 15cm (6in). Boundweave on opposites is woven, as the name implies, with each background pick woven on the opposite shafts to the pattern pick. It takes two picks, the pattern and the background, to make one complete row.

Then weave Section I, the background, for 2.5cm (1in).
Colour B. The circled picks are woven for 13cm (5in). Weave
   Section I the background, for 2.5cm (1in).
Colour C. The circled picks are woven for 10cm (4in), followed by
   Section I as above.
Colour D. The circled picks are woven for 8cm (3in), followed by
   Section I.
Colour E. The circled picks are woven for 5cm (2in), followed by
   Section I
Colour F. The circled picks are woven for 2.5cm (1in).

Finishing
Weave Section I in the background weft for 8cm (3in) as the top border, part of which will become the hem. Hemstitch the end of the hanging, cut it from the loom, allowing about 5cm (2in) of warp at each end, to prevent unravelling. Hem the top end under 5cm (2in), tucking the warp ends into the hem.

Hem the lower end under 4cm (1.5in), leaving the rya knots to form the lower fringe. Press the complete hanging using a damp cloth and a hot iron. Put a narrow wooden rod through the top hem, and plait a braid (See Chapter Nine, page 122 for instructions) for a hanger.

PROJECT FOURTEEN: TAPESTRY HANGING

This project can be woven on a rigid heddle loom, a four-shaft table loom, or a four-shaft jack loom. The width of the loom should be no less than 59cm (23in).

Warp: 8/3 cotton, 4515m/kg (2240yds/lb)
Weft: 2-ply rug wools, 1430m/kg (710yds/lb)
Sett: 4 ends per 2.5cm (1in)
Width:
    finished article: 56cm (22in)
    add draw-in: 2.5cm (1in)
    total warp width: 58.5cm (23in)
Length:
    finished hanging: 76cm (30in)
    warp take-up: 2.5cm (1in)
    no fringe allowance
    total length of hanging: 79cm (31in)
    loom wastage: 61cm (24in)
    total length of warp: 140cm (55in)
Total number of warp ends: 92 ends
Weave structure: Weft-face
Threading: 1, 2, 3, 4, straight draw
Sley: In an 8-dent reed, sley an end in every second dent.
Selvedge: Double the two outside ends.
Weight: 400gms (14oz)

Weaving

Weave a heading. Place a stick across the warp, then weave for 2.5cm in rug wool, bubbling the weft as in **Fig. 10:6**. Remove the stick, and hemstitch the end, following the instructions on page 122. Put a fringe of rya knots across, following the instructions on page 166 in the previous project.

The design for this type of tapestry hanging can be drawn out first as a cartoon on squared paper, or it can be woven free-hand, making the design up as you go along. However, because you do not see all of the hanging at once, as it is wound around the front roller, it is a good idea to have even a rough sketch worked out beforehand. You can also place tracing paper over a photograph or drawing, and make a cartoon this way.

The shapes are joined as in **Fig. 10:19**. Only two types of joining methods are used. The tree trunk is woven as a straight join, and the other shapes woven as diagonal joins. The tree trunk joins are sewn together afterwards. Build up each shape, one at a time, making sure you build up the areas that slope inwards first, otherwise the shed becomes locked in. Use small shuttles or wind the yarn into small hanks and use one for each shape.

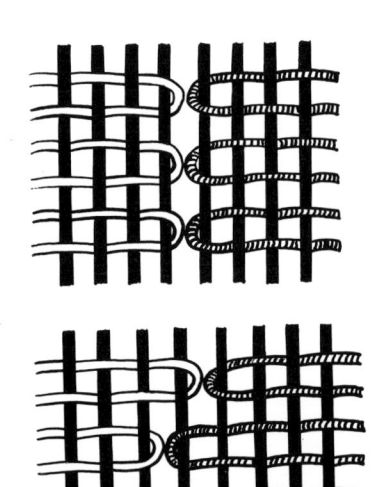

Fig. 10:19 Joining shapes

The curves can be marked on the warp with felt pens, and then weave up to just beyond these marks, as subsequent picks will continue to push down the shapes. As the fell of the cloth is not in a straight line, the beater cannot be used, but a kitchen fork makes a good beater. Keep the warp tension tight, so the weft picks will slide down the warp. Do not build up any one shape more than 13cm (5in) above the rest of the weaving. The weft ends are trimmed to about 2.5cm (1in) and left hanging out from the back of the weaving, this being an acceptable finish in tapestry weaving.

The green leafy section of the tree is woven as raised loops. Take a thick wooden knitting needle, or a piece of wooden dowelling about 1cm (0.5in) in diameter. Put a doubled weft pick through the shed, then with the dowelling or knitting needle, pick up a loop of weft between each warp end of the top layer of the warp. Twist the loop as it slides onto the dowell to lock it in Continue the loops in the raised areas, changing sheds as usual. Some areas of the leaves are looped using two different colours.

The sky area was woven with a white skein of carpet wool dyed randomly with a blue dye giving a realistic, streaky effect to the sky. Weave a 5cm (2in) heading at the top of the hanging, hemstitch the ends according to the instructions on page 122, and cut the weaving from the loom.

Remove the first heading, then hem the first 2.5cm (1in) under, leaving the rya fringe to form the fringed end. Hem the top 5cm (2in) under and press the weaving with a damp cloth.

Place a piece of wooden dowell across the top hem, and plait a braid which is then attached to the dowell at each end to hang the tapestry from.

14. Tapestry hanging designed and woven by Jane McKenzie

WEAVING PROJECTS • 169

PROJECT FIFTEEN: WARP-FACE HANGING

This project can be woven on a four-shaft table loom, or a four shaft jack loom. The width of the loom should be no less than 46cm (18in).

Warp: White polypropylene, 5/3 2703m/kg (1344yds/lb)
Weft: White cotton multi-strand 460m/kg (239yds/lb). I wound this yarn into six hanks and dyed one hank purple, and the others violet, blue, turquoise, and green, with Earth Palette dyes. The sixth hank I left white. If you do not have this type of yarn available, you can make your own multi-strand yarn by taking all your scrap cotton and linen yarns, and winding them together. The multi-strand yarn I used had appoximately 40 threads in it. Some yarns will take the dye differently to others, and this adds to the variation in colour depth. Each coloured hank measured approximately 12m (13yds).
Sett: 30 ends per 2.5cm (1in)
Width:
    finished article: 43cm (17in)
    add draw-in: 3cm (1in)
    total warp width: 46cm (18in)
Length:
    finished hanging: 68cm (27in)
    warp take-up: 8cm (3in)
    fringe allowance: 15cm (6in)
    total length of hanging: 91cm (36in)
    loom wastage: 61cm (24in)
    total length of warp: 152cm (60in)
Total number of warp ends: 540. Check that you have enough heddles!
Weave structure: Warp-face weave
Threading: See **Fig. 10:20**.
Sley: In a 10-dent reed, sley three ends per dent. With an 8-dent reed, sley 4, 4, 4, 3, ends in each dent across the reed width.
Selvedge: There is no selvedge threading.
Weight: 440 gms (15.5oz)

Warping
Wind the warp in two or four portions, with a cross at both ends of the warp, as described on page 69, as this is a very solid warp.

Threading the heddles
There are two blocks to this pattern: Block A on shafts 1 and 2, and Block B on shafts 3 and 4, with 30 ends in each block. The profile draft is a short way of showing the threading, with each block from the pattern draft in **Fig. 10:21** threaded twice, and ending in Block A. Shafts 1 and 2 need 30 more heddles each than the other two shafts.

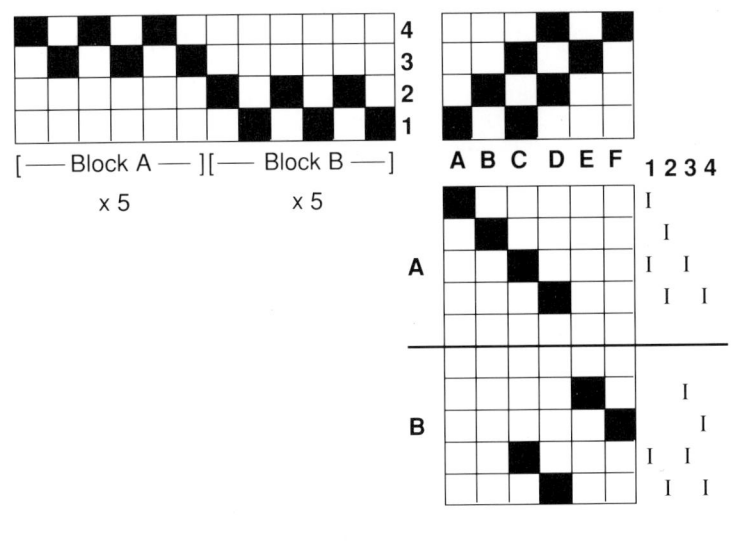

Fig. 10:20

Fig. 10:21 Profile draft

Weaving

Because of the weight and close sett of the warp, the warp sticks together and all the shafts rise when only two are meant to. Raise the shafts as normal, then push back down by hand the shafts that are supposed to be lowered. This does not take long, as the actual weaving of this hanging is very quick. When the shed becomes clear, put a warp stick through the shed, and beat it towards you, leaving an absolutely clear shed for the shuttle to pass through.

Weave a heading in plain weave, lifting shafts 1 and 3, 2 and 4. Put a narrow stick through the shed and weave five picks in the white multi-strand yarn, lifting the same shafts as for the heading, and finishing on shafts 2 and 4, on the right-hand side. Tuck the end of this weft into the next pick, on the right. Make sure you have left enough warp for a 15cm (6in) fringe. The ends will not need stitching or knotting.

Block A

Wind the 12m (13yds) of purple multi-strand yarn onto a ski shuttle and begin weaving Block A, from the right, overlapping the purple weft with the white in the first pick. Weave this block five times, that is 20 weft picks, separating the warp as described above and beating heavily. Finish on shafts 2 and 4 then cut the end of this weft about 5cm (2in) out from the right selvedge. Cut the weft floats down the centre of each float.

Block B

Divide the violet weft into two equal portions, and wind each portion onto a separate shuttle. Take one shuttle, lift shaft 3 and put this weft

15. Warp face hanging designed and woven by Anne Field

through from right to left, leaving a 2.5cm (1in) tail protruding from the raised group on the right side of the weaving. Lift shaft 4, and return the weft from left to right, leaving a 5cm (2in) loop of weft protruding from the raised group of ends on the left.

Lift shafts 1 and 3 and tuck the purple weft end left over at the right side into this shed. Take the second, filled shuttle, and put it through the shed from right to left, overlapping the end with the purple weft end. Lift shafts 2 and 4, and weave back from left to right.

Repeat this four-pick sequence five times, 20 picks in total. The shuttle that forms the floats leaves a 5cm (2in) loop at each edge. Finish with the weft on this shuttle protruding from the last raised group and cut this weft, leaving a 2.5cm(1in) tail. When the sequence is complete, cut the weft floats as before. The background weft is tucked into the next background weft pick, as at the end of Block A.

Look closely at the structure. You can see that when the weft floats over the surface, the warp-face background spreads out to take up the space. A warp-face structure is necessary for this type of weaving, as it is strong enough to hold the floats in position.

Repeat Block A in the blue weft, Block B in the turquoise weft, and Block A in the green weft.

Weave five picks in the green weft, repeating the five picks woven at the beginning of the hanging in plain weave. Into the next shed, place a wooden dowel, 1cm(0.5in) longer at each end than the weaving width. Change sheds, put the shuttle with the green weft through from the opposite side, leaving about 70cm(28in) looped as a cord to hang the weaving from. Cut the green weft just short of the selvedge and weave four picks in a rug wool or cotton to give a firm edge.

Before cutting the weaving from the loom, run a line of PVA glue across to hold the edges together, about 2.5cm (1in) from the last weft pick. When the weaving is off the loom, fold the top heading to the back, and sew a length of tape across to hide the warp ends. The green weft is looped twice around the dowelling to hide the ends of the wood, and the hanging suspended from this cord.

Trim the lower fringe to 15cm (6in). The hanging does not need washing or pressing.

PROJECT SIXTEEN: DOUBLE CORDUROY RUGS

This project can be woven on a four-shaft jack loom. The loom should not be less than 970mm (38in) wide.

Warp: Strong cotton, 2000m/kg (994yds/lb)
Weft: 2-ply rug wool, 1430m/kg (710yds/lb)
Sett: 6 ends per 2.5cm (1in)
Width:
    finished article: 74cm (29in)
    add draw-in: 2cm (1in)
    total warp width: 76cm (30in)
Length:
    finished rug: 152cm (60in)
    warp take-up: 3cm (1in)
    total length of rug: 155cm (61in)
    number of rugs   1
    loom wastage: 61cm (24in)
    total length of warp: 216cm (85in)
Total number of warp ends: 180 + 8 (selv) = 188
Weave structure: Pile rug, derived from overshot floats, which are cut.
Threading: See **Fig. 10:23**
Sley: With an 8-dent reed, sley /*/*/*/ /*/*/*/ /
Selvedge: See **Fig. 10:22**. The warp ends are doubled and tripled in the heddles, as well as the reed, to give a strong edge to the rug. The 20-thread warp repeat should not be broken, as this complicates the sequence of weft floats. Hence the total number of warp ends should be divisble by 20, plus 8 for the selvedge.
Weight: 3.5kg (7.7 lbs), for each rug.

Warping
Wind the warp under tension, using wooden slats, Venetian blind slats, or strong corrugated cardboard to separate the layers, as the warp tension should be firm. The warp should be wound in four sections, to keep the tension even and prevent build-up.

Weaving
The weaving instructions for this sound complicated, but the ryhthm is soon mastered, and weaving is very quick. A complete rug can be woven in about 10 hours.

    Weave a heading, then leave a gap and weave the rug heading for 5cm (2in) in the doubled rug wool. This hem will be turned under when the rug is off the loom. The heading is woven in plain weave, using treadles A and D. Bubble this heading, as shown in **Fig. 10:6**, to prevent draw-in, and also remember to bubble the plain weave picks in the body of the rug itself.

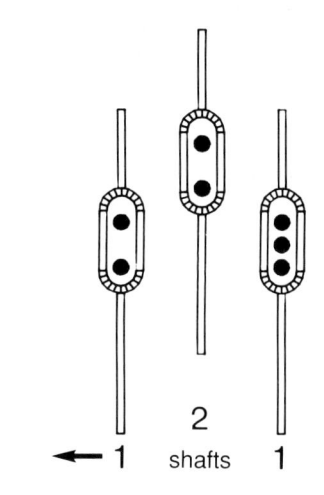

Selvedge threading for heddles

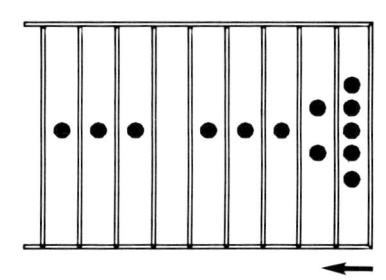

Selvedge threading for reed

Fig. 10:22 Selvedge threading

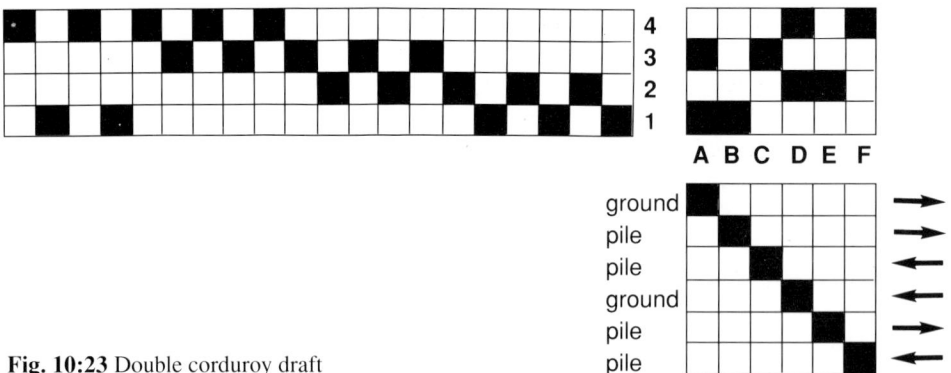

Fig. 10:23 Double corduroy draft

There are two wefts, a ground weft and a pile weft. The ground weft is not seen, but adds strength to the rug, and provides a base for the pile structure.

Ground weft: Two strands of 2-ply rug wool, in a matching colour to the pile. A rug or ski shuttle holds the weft.

Pile weft: Six strands of 2-ply rug wool. A ski shuttle is best for holding this considerable amount of yarn. Put all the balls or cones of wool in a box to prevent tangling.

Weaving sequence
The shuttles must be thrown in the direction indicated. You can choose to weave either the red/brown rug or the blue rug (see Photo 16, page 176) on this warp. The weaving instructions are the same for both rugs.

Red/Brown rug
Two pattern repeats of the darkest weft (colour A), which is approximately 10m (11yds) of weft wound on to the shuttle. Follow this by one repeat with half colour A, mixed with half the next colour, colour B (5m (5.5yds) of each). (See inset to Photo 16, page 176.) Then use two repeats of the solid colour B, and one repeat of colours B and C together, and so on. There are eight colours in all.

Blue rug
The dark blue weft comes in on shaft 3, because this pile pick does not reach either selvedge, and will not leave untidy edges to the finished rug. The other three pile picks are in the light blue weft.

Weaving
Pick 1: Lift shaft 1 and 3 (treadle A). Throw the ground weft from left to right.
Pick 2: Lift shaft 1 (treadle B). Throw the pile weft from left to right. Pull up the floats to the length of pile required. Leave 5cm

(2in) of the end of the weft hanging out in the first space between the raised warps at the left selvedge. Cut the right end about 10cms (4in) from the selvedge. On this, the very first pick, take a separate piece of weft of half the normal thickness, loop it around the left selvedge warp ends, and back into the shed. This is only done once, at the beginning of the rug.

Pick 3: Lift shaft 3 (treadle C). Pile weft from right to left. Pull up the floats and leave a tail protruding from the right raised warp group, and cut the weft 5cm (2in) out from the warp group on the left.

Pick 4: Lift shafts 2 and 4 (treadle D). Ground weft from right to left.

Pick 5: Lift shaft 2 (treadle E). Tuck the weft end hanging at the right side after Step 2, under the first warp group. Throw the pile weft from left to right, leaving a 5cm (2in) tail on the left. Pull up the floats. Cut the weft between the last two warp groups on the right.

Pick 6: Lift shaft 4 (treadle F). Pile weft from right to left, and pull up the floats. Leave a 5cm (2in) tail protruding from the warp group on the right selvedge. Do not cut the weft.

Repeat these picks, until you have woven about 8cm(3in). Use a weighted rug beater to beat this 8cm (3in) firmly.

Fig. 10:24 Double corduroy

Cutting instructions
After you have woven and beaten down 8cm (3in), the loops should be cut. Cut the pile after a ground weft pick. Begin on the right side, and slide the scissors vertically, up the rug pile, under the floats on each of the four blocks.

Red Rug
For an even pile, as in the red/brown rug, cut each block of floats, in the centre of the float. There will be four vertical cuts, to each block of 20 warp ends.

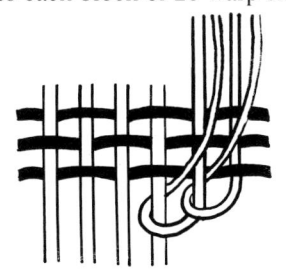

Fig. 10:25 Half Damascus edge

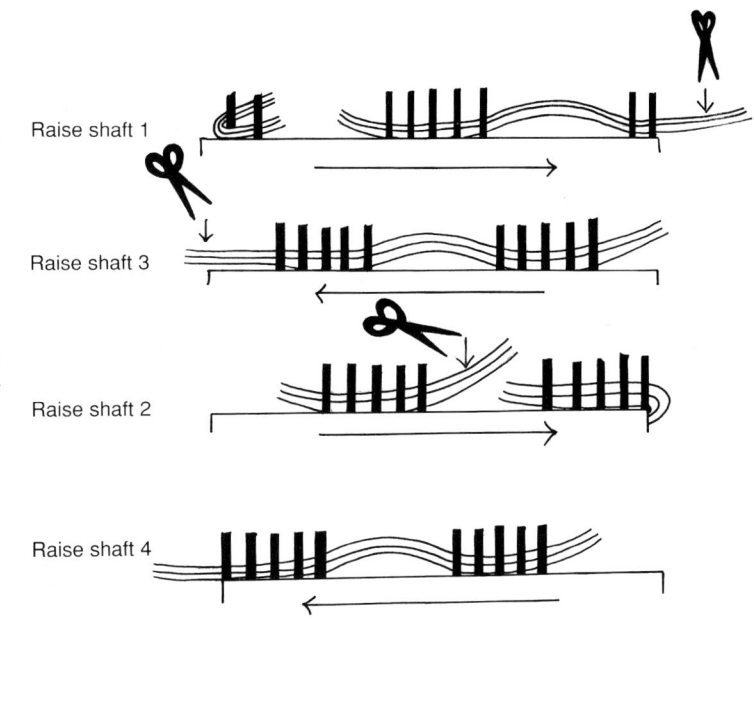

WEAVING PROJECTS • 175

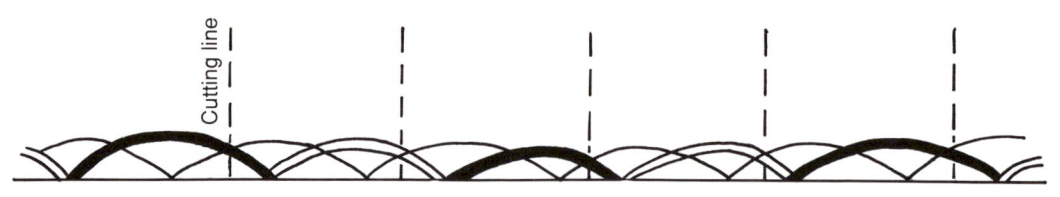

Fig. 10:26 Cutting for an uneven pile

Blue rug

For an uneven pile, as in the blue rug, cut the floats unevenly. Cut the dark blue floats to the right of centre, and also catch and cut the float directly behind in pale blue in the centre of the float. Then make the second vertical cut, to the right of a pale blue float, and in the centre of the pale blue float directly behind. This sounds complex, but makes sense when you see the floats on the rug itself. (**Fig. 10:26**)

Weave for 155cm (61in), then weave a 5cm (2in) heading to match the beginning of the rug. Cut the rug from the loom, leaving plenty of warp to prevent unravelling.

Finishing

To give added strength to the rug ends, work a Half Damascus edge (**Fig. 10:25**), trim the warp ends, and hem under the 5cm (2in) heading.

Variations

There are many interesting variations of double corduroy rugs which can be woven. Read Peter Collingwood's excellent book *The Techniques of Rug Weaving*, published by Faber and Faber.

The subtle gradation of colours for the red/brown rug: from right to left, dark brown (colour A) through to bright red (colour H).

16. Double corduroy rugs designed and woven by Marion Gilbert

THE ASHFORD BOOK OF WEAVING

PROJECT SEVENTEEN: EIGHT-SHAFT FABRIC

This fabric can be woven on the eight-shaft jack loom. The loom should not be less than 970mm (38in) wide.

Warp: Cotton, 10/3 4515m/kg (2240yds/lb)
Weft: Slub cotton and rayon. 60% cotton, plyed with 40% rayon. 3125m/kg (1553yds/lb) Sample at end of warp was woven in a blue linen weft, 8333m/kg 4142yds/lb)
Sett: 16 ends per 2.5cm (1in)
Width:
- finished article: 92cm (36in)
- add draw-in: 5cm (2in)
- total warp width: 97cm (38in)

Length:
- finished fabric: 8m (8.5 yards)
- warp take-up: 0.8m (0.8yd)
- total length: 8.8m (9.3yds)
- loom wastage: 61cm (24in)
- total length (rounded up): 9.5m (10yds)

Total number of warp ends: 608
Weave structure: This weave has alternating blocks of twill and plain weave.
Sett: As for a balanced plain weave
Threading: See **Figs. 10:27 and 10:28**. A profile draft is a short way of writing out a threading draft. Beginning from the right, you can see from **Fig. 10:28** that Block A is threaded twice (16 ends), Block B four times (32 ends), and so on across the warp width. As the fabric is to be cut afterwards, to make up into a garment, it is not important to balance the blocks to finish with the same block on the left as on the right.

17. Eight-shaft fabric designed and woven by Anne Field

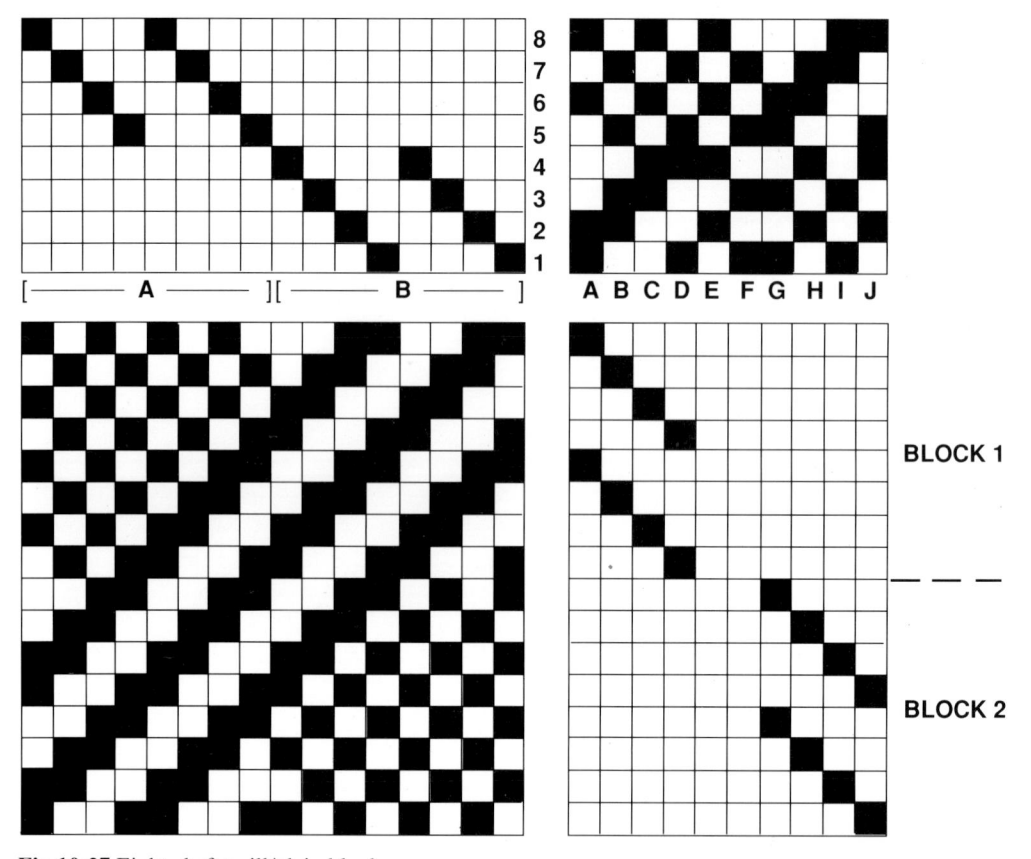

Fig 10:27 Eight-shaft twill/plain blocks

Fig. 10:28 Profile draft for threading

Sley: With an 8-dent reed, sley 2 in each dent.
Selvedge: Double the outside ends in the reed.
Weight: 2.3kg (5lb)

Weaving
Weave a heading in plain weave, using treadles E and F. Leave a gap, and weave a narrow border, for 2.5cm (1in), also in plain weave. Check that you are beating with 16 picks to 2.5cm (1in). Hemstitch this edge. I have placed the plain weave treadles in the centre to separate the two blocks when weaving, which lessens mistakes.

Treadles A, B, C, D, used in that order, give plain weave blocks in the areas threaded on shafts 5, 6, 7, 8, and twill blocks in the areas threaded on shafts 1, 2, 3, 4 (marked Block I on the treadling draft). Treadles G, H, I, J, used in that order, give plain weave blocks in the areas threaded on shafts 1, 2, 3, 4, and twill blocks in the areas threaded on shafts 5, 6, 7, 8 (marked Block II on the treadling draft).

When transferring from one block to another, there will be some three-thread floats. As the sett is 16 per 2.5cm (1in), this size float is acceptable for fabric.

Each block is woven for 10cm (4in). If the blocks are any longer than this, the difference between the twill and plain weave sections will show up, and cause the fabric to hang badly.

Continue weaving these blocks for 8.8m (9.3yds), measuring every 0.5m (2 feet) and marking this measurement with a tie to keep track.

Finishing

When the complete length is woven, hemstitch the ends, cut the weaving from the loom, and check for any mistakes or skipped threads. Mend these, then wash the fabric in warm, soapy water, agitating the fabric thoroughly. The fabric could be placed in a washing machine, on the 'gentle' cycle, for this washing process. Rinse well, spin off the excess water in the spin cycle of the washing machine, and hang out to dry. Press while still slightly damp. The fabric can also be dried around a roller, with the fabric being re-rolled every day.

Sewing

If the fabric has been correctly beaten and washed, the cloth can be cut and treated as normal, store-bought fabric. There is a right and wrong side to the fabric. On the right side, there will be no three-thread floats travelling vertically.

Variations

On the end of this warp I wove with a different coloured weft, to make the blocks stand out more. I used a fine, dark blue linen weft for this section, and wove each block 5cm (2in) long. This is the fabric shown in the lower portion of the photograph. The cream weft is more subtle than the blue weft, but both have a fascinating texture, with the twill blocks reflecting the light in a different manner from the plain weave blocks. I could also change the direction of the twill blocks, and have some running to the right and some to the left.

PROJECT EIGHTEEN: EIGHT-SHAFT STUFFED CUSHION IN DOUBLE WEAVE

This project can be woven on an eight-shaft table loom, or an eight-shaft jack loom. The width of the loom should be no less than 410cm (16in). This cushion was based on an idea from 'Handwoven' Sept/Oct 1987; a bedspread designed by Wendy Mckay.

Warp: Fine 2-ply wool.
    Apricot Berga 10,000m/kg (4970yds/lb)
    Grey 10,000m/kg (4970yds/lb)
    Blue 10,000m/kg (4970yds/lb)
Weft: Same as warp
Stuffing: Dacron or wool batting
Sett: 16 ends per 2.5cm in each layer, 32 ends in doubled layer
Width:

finished article:	40cm (15.5in)
add draw-in:	3cm (1.5in)
total warp width:	43cm (17in)

Length:

finished cushion:	79cm(31in)
warp take-up:	8cm (3in)
total length of cushion:	87cm (34in)
number of cushions:	1
loom wastage:	91cm (36in)
total length of warp:	2m(2yds) (rounded up)

Total number of warp ends: 552 (the narrow or tie-down stripes are sett closer than the squares)
Weave structure: Plain weave

Warping

Wind the warp with two crosses, following the description on page 69. Also wind the warp with two ends at once, as described on page 70. Follow the colour sequence in **Fig. 10:29**, that is, in the first section, Block I, wind 24 ends of grey with two ends coming from two cones or balls of yarn. The next section, in Block II, is wound with one grey, one apricot (40 ends of each), a total of 80 ends in all. The next section is wound with 80 ends of grey and so on, until you have a total of 552 ends wound.

Threading

See **Fig. 10:30**. Check that there are plenty of heddles on your loom. More are required on the back four shafts than on the front four.

Follow the threading draft in **Fig. 10:30**, and the colour sequence in **Fig. 10:29**. If the threading is done in steps, and each step is checked before moving on to the next, there will be no problems, and what seems a difficult task is broken up into manageable steps.

18. Stuffed cushion in double weave woven by Jane McKenzie

Thread each colour block, check, then move onto the next colour block.

If you are using the eight-shaft table loom, take particular care not to confuse shafts 4 and 5, as these central shafts seem to get easily mixed up.

The first block in the threading draft, reading from right to left, indicates that you thread 24 grey ends on shafts 1, 2, 3, 4, (tie-down block x6). The second block, A, has grey and apricot threaded alternately on shafts 5, 6, 7, 8, with grey on shafts 5 and 7 and apricot on shafts 6 and 8. This block has 80 ends. Continue across the draft, keeping the grey ends on shafts 5 and 7 and the apricot/blue ends on shafts 6 and 8 in blocks A and C. If you have wound your warp in the correct colour sequence according to **Fig. 10:29**, you will have no problems.

Fig. 10:29 Warp colour sequence

	40	40	40		40	40	40		
24	1	1 1	1	24	1	1 1	1	24	Grey
	1						1		Apricot
			1		1				Blue
[I][		II	][I][		II	][I]			

Block I sleyed /5/5/4/5/5/
Block II sleyed /4/4/4/4/

WEAVING PROJECTS • 181

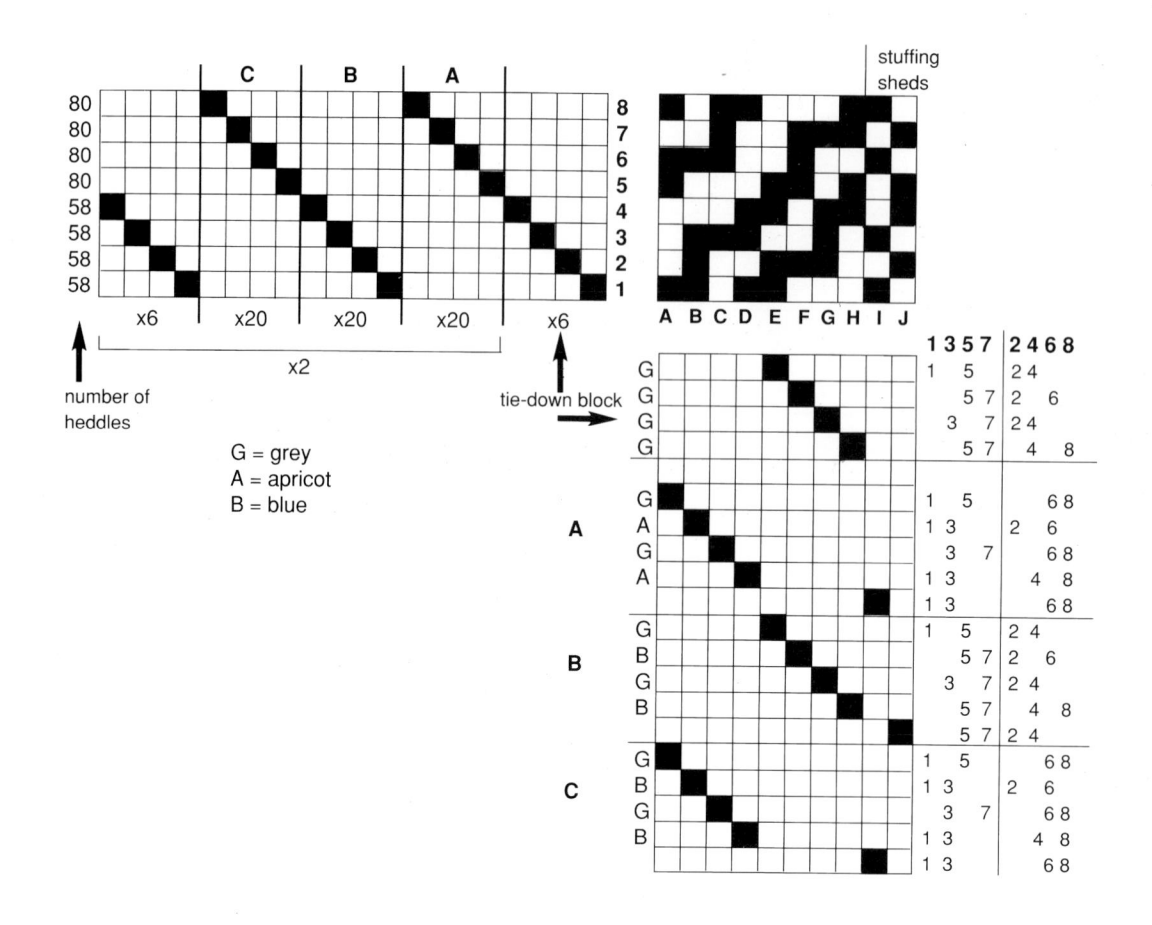

Fig. 10:30 Eight-shaft double weave draft

The sequence of blocks is: tie-down, A, B, C, tie-down, C, B, A, tie-down.

Sley: On an 8-dent reed, Block I, from **Fig. 10:29**, (the tie-down blocks) are sleyed /5/5/4/5/5/ for these 24 ends. Block II is sleyed four per dent.

Selvedge: Do not sley the ends any closer at the selvedge.

Weight: 100gms (2.8oz)

Weaving

This is a very fine piece of weaving, and requires patience, but you will be rewarded with a very special cushion at the end of the project. Follow the treadling draft in **Fig. 10:30** if you have a jack loom. If you have a table loom, follow the lifting instructions on the right side of the treadling draft. Again weave and check one square at a time, and, if possible, do one square without interruptions.

Weave a heading of a few picks, using the tie-down section of the draft.

Read the draft from the top, and begin with the grey tie-down block. Weave this section for 2.5cm (1in), beating hard. The colours for the weft are shown to the left of the treadling draft.

Then weave Block A for 6cm (2.25in). Open the stuffing shed, and push in the dacron stuffing which has been cut into 6cm (2.25in) squares. Make sure the stuffing is flat in the corners. Beat the next few picks harder after the change of blocks to prevent the stuffing from showing through. Beat the tie-down sections harder than the other sections.

The blocks are woven in the following order (the same order as in the threading):

Tie-down
A
B
C
Tie-down (weave this block the same width as the lengthwise tie-down block)
C
B
A
Tie-down.

Make this last tie-down block just over twice the length of the central tie-down block. Repeat exactly the same blocks as for the back of the cushion, beginning with Block A. Remove the weaving from the loom, and zig-zag the ends on the sewing machine.

Finishing

Wash the cushion cover in warm soapy water, rinse, dry lying flat, and press. Sew a line of machine stitching along the fold, on the wrong side. to make a false seam. This will make all the seams match. Then sew around the other two sides, also on the wrong side, leaving the fourth side open for the cushion insert. This fourth side can be closed with a zip, velcro, or by hand stitching.

19. Jersey designed and woven by Jane McKenzie

PROJECT NINETEEN: WOVEN JERSEY

This project can be woven on an eight-shaft table loom, or an eight-shaft jack loom. The width of the loom should be no less than 76cm (30in).

JERSEY

Warp: Crucci Lambshair, 3125m/kg (1553yds/lb). 250g (9 oz) were needed for the warp.
Weft: Mohair, 2325m/kg (1156yds/lb). 250g (9 oz) were needed for the weft.
Sett: 8 ends per 2.5cm (1in)
Width:
    finished article: 71cm (28in)
    add draw-in: 5cm (2in)
    total warp width: 76cm (30in)
Length:
    finished fabric: 220cm (87in)
    warp take-up: 15cm (6in)
    total length: 235cm (93in)
    loom wastage: 70cm (28in)
    total length of warp: 3m (10 feet) (rounded)
Total number of warp ends: 240
Weave structure: Three-thread herringbone. (sett as for a balanced 2/2 twill)
Threading: See **Fig. 10:31**.
Sley: In an 8-dent reed, sley one per dent
Selvedge: Place two ends together in the two outside dents
Weight: 300gms (10oz) for complete jersey
Warping: Warp with two crosses, as described on page 69.
Threading: Note that shafts 2 and 4 have more heddles.

Weaving

Weave a heading, then leave a small gap, and weave the fabric, following the draft in **Fig. 10:31**. Check that you are weaving with eight picks to 2.5cm (1in). Measure and mark each 30cm (12in). Hemstitch or blanket stitch the ends to prevent unravelling during washing.

    Weave the full length of the warp, remove the weaving from the loom, check for any mistakes or skipped threads, and mend these. Then wash the fabric in warm, soapy water, rinse, and dry. Do not use a tumbler drier, as this causes excessive shrinking.

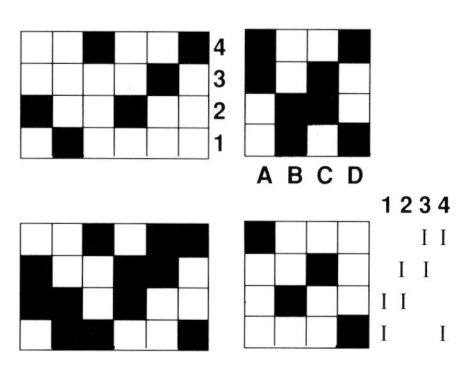

Fig. 10:31 Three-thread herringbone

BROCADE INSERT

Warp: Same as for the warp in the body of the fabric, the Crucci lambshair.
Weft background: Same as warp
Weft brocade: Anny Blatt novelty yarn (44% mohair, 32% acetate, 13% wool, 7% nylon, 4% polyester)
Amount: 150g of lambshair and one ball of the novelty yarn (Anny Blatt) are needed for the insert and knitting the ribbed bands.
Sett: 8 ends per 2.5cm (1in) of the background yarn
Width:
    finished article: 38cm (15in)
    add draw-in: 8cm (3in)
    total warp width: 46cm (18in)
Length:
    finished piece: 51cm(20in)
    warp take-up: 5cm (2in)
    total length of piece: 56cm (22in)
    loom wastage: 61cm (24in)
    total length of warp: 1.25m (4 ft) (rounded up)

Fig. 10:32 Eight-shaft brocade

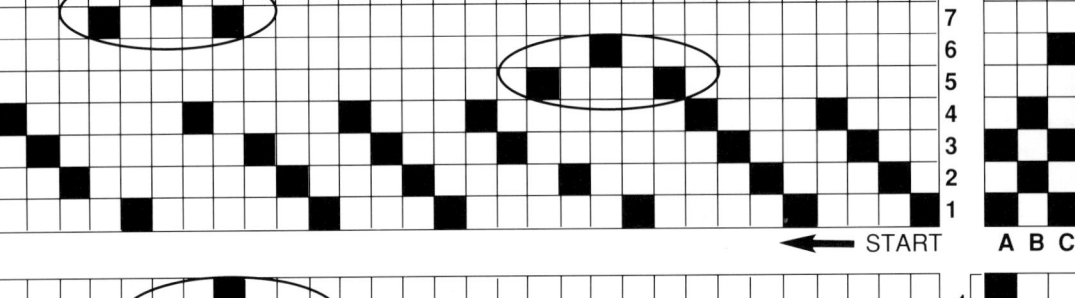

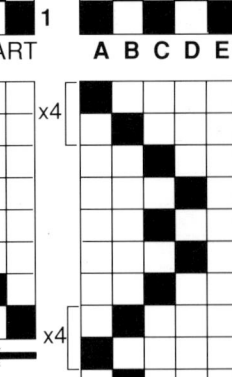

Total number of warp ends: 144 ends of the background warp, 36 ends of the novelty yarn.

Weave structure: Plain balanced weave, with brocade insert

Warping: Wind the first eight ends in the lambshair, then join and wind three ends in the novelty yarn. From then on wind 12 ends of the lambshair and 3 ends of the novelty yarn alternately, until you have 144 ends of lambshair, and 36 ends of the novelty yarn.

Threading: See **Fig. 10:32** The background is threaded as plain weave on the first four shafts, as a straight draw. The brocade insert is threaded on shafts 5 to 8, with Block I on heddles 5 and 6, and Block II on 7 and 8. The brocade ends are circled, and are threaded in the novelty yarn. Thread the pattern in **Fig. 10:32** three times (lambshair yarn 3 x 48 =144; novelty yarn 3 x 12 = 36).

Sley: In an 8-dent reed, sley one end of lambshair per dent. The novelty yarn is sleyed through the same dent as the adjacent warp end on the first four shafts.

Selvedge: Double the outside two ends in one dent.

Weaving

Follow the treadling draft in **Fig. 10:32** if you have a jack loom, and the lifting sequence (left) if you are weaving on an eight-shaft table loom.

Weave a heading, then leave a small gap and weave the fabric, hemstitching or blanket stitching the ends to prevent the fabric unravelling while washing.

LIFTING SEQUENCE

1 3 5 7	2 4 6 8
1 3	
	2 4
1 3	6
5	2 4
1 3	6
5	2 4
1 3	6
	2 4
1 3	
	2 4
1 3	8
7	2 4
1 3	8
7	2 4
1 3	8
	2 4
1 3	
	2 4

Count the number of background picks to 2.5cm (1in), to check that you are weaving a balanced weave, with 8 picks to 2.5cm (1in). The brocade sections will float over the surface of the fabric. Remove the weaving from the loom, and check and mend any mistakes.

Wash the fabric in warm, soapy water, rinse, and dry, lying flat. Press while still slightly damp on the wrong side of the fabric. Cut the brocade floats halfway across the floats.

Making up

See **Fig. 10:33**. Cut out and zig-zag the cut edges to hold the weaving firmly in place. Sew the pieces together, using the stitch on your sewing machine that is used for sewing stretch fabric, such as sweatshirt fabric.

Turn to Chapter Nine, Pages 125–126, to find the instructions for knitting directly onto a garment. On the neckband, 92 stitches were picked up and knitted in 2/2 rib, using 3.25mm needles. The American equivalent is size 3, and the English equivalent is size 10. On the wristbands, 48 stitches were picked up, and the waistband had 196 stitches. Two stripes, of 2 rows each, using the novelty yarn, were knitted into the bands. These stripes tie in the brocade warps with the garment proper.

Fig. 10:33 Pattern for cutting out jersey

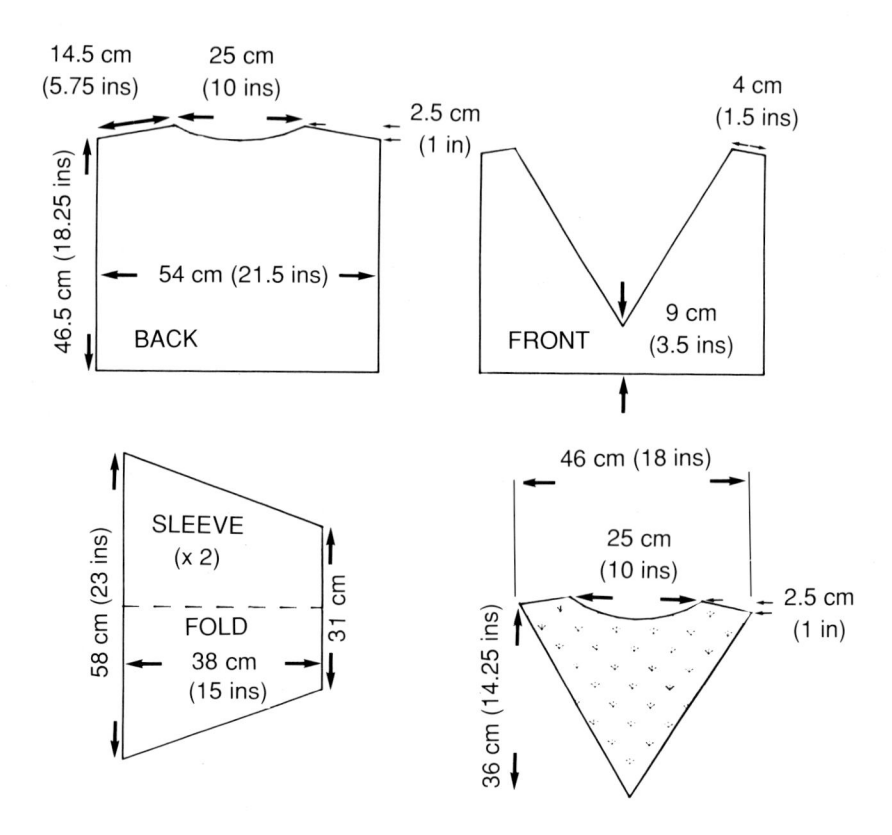

20. Double width knee rug woven by Anne Field

WEAVING PROJECTS • 189

PROJECT TWENTY: DOUBLE WIDTH KNEE RUG

This project can be woven on a eight-shaft table loom. The width of the loom should be no less than 610mm (24in). This knee rug, afghan or throw, makes a rug twice as wide as your loom, by weaving two layers at the same time and joining them on one side. At the end of this project I will describe how to weave the same knee rug, in plain weave, on a four-shaft loom.

Warp: 2 ply wool, 1786m/kg (888yds/lb), in blue and grey. This wool is very soft.
Weft: Same as warp
Sett: 6 ends per 2.5cm (1in) in each layer, 12 ends in doubled layers
Width
    finished article: 97cm (38in)
    add draw-in: 15cm (6in)
    total warp width: 112cm (44in)
Length:
    finished knee rug: 155cm (61in)
    warp take-up: 20cm (8in)
    fringe allowance: 15cm (6in)
    total length of knee rug: 190cm (75in)
    loom wastage: 61cm (24in)
    total length of warp: 251cm (99in)
Total number of warp ends: 264
Weave structure: Balanced 2/2 twill
Warping: Wind the warp with two crosses, and place your counting tie around each bundle of 12 ends (6 for the upper layer and 6 for the lower layer). The warp will need to be wound in two sections.
    Wind 48 ends in grey, 48 in blue, 36 in grey. This is half the warp. The other half has 12 grey, 48 blue, 48 grey, 24 blue ends. When you put these two warps on the loom, make sure the 36 grey and the 12 grey ends are in the centre of the warp.
Threading: Follow the threading draft. The circled end, on shaft 5, is missed out once, on the left side. Just leave this spare end hanging from the back of the loom.
Sley: There are six ends per 2.5cm (1in) in each layer. This makes 12 ends per 2.5cm (1in) in the reed. Sley two in each dent for three dents, then miss one dent, across the warp width for an 8-dent reed.
Selvedge: Do not sley the ends any closer together at the selvedge.
Weight: 450g (1 lb)

Weaving

Do not weave a heading. Fill one ski shuttle with the blue yarn, and the other with the grey. Begin with the grey yarn, and follow the lifting sequence in **Fig. 10:34**. Follow the arrows carefully.

U= upper layer
L = lower layer

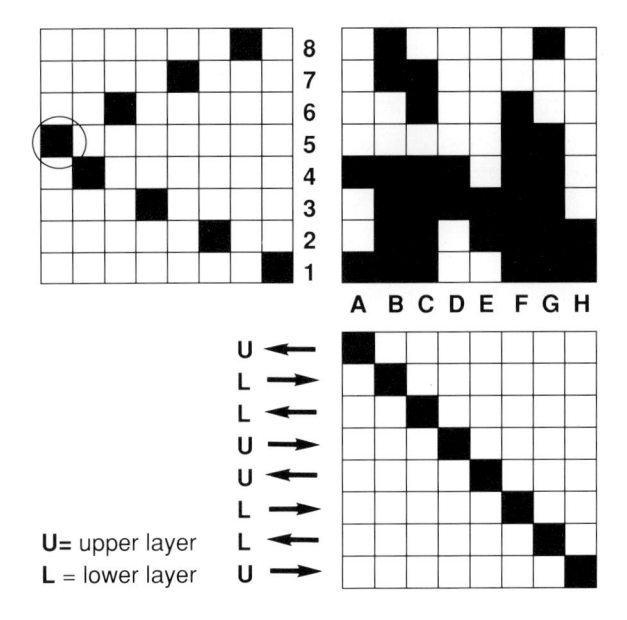

Fig. 10:34 Twill double weave

Begin on the right side, lift shafts 1 and 4, and throw the shuttle from right to left. This is the first pick in the upper layer.

Lift all the first four shafts, 1,2,3,4, to keep the upper layer out of the way while you weave the first pick in the lower layer, from left to right, by lifting shafts 7 and 8. When the cloth is opened out, this will be one continuous pick across the whole width. Drop shaft 8, lift shaft 6, and weave from right to left in the lower layer. Lift shafts 3 and 4, for the continuation of this pick, from left to right in the upper layer. This is the first two picks. Weave the next four picks, following on from the draft.

When you have woven this far, you should have four picks in both layers. Peek at the fold, and you will see the twill continuing on around the bend. If you have a doubled warp end here, you have forgotten to remove that circled end from shaft 5, but do not worry – you can remove this warp thread when the weaving is taken from the loom. Be careful not to pull the folded warps on the left in too much, or the threads will cram up. The open side can be seen by lifting up the upper layer on the right. I need to reassure myself that it is correct by taking a look here now and then.

Weave 24 picks in the grey yarn, counting the picks so you have six to 2.5cm (1in), for a balanced twill. You will find the extreme right warp end in the upper layer is not caught by the shuttle. I just snip this end off and leave it hanging over the back of the loom, as it is a nuisance to take the shuttle under and over this end separately.

Measure and mark every 30cm (12in), and weave with 24 picks in each colour, until you have woven 175cm (69in). As this wool is soft, I have allowed extra length for shrinkage. Leave about 15cm (6in) for a fringe, and cut the weaving from the loom.

WEAVING PROJECTS • 191

U = upper layer
L = lower layer

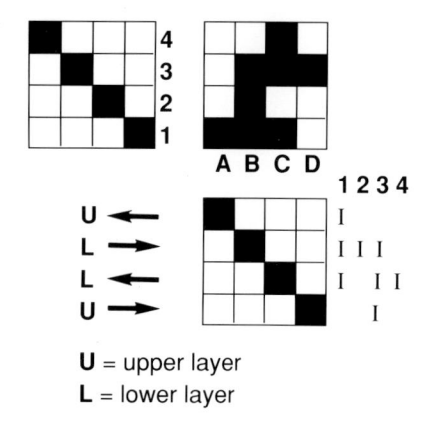

Fig. 10:35 Four-shaft double weave

Check for any skipped threads, which will probably be in the lower layer, where you cannot see them while weaving. Mend these, then make the fringe, using the twisted fringe described in Chapter Nine, page 123, **Fig. 9:I**.

Wash the knee rug in warm, soapy water, and press while still slightly damp. Because the wool is so soft, the threads will spread out to make the fold less obvious.

Folded knee rug in plain weave, on a four-shaft table loom

The principle is the same, but as this loom has only four shafts we cannot weave twill, but must make a plain weave. Because the yarn is so soft, we can use the same sett as for the twill knee rug.

Follow the instructions for making the warp as above, but thread with a straight draw, 1, 2, 3, 4.

There are only four picks to weave, to make two complete full width picks. The size of the checks, and the finishing are the same as for the twill knee rug.

APPENDICES

1. CARE AND MAINTENANCE OF YOUR LOOM

Maintenance and storage
1. Tighten any nuts that may have worked loose.
2. Check loom tie-up cords to ensure they have not stretched.
3. Do not store loom in a damp place as the wood may warp. Keep covered from direct sunlight.
4. Make sure there is no direct heat on the loom, as it dries the warp yarn and may damage it. The yarn needs a certain degree of humidity to keep its stretching and flexing ability.

Reeds
There are two types of reeds; carbon and stainless steel. All of the older Ashford looms will have carbon reeds, however later models can have the stainless steel reeds, or you may be offered the choice.

Carbon reeds: These can rust, but if care is taken they will last for a long time. If you live in an area where rust is no problem, a carbon reed will be quite satisfactory. If you will not be using a reed for a while, spray it with a fine oil, wrap it in plastic, and store it in a dry area.

It is very difficult to remove rust from a reed. The sides can be cleaned with steel wool, but it is difficult to get into the dents. If you have cleaned or oiled a reed, put on a dark warp for your first warp and assume that the first .5m (1-2 feet) will be wasted.

Handle the reed as little as possible, as even the moisture on your fingers can cause rust.

Stainless steel reeds: These may be more expensive, but are worth it if you live in a humid area prone to rust. If you spray water on your warps, as is sometimes done with linen, or when dyeing on the loom, a stainless steel reed is necessary.

New reeds: With a brand new loom, you may find the reed manufacturer has left a fine coat of oil on the reed to protect it. This may have attracted dust, and this film will rub off onto your first warp. Again, it is probably quicker to clean the reed by using a dark warp and using the first portion to clean the reed. A pipe cleaner is also useful for cleaning between the dents.

Accessiblity
The loom needs to be accessible on all sides and placed on a level floor.

Lighting
It is important to have your weaving well lit. I can well remember the frustration because I wove one evening in poor light, and did not notice that the colour had changed slightly between one batch of yarn and another. The next morning, in clear light, the colour change was obvious. On the Ashford jack loom, it is easy to clamp a light to the loom castle, which gives direct light onto your weaving. Whatever the loom you are using, it is important to have good side light rather than from behind or in front.

2. ADDITIONAL EQUIPMENT

Ashford Table Loom Stand
A loom stand can be bought from your Ashford stockist to hold a four-shaft or eight-shaft table loom. This saves valuable table space, as the loom is bolted directly to the stand. The loom in the photographs in Chapter Three uses such a stand. The stand can be adjusted to different heights to suit the individual weaver, who can then sit down to weave. If you are not using the stand, clamp the loom firmly to a solid table, with the clamps included with the loom. This will prevent the loom moving as you beat.

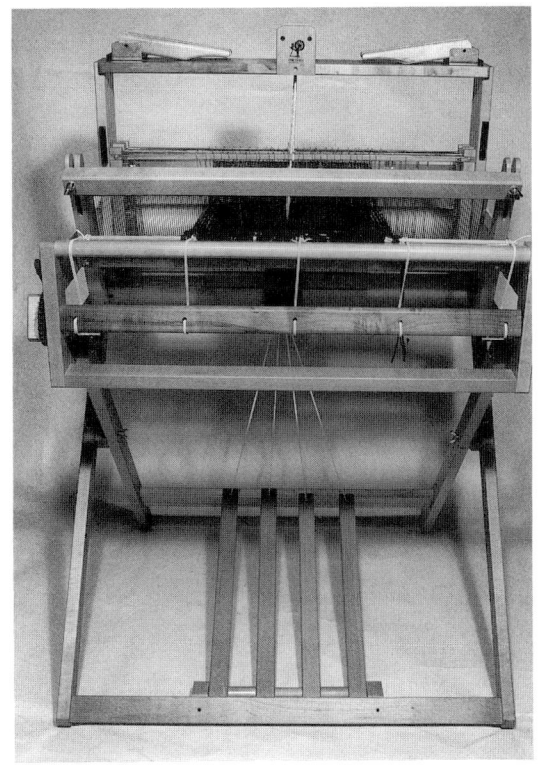

Ashford Table Loom Treadle Kit
This kit converts the Ashford four-shaft table loom into a treadle-operated loom, and fits both 610mm (24in) and 810mm (32in) looms. This kit is used in conjunction with the Ashford loom stand.

The treadle kit has four treadles, one to each shaft in a direct tie-up. When a treadle is depressed, the attached shaft will rise. To raise two or more shafts at once, use two feet on the corresponding treadles.

Converting the table loom to a floor loom means you will use your feet, not your hands to operate the shafts. You can then throw the shuttle from one hand to another, without having to put the shuttle down to operate the shafts. This will give a better rhythm to your weaving, may place less strain on your shoulder muscles, and certainly makes the weaving faster.

Ashford table loom treadle kit

Ashford Loom Bench
With a floor loom you will be sitting down to weave, and a seat or bench of the correct height is important. An Ashford loom bench, with adjustable heights is available. A bench is more comfortable than a seat, as you can slide along the bench while throwing and catching the shuttle.

It is important that you sit at the correct height while weaving. The breast beam should be about your waist height when sitting at the loom, so therefore is somewhat misnamed. Adjust the height of your loom bench by removing the bolts and moving the pegs up or down.

Ashford loom bench

3. ASHFORD DISTRIBUTORS

Australia:
Ashford Handicrafts Ltd, Traveller's Rest, Snowy Mountain Highway, Cooma NSW 2630. Tel. 008-026397, 064-524422. Fax 064-524523. Ashford weaving looms and spinning wheels are sold throughout Australia. For the name of your nearest dealer please contact our branch office for details.

Austria:
Alles Zum Gesunden Bauen and Wohnen, Ing Volkmar Baurecker, Hirrshgasse 22A, 4020 Linz. Tel. (0732) 277285

Belgium:
Artisans, Boulevard Paul Janson, 11-13, 6000 Charleroi. Tel. (071) 316505

Canada:
Treenway Crafts Ltd, 725 Caledonia, Victoria BC, V8T 1B4. Tel. (604) 383-1661
Samson Angoras, RR1 Brantford, Ontario N3T SL4. Tel. (519) 788 5650

Denmark:
Elsa Krogh, Havndalvej 40, 9550 Mariager. Tel. (98) 542253
Spindegrej, Fjellebrosvejen 25, 5762 V. Sterninge. Tel. (09) 244030
Kip Garn, Hersegade 12, 4000 Roskilde. Tel. 02372349

Finland:
Toijalan Kaidetehdas KY, PL 25, 37801 Toijala. Tel. (937) 21095

Germany:
Fredrich Traub KG, D-7065 Winterbach, Schorndorfer Str Be 18. Tel (07181) 77055

Ireland:
Craftspun Yarns Ltd, Johnstown-Naas, County Kildare. Tel. (045) 76881

Japan:
Ananda Co Ltd, 1221 Shimojo, Nagasaka-Cho, kitakoma-Gun, Yamanashi. Tel. 0551 324215
Ocean Trading Co Ltd, 8th Floor, 1-2, Kyoto Toshiba Bldg, 25 Hira-machi, Saiin, Ukyo-ku, Kyoto. Tel. (075) 314 8720
Mariya Handicrafts Ltd, Kita-1, Nishi-3, Chuo-Ku, Sapporo 060. Tel. (011) 221 3307

Sanyo Trading Co, Minamisenju, 5-9-6-905 Arakawa-ku, Tokyo 116. Tel. (03) 801 9020
shida Noriko, 502 Daitshu Building, Imagawa 2-1-67, Fukuoka

Korea:
Haelim Trading Co Ltd, CPO Box 1653, Seoul. Tel. 752 8271
Fine Corporation, CPO Box 6718, Seoul. Tel. (02) 7791894

Netherlands:
Falkland Natuurgarens, Bosstraat 33, 3971 XA Drieber-gen. Tel. 03438-18155

New Zealand:
Ashford Handicrafts Ltd, PO Box 474, Ashburton. Tel. (03) 308-9087, Fax (03) 308-8664

Norway:
Spinninger, Boks 36, 1362 Billingstad. Tel.(02) 846022

Papua New Guinea:
Eastern Highland Cultural Centre, c/- Mrs Anne Montgomery, Box 37, Kaimantu.

Sweden:
Gundruns Ullbod, Ulunda 5462, 19991Enkopenj. Tel. (0171) 39995

Switzerland:
Spinnstube, Sch miedengasse 6, 2502 Biel. Tel. (032) 22 2960
Spycher – Handwerk, 4953 Schwarzenbach, b. Huttwil. Tel. (063) 721152.

United Kingdom:
Haldane & Co, Gateside by Cupar, Fife KY14 7ST. Tel. (03376) 469, Fax (03376) 507
Ashford weaving looms and spinning wheels are sold throughout the UK. For the name of your nearest dealer, please contact our UK distributor Haldane & Co for details.

United States:
Crystal Palace Yarns, 3006 San Pablo Ave, Berkeley CA 94702. Tel. (415) 548 9988

4. BOOKS FOR FURTHER STUDY

Chapter One: The Inkle Loom
Atwater, Mary Meigs. *Byways in Handweaving*, Macmillan Company, 1970 USA.
Bradley, Lavinia. *Inkle Weaving*, Routledge & Kegan Paul, 1982.
Holland, Nina. *Inkle Loom Weaving*, Watson-Guptill Publications, 1973
Tacker, Harold and Sylvia. *Band Weaving*, Studio Vista, 1974.
Weaving and Spinning, Excalibur Books 1975

Chapter Two: The Rigid Heddle Loom
Davenport, Betty Linn. *Hands On Rigid Heddle Weaving*. Interweave Press, USA 1987.
Davenport, Betty Linn. *Textures and Patterns for the Rigid Heddle Loom* Dos Tejoras, St Paul, USA. 1980.
Field, Anne. *Weaving With The Rigid Heddle Loom* A.H. & A.W. Reed Ltd, New Zealand, 1980.
Swanson, Karen. *Rigid Heddle Weaving* Watson-Guptill Publications, NY 1975.
Xenakis, David. *The Xenakis Technique* Golden Fleece Publications, USA, 1980.

Chapter Three: The Four-shaft Table Loom
Atwater, M.M. *The Shuttlecraft Book of American Handweaving* Macmillan. 1972, USA.
Black, Mary. *New Key to Weaving*, Bruce Publishing Co, 1949 . N.Y.
Collingwood, Peter. *The Techniques of Rug Weaving*, Watson-Guptill, 1968, USA.
Field, Anne *The Four-Shaft Table Loom*, 1986. Shoal Bay Press Ltd, New Zealand.
Frey, Berta. *Designing and Drafting For Handweavers*, Collier Books 1958, UK.
Kurtz, Carol. *Designing for Weaving*, Hastings House, 1981, USA.
Moorman, Theo. *Weaving as an Art Form*, Van Nostrand Reinhold, 1975 USA.
Porter Davison, Marguerite. *A Handweaver's Pattern Book*, published by the author, USA. First published 1944.
Selander, Malin *Weaving Patterns*, Studio Books, Longacre Press, UK.
Selander, Malin *Swedish Handweaving*, Studio Books, Longacre Press, 1961, UK.
Tidball, Harriet, *The Weavers Book*, Macmillan, 1961, USA.
Tovey, John. *Weaves and Pattern Drafting*, Batsford, 1969, UK
Weigle, Palmy. *Double Weave*, Watson-Guptill, 1978, USA.
Wilson, Jean. *Weaving is Creative*, Van Nostrand Reinhold, 1972 USA.

Windeknecht, Thomas and Margaret, *Colour and Weave*, Van Nostrand Reinhold, 1981, USA.

Chapter Four: The Four-shaft Jack Loom
Fannin, Allen. *Handloom Weaving Technology*, Van Nostrand Reinhold Co, 1979.
Tovey, John, *The Technique of Weaving*, B.T. Batsford Ltd, UK. 1965.
Worst, Edward. *Weaving with Foot-power Looms*, Dover Publications, Inc. NY. 1974 edition.

Chapter Five: Eight-shaft Table and Jack Looms
Best, Eleanor, *Weaves – A Design Handbook*, Bestudio 7130 Eastwick Lane, Indianapolis, Indiana 46256. USA 1987
Laughlin, Mary Elizabeth. *More than Four*, McMinnville, Oregon, USA 1976.
Phillips, Janet. *The Weaver's Book of Fabric Design*, Batsford, 1983. UK.
Straub, Marianne, *Handweaving and Cloth Design*, Pelham Books Ltd, 1977 UK.
Voiers, Leslie. *Looking at Twills*, Harrisville Designs 1983. USA.
Wertenberger, Kathryn. *8, 12 . . . 20*, Interweave Press, 1988 USA.
Worst, Edward F. *Weaving with Foot-Power Looms*, Dover Publications, reprinted 1974. N.Y.

Chapter Six: Choosing Your Yarns
Cook, J. Gordon. *Handbook of Textile Fibres: Natural Fibres, Vol. 1*, and *Man-made Fibres, Vol.2*. Merrow Publishing Co., UK, 1959
Hochberg, Bette. *Fibre Facts*, published by the author. 3400 Paul St, Apt. 303 Santa Cruz, California 95065. USA.
Quinn, Celia. *Yarn: A Resource Guide for Handweavers*, Interweave Press.
Pizzuto, J.J. *Fabric Science*, Fairchild, 1980.
Roth, Bettie G. & Schulz, Chris. *Handbook of Timesaving Tables for Weavers Spinners and Dyers* published by the authors, P.O.Box 951, Elk Grove, California, 95624, USA.
Thomson, Helen. *Fibres and Fabrics of Today*, Whitcoulls, New Zealand, 1966.
Welford, T. *The Textile Student's Manual*, Pitman, UK 1947.

Chapter Seven: Designing Woven Projects
Bateson, Vivienne, *Woven Chic*, Bell & Hyman UK 1984
Beeston, Mary, *Spinning and Weaving*, Support Yourself series, Fontana Books, Sydney, 1986
Kurtz, Carol. *Designing for Weaving*, Hastings House. NY 1981.

Phillips, Janet. *The Weaver's Book of Fabric Design*, Batsford, UK. 1983.
Regensteiner, Else. *Weaving Sourcebook*, Van Nostrand Reinhold Co., NY 1983.
Sutton, Ann. *The Structure of Fabrics*, Lark Communications, USA 1982.

Chapter Eight: Pattern Drafting
Davison, Marguerite P. *A Handweaver's Pattern Book,* Published by the author, Pennsylvania, USA, 1944.
Frey, Berta. *Designing and Drafting for Handweavers,* Collier Books UK 1958.
Tovey, John. *Weaves and Pattern Drafting* Batsford. UK 1962.

Chapter Nine: Finishing Techniques
Baizerman and Searle, *Finishes in the Ethnic Tradition,* Dos Tejeoras. Minnesota, 1978.
Gordon, Beverley. *The Final Steps: Traditional Methods and Contemporary Applications for Finishing Cloth by Hand*, Interweave Press, USA 1982
West, Virginia. *Finishing Touches for the Handweaver,* Charles T. Branford Co. 1968 USA.
Wilson, Jean. Joinings, *Edges and Trims . . . Finishing Details for Handcrafted Products*, Van Nostrand Reinhold, NY 1983.

5. GLOSSARY

Cloth beam: beam or roller on floor loom that stores the woven cloth.
Beaming: winding the warp onto the warp beam.
Beater: frame holding the reed.
Bobbin: reel or spool to carry the weft thread.
Breast beam: bar at the front of the loom which guides the woven fabric onto the cloth beam.
Dent: single space in a reed.
Draft: diagram of threading order.
Draw-in: amount weaving will narrow while being woven.
End: a warp thread.
E.P.Cm: ends per centimetre.
E.P.I: ends per inch.
Fell: the edge of weaving at the last weft pick.
Floats: pattern threads that pass over more than one warp end.
Fulling: finishing process for woollen fabric.
Heading: the first few rows in a new warp.
Heddle: wire or cord holder of the warp ends on the loom.
Jacks: levers connected to shafts and lamms which move the shafts.
Lamms: levers connected to treadles and shafts to centralize the shedding action.
Pawl: metal tongue that engages with a ratchet to form a brake.
Pick: a single row of weft thread.
Raddle: bar with pegs to separate the warp while winding it onto the warp beam.
Ratchet: toothed wheel which prevents a roller from turning when engaged with a pawl.

Reed hook: thin, flat hook for threading the warp through the reed.
Rigid heddle: comb-like piece, with holes and slots, which carries the warp.
Shafts: frames on which heddles are hung (also called harness).
Selvedge: outside warp ends that strengthen the fabric edges.
Sett: number of warp ends per centimetre (in).
Shed: opening formed in the warp, through which the shuttle passes.
Shuttle: holder for weft thread.
Sley: number of warp ends in reed dents.
Tapestry: a weft-face weave, in which an interrupted weft completely covers the warp.
Threading hook: fine metal hook for drawing warp ends through the heddles.
Treadles: pedals used on a floor loom to move the shafts.
Tie-up: tying of lamms to treadles.
Twill: weft threads forming a diagonal pattern.
Warp: lengthwise threads.
Warp beam: beam or roller on a loom which holds the warp.
Warping board: wooden frame with pegs which holds the warp at tension while making the warp.
Warping mill: reel used to hold the warp ends at tension while winding the warp.
Wastage: length of warp that cannot be woven.
Weft: the threads running the width of the loom.

INDEX

Acetate 108–09
Acrylic 109
Added fringe 123
Added warp ends 123
Afghan 139
Angora rabbit 107
Apron 77

Back beam 71, 87
Back roller 21
Balanced weave 25, 49
Beater 43, 73, 87
Beating 37
Binder weft 65–66, 80–82
Blanket stitch 121
Blended yarns 109–10
Block switching 42
Bobbins 84
Bobbin winder 84
Boundweave on opposites 167
Braces 160
Brake lever 76–77
Braids 16–20
Breast beam 71, 87
Brighton honeycomb 101–02
Brocade 186–87
Broken warp ends 38–39
Brooks bouquet 135
Bubbling the weft 138
Burning test 105

Camel hair 107
Cartoon 168
Cashmere 107
Calculating sett 24–25, 49–50
Castle 45
Chaining 132
Chaining the warp 54
Clamps 24, 34
Closed shed 34
Cloth beam 71, 87
Cold water dyes 151
Cloth finishing 106
Cocoon jacket 153–55
Computers in weaving 118
Conversion to metrics 51
Crossover shawl 156–59
Cotton 107–08
Cottolin 108, 134
Cross sticks 55, 79
Curtains 115
Cushions 111, 137–39, 180–83
Diagonal joins 168
Differential rise and fall 88–89
Direct tie-up 196
Distorted warp 147–48
Double corduroy rugs 173–76
Double weave 96–100, 180–83
Draw-in 26, 50
Draw down 62, 76, 92, 120

Eight-shaft jack loom 85–102
Eight-shaft table loom 85–102
End 24
Exhibitions 117
Extended twill 90

Fell of the cloth 39
Fibreglass 108
Finger crochet 126
Fleece cushions 137–39
Fleece tablemats 139
Floats 41, 92
Folded cloth 191, 192
Four-shaft jack loom 71–84
Four-shaft table loom 45–70
Friction brake 76–77
Fringes 122–24

Ground weft 174

Hanna yarn 131, 154
Heading 35, 66
Heddle 45, 75
Hemstitching 121–22
Herringbone 185

Inkle loom 13–20

Jacks 72
Jackets 147–49, 154–55
Jute 108

Knee rug 116, 139–41, 190–92
Knitted fringe 124
Knitting a bias edging 125
Knitted ribs 126
Knots
    overhand 122
    reef 30, 122
    slip 32
    snitch 55
    triple twist 33

Lamms 72
Leash 14, 19
Leno 134
Lifting sequence 62
Lighting 195
Linked weft 132
Linen 108
Loom bench 196
Loom treadle kit 196
Loops 169
Loose warp ends 35, 56
Lurex 108

Measuring 39
Missing warp ends 35
Mistakes in the heddles 61
Mistakes in the reed 61

Mock Leno 42–43
Mohair 107

Norse kitchen draft 163
Nylon 109

Overshot weaves 94, 162–64

Pattern drafting 62, 118–20
Pawl 57
Peruvian stitch 125–26
Philippine edge 123
Pick 34
Pick-up stick 40
Pick-up stick weaving 40–43
Pirn 84
Plaiting 122–23
Plied yarn 110
Polyesters 109
Profile draft 170–71, 177–78

Queens cord 166

Raddle 47, 55, 79
Random warp stripes 142–44
Ratchets 31, 45, 57, 76
Reed 43, 195
Records 40
Repeating units 118–19
Replacement heddles 61
Rising shed loom 47, 73
Rugs 75
Rya knots 166

Sampler 43–44, 51, 63
Scarves 112, 131–33
Selvedge 35
Separating articles 37–38
Sett 24–25, 49–50, 129
Shrinkage 50
Shuttles
    Boat 84
    End delivery 84
    Rug 47, 83
    Ski 47, 83
    Stick 36, 83
Shuttle race 72, 73
Silk 106–07
Sley 59
Sleying for other setts 59
Singles 110
Static electricity 109
Stole 150–52
Stitched double weave 100
Straight draw 58
Surface weave 145–46

Tabby 49
Tablemats 113–14, 134–36
Take-up 26, 50

APPENDICES • 199

Tapestry 168, 169
Tension 33–34, 60
Terylene 109
Tex 110
Texsolv 43
Threading 58
Threading hook 58
Throw 139
Tie and dye 169
Tie-up 75–76, 85, 87–88, 119
Treadles 75–76
Treadling quadrant 75–76, 119
Triple knotted fringe 122
Turnbuckle 77
Twill
   2/2 64, 140

1/3 64, 82
3/1 64, 81
point 119
Swiss 64, 82
zig-zag 65, 81
Twisted fringe 123

Upholstery 114, 142–44

Walking the treadles 75
Wall hangings 116–17, 165, 170–72
Warp 22, 48
Warping 27, 51, 78–80
Warping board 47
Warping mill 51, 68

Warping pegs 23, 27
Warp beam 71
Warping with two crosses 69–70
Warp-face weave 49, 170–72
Warp take-up 26, 50
Weaving with handspun wool 139–41
Weft 24
Weft-face weave 25, 49
Winding with two threads 70
Wool 105–06
Woollen yarn 105
Worsted yarn 105
Woven jersey 185–89